Trials on Trial
The Pure Theory of Legal Procedure

GORDON TULLOCK

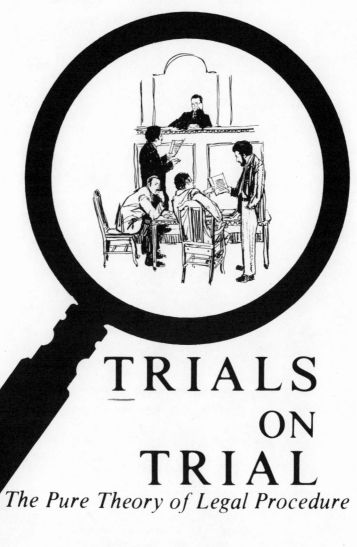

TRIALS
ON
TRIAL
The Pure Theory of Legal Procedure

New York COLUMBIA UNIVERSITY PRESS *1980*

Library of Congress Cataloging in Publication Data
Tullock, Gordon
Trials on trial.

Includes bibliographical references and index.
1. Procedure (Law)   2. Law—Interpetation and
construction.   3. Procedure (Law)—United States.
4. Procedure (Law)—Economic aspects.   I. Title.
K2205.4.T84   347'.05   80-13113
ISBN 0-231-04952-8

Columbia University Press
New York   Guildford, Surrey

Contents

Acknowledgments

I should like to thank the editors of *Kyklos* for permission to use material which originally appeared in their publication. The manuscript was also greatly helped by detailed and exhaustive comments by Juergen Backhaus, Walter R. Lane, and Charles K. Rowley. Mrs. Iris G. Bowman typed the manuscript and was a great help in various ways with its preparation.

Prelude for Lawyers

Although I graduated from the University of Chicago Law School, and until a couple of years ago was a member of the Illinois bar, most of my work has involved economics. This book is an example, applying as it does, essentially economic tools to the analysis of legal procedure. Since it is written by a man who was trained in law and in fact had only one brief formal course in economics, it should be intelligible to lawyers. Many lawyers, however, will find the approach and the methodological tools used strange, and the point of this prelude is to introduce the method. Economists and those lawyers, quite common today, who are familiar with economics should skip it.

Lawyers who have no economic background are not as much disadvantaged over economists, or economically trained lawyers, in reading this book as by many others. In general the tools that I have used, although economic in spirt, do not directly come out of any economics book. There are some cases in which I have used diagrams and lines of reasoning which would be familiar to the average economist but, in general, I have had to invent new techniques. Thus, the lawyer without economic training will find much that is unfamiliar, but so would an economist.

It is sometimes alleged that economics is a particularly precise way of dealing with legal topics. As a matter of fact, it could just as well be said that it is an exceptionally vague way. All scientific activity involves abstracting part of a problem and considering only that part. Thus there is, if the project is successful, a more precise examination of part of reality, with, as a sort of cost, greater vagueness with respect to other parts of reality. Economic analysis of the law is no exception to this rule.

Lawyers should be fairly familiar with abstractions, since they engage in abstraction themselves. First, they characteristically study the law out of decisions by upper courts. This decision, of course, does not tell one everything that happened in the lower court, let alone everything that happened in the real world, which led to the lawsuit. The judge has undertaken a major work of abstraction and only includes in his opinion those matters which he thinks are most important. Second, the lawyer then performs another act of abstraction by deciding what the "rule" of the case is. The rule is, of course, only a very tiny bit of the reality with which the case started. Naturally, I do not criticize this activity on the part of lawyers. I mention it only to indicate that it is not only the economists who engage in abstraction.

In both scientific activity and in the law, the reasons for abstraction are straightforward. The human mind is not capable of dealing with more than a rather limited number of propositions at the same time. If we are to think about any real-world problem, we have to simplify it by abstracting the most important considerations and considering them in isolation. If we are successful in obtaining either a scientific law, or the rule of a complicated chain of cases, we then feel that this can be used in the future to deal with other similar situations. But, in each future situation, it will be necessary to add in a lot of detail to find out how the rule applies in that particular situation.

All of this involves one of the fundamental themes of Western thought, at least since the Greeks. This is the idea that a phenomenon can be broken down into smaller pieces. Some of these smaller pieces will be laws or rules, which means simply that we believe they are principles that apply over very, very many cases. The rule of *Erie vs. Tompkins*, for example, has had effect in an immense number of law cases, even though, in each case, the other circumstances surrounding the decision differed from any other. Similarly, the proposition that demand curves slant downward turns out to be important for an immense number of economic examinations of the world. Combined with other details from the specific situation under examination, it can shed a great deal of light on the probable outcome.

To take a somewhat similar example from physics, when Galileo wrote about gravity, he ignored the friction of the air, although in his day there was no way of obtaining even a moderately good vacuum. This was not because he did not know that a feather fell slowly because of air resistance. It was because he thought that the force of gravity acted on the feather in much the same way as it acted on a lead weight. The difference was in something else, i.e., air resistance which he, at that time, could not measure.

As a matter of fact, when he performed his actual measurements, he rolled weights down an inclined plane. He did not, of course, think that the friction of the inclined plane was the same as the friction of the air. But he did think that the gravitational force acting on an object is the same regardless of what kind of friction it is subject to.

All this may seem tedious to the reader. I can only say that some lawyers to whom I have talked have objected to economics on the grounds that it is abstract. The above paragraphs are my defense against this charge.

Economists make a great deal of use of both mathematical equations and geometric figures in analyzing the real world. I am somewhat old-fashioned in that I tend to use figures a great deal and mathematics very little. The legal reader may find this an advantage, since I believe the figures in general are easier to follow. The basic restriction on the use of geometry rather than algebra is that one is largely confined to two-dimensional figures, and one may want to deal with situations so complex that they do not go well in two dimensions. In this case, algebra of course provides an out. I have, in general, simplified things down so that I can get by with my two-dimensional figures. I find that some people find various forms of algebra easier to follow than essentially geometric figures, but most people seem to find the figures easier. I hope that most of my legal readers will find that my specialization on figures is a help rather than a hindrance.

A figure (or an equation) is essentially an analogy to the real world. We choose some set of symbols, it can be lines or algebraic terms, whose behavior is very well known and which represents some real-world phenomena. It is, of course, a legitimate complaint against such a "model" that it does not fit the real world with a sufficient degree of closeness. It always is worthwhile to examine models carefully to find out whether they do fit the world, but I think that most of the ones that I use in this book will pass the test.

Turning then, to the actual models themselves, may I ask the reader to turn to the very first diagram in the book on page 27. This will do as a sample of the way we make use of these models. Cases sometimes have very good evidence and sometimes bad. In this diagram, cases are arranged on the axis on the bottom in terms of how good their evidence is, with those for which the evidence will lead inevitably to the right conclusion on the part of whatever decision maker we are using at the left end, and those in which it is so bad that it will inevitably lead to the wrong decision at the right end. Lawyers frequently talk about cases in which the outcome was wrong, but they do not seem to like to think about them in a rigorous way. Hence, I rather anticipate a certain amount of puzzlement by the average lawyer looking at this diagram, but I hope he will be willing to conceive that in some cases, the evidence is more deceptive than in others and that is all that is necessary for the assumption of the arrangement of the cases on the horizontal axis. In the real world, we will not know which cases are more deceptive than others, but since I am not suggesting that one locates any particular case at any point on the axis, we do not have to know that; all we have to know is that some are more deceptive than others.

The vertical axis shows the percentage of cases of any given degree of deceptiveness, or nondeceptiveness, of evidence where the court will come out with the right decision. The line P then simply shows the percentage of right decisions that may be expected with each degree of accuracy, or deceptiveness, of the evidence. I have drawn it in a way which seems familiar to economists, but there is no strong reason why the lawyer who objects to that may not draw another line of his own. There are only two restrictions. First, if one is not careful, the line will be drawn in such a way that the courts are wrong more often than they are right; and under those circumstances, of course, we would be well advised to substitute flipping coins for the court process. A second restriction is that since the evidence gets more deceptive as one moves from left to right, it is essential that the line be monotonically decreasing. As I said above, in some ways our "economic" reasoning is not highly precise, but vague. All I need for the conclusions I draw from this diagram is that that line be drawn so that it meets the above two conditions.

Throughout this book, I assume that lawyers are skilled enough so that although they are not able to tell whether the evidence in the case is deceptive or not, they can estimate the outcome of the case in a probabilistic sense. That is, they can say the plaintiff has a 2 out of 3 chance of winning. This means that assuming, for example, that we are confining ourselves to a universe of cases in which the plaintiff is right, the lawyers would be able to tell, with respect to any given case, the probability that the plaintiff was going to win—and this would correspond to our probability of an accurate outcome. This being so, they can advise their client as to whether proceeding with the case would be worth the cost. In order to transfer this information to a diagram, it is essential to draw in the cost of the plaintiff and of the defendant, and I have done so in figure 3.1 in a very simple form. From the diagram, we can tell which cases the plaintiff would not press, cases where the defendant would pay up without going to court, and finally those cases in which there would either be a trial or some kind of compromise out-of-court settlement. The reasoning is easy, and the diagram, in my opinion, makes it easier to follow.

But this is merely one sample; going through the book, the reader will find there are many others. They look impressive at first glance, but do not be fooled. They are simple. It is true, however, that there is some skill in both drawing and using these figures; and the lawyer who has not encountered them before will probably find he has less than complete fluency in dealing with them until he has worked his way well into the book. In general, he should assume that if one of the figures appears to be wrong, it is because he misunderstood, not because it is in fact wrong. That is not because I am always right, but simply because I am working in a field in which I am fairly expert, and the lawyer who has not dealt with these things before will not be an expert. Further, this is only the first assumption. The prospect that I have made a mistake is always a real one, and there is no reason why a lawyer who does not have previous knowledge in economics cannot detect it. I simply suggest caution before the reader decides that I am wrong, not acceptance of my accuracy as a matter of faith.

The point of this brief prelude has been to give the noneconomically trained lawyer at least a little bit of introduction to the methods used in this book. I have not argued that the methods are valuable themselves; it seems to me that in this case, the test is in the reading. If the reader finds that he has learned nothing, it follows that the methods were not worthwhile. I hope that is not the ultimate conclusion.

Trials on Trial
The Pure Theory of Legal Procedure

Chapter 1

Why Have Law?

The point of the law is to control individual and group behavior. Further, it is but one of many techniques for controlling such behavior. We can keep people from stealing our furniture by building very good doors with excellent locks and putting bars on the windows, or by supporting a police and court system which will attempt to catch the perpetrators if they engage in this theft and, if it does catch them, will impose a sanction severe enough so that they are unlikely to adopt the profession of burglary. The first makes no use of the law, and the second depends on it. Similarly, indoctrination, lecturing, giving sermons, etc., are all extra-legal efforts to control behavior. The characteristic legal method of control is the use of a sanction, or the threat of a sanction, to insure compliance with the law, contract, or judicial order.

The imposition of this sanction requires that we know who has violated the law or contract. Frequently this is a very simple problem; the judge has ordered John Jones to sit down and be quiet, and John Jones jumps up and calls the judge a dirty name. The judge has no difficulty determining who did it. In many cases, however, the problem is a very difficult one. The question of who murdered Mrs. Jones or, indeed, whether she was, in fact, murdered or committed suicide may be extremely difficult to answer. Similarly, in a contract case, both Mr. A and Mr. B may be accusing the other of having violated the contract between them. To apply the law, we must first find out if the contract was violated and by whom. For this purpose, law codes are normally implemented by an institutional structure which determines who murdered Mrs. Jones and then imposes the legally prescribed penalty. It is the purpose of this book to examine the pure theory of this procedural portion of the law.

In Anglo-Saxon countries, and to a lesser extent in other countries, the court procedure also involves another decision-making process.

Frequently, the law is not clear with respect to the case at hand, and hence it is not possible, strictly speaking, to apply the law—because no one knows what the law is. In general, this is a defect in legal design, but it is doubtful that any legal system can be designed in such a way that all conceivable cases which arise will be clearly covered by an appropriate section of the code. It is true, of course, that one could do very much better than Anglo-Saxon law does in this regard.

The decision as to what should be done if the law is unclear, or if the contract which is drawn up between the two parties does not seem to cover the contingency which has arisen, must be determined in the actual judicial proceedings. We are, however, going to defer consideration of this kind of problem until the latter portion of this book (see chapters 11 and 12). In general, we shall begin with those cases in which the law itself is clear and the only issue is factual. The question is, did Mr. Jones, or did he not, shoot his wife; not whether shooting his wife is an illegal act, nor even whether shooting his wife was first-, second-, third-, or fourth-degree homicide.

I realize that by dealing with cases in which the law is definite and the only problem is factual, I am deviating sharply both from what is taught in law schools and the bulk of what is called "legal scholarship." In law school you learn mainly what the law is, with (at least in the law school I attended) special emphasis on the areas where the law is ambiguous. Indeed, you spend much class time in debating what the law actually is, or should be, in various areas where it is unclear. The examinations at the end of the term characteristically involve giving the student a series of difficult cases in which the professor himself is not absolutely sure of the law, and the student is supposed to make a strong argument for his own point of view. Indeed, in my law school, the professor was supposed to reserve his very best grades for those students who argued that the law was different from what the professor had thought but did so in an extremely convincing and brilliant manner.

Legal scholarship is very largely devoted either to attempts to determine what the law is with respect to some given point, or to urging that the law be changed. I suspect that this primary focus of legal scholarship is one of the basic reasons that the law schools—taught, almost by definition, by legal scholars—concentrate so heavily on these problems.[1]

I have no great quarrel (although, as I shall mention in a moment, I do have a minor quarrel) with this concentration for either legal scholarship or legal training. It would be almost impossible, for example, to train lawyers in the facts of individual cases, because the cases they are going to try have not yet occurred. However, they can be taught the law which covers a large number of cases, and then, when the cases come up to them in practice, apply that general rule.

My only quarrel with this has to do with the absence of training in the actual determination of the fact in a scientific or empirical sense. I would like to have the students in our law schools, in addition to studying the legal rules, be given courses on fingerprints, ballistic identification, statistical theory with applications to detection of forged signatures, etc. I realize that these matters are not relevant in most law cases. It is also true, however, that any given individual legal rule is not relevant in most law cases; and it seems to me that some time devoted to these subjects in law school would pay off as well, or better, than the courses we now have on individual legal rules.

The concentration on the legal situation where the law is vague or muddled is, in the better law schools, perhaps overdone; but, still, it is not by any means an irrational concentration. It is my opinion—and this is based on discussion with lawyers—that most of the legal problems which turn up in court are fairly simple and straightforward. Cases where there is real doubt as to the law, or where there is some possibility that a brilliant legal argument might change the law, are relatively rare.

Note that we are very fortunate that this is true. If the law actually were vague enough so that most of the time most people did not know what the law was, it could not perform its social control role very well. To obey the law, or, for that matter, to carry out a contract, one must first know what the law is or what the contract says. If the law or the contract is vague, so that even skilled legal counsel cannot say with certainty what your legal duties are, then you are prevented from implementing the law by simple ignorance.

It is true, however, that on occasion the law will be unclear with respect to a given subject. In my opinion, even though this is rather rare in Anglo-Saxon practice, it could be made more rare; but the fact remains that we will never be able to draft a law code such that every single thing which *could* occur will be either unambiguously legal or unambiguously illegal. Hence, lawyers should receive at least some training on what to do in cases where the law is unclear. Whether they should be trained to argue for change in the law is not quite so clear, because it is not really obvious that this is a good way to change the law. I should like, however, to postpone discussion of this problem until much later (see chapter 12). I realize that from the conventional standpoint, I have just waved a red flag in front of a bull and then quietly announced that he may not charge for another two hundred pages; but, after all, it is my book, and I think that organizationally it works out better this way.

Nevertheless, although I have no objection to students in law school or legal scholars dealing with the problems with which they now deal, the bulk of this book is to be devoted to determination of what happened *in fact* with respect to some area in which the law is clear. I should like to emphasize that this is not because I believe the law is always clear, but because I want to talk about one thing at a time; the trial of the fact is an important issue, and it is one which I believe has been underemphasized in most discussions of jurisprudence.

For those lawyers who are primarily interested in legal problems rather than factual problems, however, the book (and even the portion on the trial of the fact) still will hold considerable interest. The tools I am going to develop for analysis of the determination by the court of what actually happened can (and will) be used for a discussion of the problems of determining what the law is, or urging that the law be changed, or last but by no means least, for constitutional problems. In any event, I shall devote a good deal of time to trial of the fact and turn to other matters only later.

Before turning to the substance of the book, however, a brief digression is necessary to explain what I am *not* talking about. This book is not a contribution to that branch of legal "learning" called the law of evidence or the law of procedure. Indeed, it is not only not a part of it, it is an attack on it. It is my opinion that the bulk of the procedural rules used in Anglo-Saxon courts are useless or positively perverse. I prefer the procedure used on the continent of Europe to the Anglo-Saxon procedure, but I believe that even the former can be improved. Further, I should say that, in my opinion, the courts of arbitration which now handle much of the litigation connected with international trade use better methods. This may rather shock some of the people participating in these courts, because the courts do make a pretense of following the official procedure of the country in which they sit, to make certain that the regular courts of law will enforce their decisions. However, in my opinion, this is almost entirely a pretense, and the actual functioning of the arbitral courts is different.

As one bit of evidence for my view that the procedure is radically different, former Supreme Court Justice Arthur Goldberg refused a presidential appointment on the grounds that in six months time he was to preside over a major international arbitration proceeding, and he had to devote full time to preparing for it. Whoever heard of a judge in an Anglo-Saxon court (or, for that matter, a Continental court) who devoted six months to the preparation of a case.[2] Indeed, under Anglo-Saxon procedure, this would probably be regarded as extremely improper, since the judge would certainly have fairly strong opinions—which would be called bias when the case actually came up before him.

Nevertheless, the arbitration tribunals in England and the United States do make some pretense of applying Anglo-Saxon procedure, and I suppose this pretense is necessary; hence, I do not expect the professionals who earn their living in these courts to publicly admit that their methods are radically different from those of our standard court system. What is needed here, as almost everywhere else in the law, is empirical research done by people whose own careers are not in any way likely to be affected if the results of their research annoys judges.

To return to my basic point, Anglo-Saxon procedure descends historically from trial by battle, and to this day it is largely devoted to assuring "fairness" between the parties. This fairness is largely defined in terms of various antique customs, but the courts occasionally introduce new rules. So far as I can see, there is no scientific backing for either the older procedures or the new ones, although the judges do occasionally make statements about how a given rule, either an old one or a new one, is justified because it somehow or other contributes to "fair" trials. Of course, the judges themselves have never been trained in scientific method and, for that matter, they tend to be elderly men.

In my case, I am not very much interested in "fairness" if that word is defined as "in accord with certain ancient customs." The objectives at which I think legal procedure should aim are accuracy and low cost. As we shall see later, it is possible to join these two objectives together in a joint function, and the purpose of any procedural rule should be to maximize this function or, putting it more accurately, to minimize the costs inflicted on society by incorrect decisions, together with the cost of the decisions themselves.

Some people feel that courts should not simply try to maximize accuracy but should be biased in one way or another. Continental courts, for example, are supposed to decide in favor of the accused in criminal cases if there is doubt. The somewhat more pragmatic Anglo-Saxons use the less generous "reasonable doubt" criterion for the same situation. This clearly expresses a desire that the proceedings be biased in favor of the accused. It is not obvious from the use of these slogans that the proceedings *are* biased in any particular way, but at least there are many people who think this kind of bias should exist.

Most people, when asked, would say that civil procedures should not be so biased but should simply come out in favor of whichever party has the preponderance of the evidence on his side. Notably, the American courts have muddled this particular rule by adding the word "fair" so that it is "a *fair* preponderance of the evidence." Either the "fair" is redundant or it means that the preponderance has to be somewhat more than simply 50.0001 percent of the evidence. Unfortunately, the rule does not tell you what to do if you do not have a "fair" preponderance either way.

Apparently, from empirical work, American courts do in fact feel— even if they do not say—that there should be some bias in favor of the defendant in civil proceedings, too. What little empirical evidence there is on this matter is discussed below (see p. 80), but the reader may wish to contemplate his own feelings if Mr. A is suing Mr. B for $100,000, and the evidence is such that, although there is just a hair indicating Mr. A is right, it is not greatly different from flipping a coin. I suspect that the reader would be strongly inclined to decide for B under these circumstances; but this is an appeal to introspection on the part of the reader and I cannot be sure what the outcome will be.

Whether such bias should or should not be introduced into the proceedings is a separate issue and will be dealt with later (see chapter 5). For the moment, we shall simply assume that pure accuracy, together with minimized costs, are the only objectives, because that is simpler. Discussing the introduction of bias adds another complication, and hence it is best deferred until the simplest model has been outlined.

The reader will no doubt notice that I am setting aside one of the major costs of inaccurate enforcement of the law, and that is the fact that the law will be violated. Currently, I am contemplating suing someone for breach of contract. I have not positively decided to do so, although in my opinion the breach is glaring, because I am not convinced that the benefit to me, discounted by the possibility that the court will go wrong, is great enough to pay for the trouble to which the proceeding would put me. In all probability, the basic reason I face this breach of contract is that the other party to the contract realized that I would be in this position and, therefore, if his breach was not completely *safe*, it was not desperately dangerous.

Clearly this is a case where the combination of cost and inaccuracy of the courts inflicts some "social cost." If we all knew that our contracts would be costlessly and accurately enforced, we could enter into many more contracts and get better performance than we now do; hence, our society would be richer. Similarly, if all laws were accurately and costlessly enforced, there would be no cases of people violating the laws because they thought they could get away with it. Thus, inaccuracy or cost does indeed inflict high costs on society in addition to those directly involved in court procedure. Nevertheless, in this book, I am going to confine myself to minimizing the sum of the cost of the proceedings and the cost of the error.

This is not because I feel that the failure of enforcement of the law due to the cost and inaccuracy of the proceedings is unimportant, but simply because this book is about legal proceedings themselves. Further, insofar as we can get the cost of proceedings down and the accuracy up, we make it more likely that people will proceed to court, either in cases of contract breach or tort or criminal action, and less likely that people will breach contracts or commit torts or crimes. Thus, there is a very large "external" saving from improving the efficiency of the courts and, indeed, it is this saving that we really aim at when we talk about improving courts and the proceedings.

It is clear that the reason we have courts is not that we want people to be convicted of crimes, but that we want people not to commit them. The whole procedure of the law is one, essentially, of threatening people with unpleasant consequences if they do things which are regarded as objectionable. The more credible the threat, the less likely it is that they will breach contract, behave carelessly with respect to other people's lives or property, or commit crimes. And it is the change in the likelihood that they will engage in this kind of antisocial behavior that justifies the law.

In general, then, we are dealing with a system in which a threat is made to control people's behavior. The severity of the threat and the likelihood that whatever unpleasant consequences threatened will in fact occur are, of course, taken into account by the people whose behavior is to be controlled; and it is this response on their part to the threat which is the real justification of the law.

But this is a discussion of the motives for the substance of the law. In this book, I propose to discuss the procedure by which we decide whether, in any particular case, the threat should be actualized by imposing whatever unpleasant consequence is called for upon a given person. He may, after all, not be the man who murdered Mrs. Jones. If he is not, then imposing the sanction on him in not very helpful, because at least one person—the person who *did* murder Mrs. Jones—knows that the actual crime was performed safely.

It could be argued, and in a way Chinese jurisprudential practice did point in this direction, that it is not so important to actually catch the criminal as it is to convince people that you have caught the criminal. Hence, the court and punishment procedure should be basically a propaganda exercise aimed at intimidating potential criminals rather than an effort to achieve accuracy. There is something to be said for this point of view; but unless a good deal of accuracy is built into the process, the intimidation procedure will not work. If every time a murder is committed, someone is selected at random, given a formal trial, and a spectacular public execution, it seems likely that, with time, the secret would come out and a great many people would realize that they do not really jeopardize their own lives very much by committing murder.

In any event, ignoring this particular issue, this book is devoted almost entirely to the problem of getting courts to behave accurately and to do so at a relatively low cost. It should be noted, however, that the problem is really not entirely the courts. The problem is the entire system of justice. No matter how accurate the courts, if the case is not brought before them, the sanctions required by the law will not be imposed. Thus, if the police fail to catch a burglar, this has the same effect on the threat potential of the law as would a court error which released him. In general, in our legal system, the police can only make this kind of negative error and not a positive error. They may arrest the wrong person and may even fabricate evidence against him, but the error of convicting him is an error on the part of the court, not on the part of the police. The error of not catching him, however, is characteristically a failure of the police.

There are some exceptions to this. Judge Sirica, to a considerable extent, took personal charge of the investigation of the Watergate cases, appointing his own expert witnesses and holding preliminary hearings which were intended to produce evidence which would later be used in the prosecution. The appellate court in Washington also took a strong role in this preliminary investigation, ordering the prosecuting attorney to undertake a totally impossible task, i.e., preventing Jack Anderson from obtaining secret information.[3] They also ordered him to press on with the prosecution, which was something that he could do.

Nevertheless, this is quite unusual. Normally, the actual investigation and initiation of prosecution is carried on by one group of officials, and then the final decision is made by another, at least in Angio-Saxon countries. In the continental countries, the procedure is different, in that the preliminary investigation for important crimes is carried on by an official who is sort of halfway between the policeman and a judge; and, in a way, the first judicial proceeding in which "pure" judges are involved is sort of halfway between our trial and our appeal.

A few words now about the general structure of the book. First, it will be basically an exercise in pure theory. This is not because I am particularly enamored of pure theory but because the necessary statistical and other empirical bases for a less theoretical work are not available. It does, however, seem undesirable that all work be theoretical, and I sincerely hope that my book will inspire both its friends and enemies to do empirical work in the area. Of course, there is room for much more theoretical work, also. Indeed, it seems to me the whole field of legal procedure would benefit from a good deal of scientific attention.

It is now only a few years since a truly scientific approach to the law began, essentially by a colonization of legal studies by economists, and so far there has been very little concern with procedure in these studies. It is my intent to expand the existing work in the economics of substantive law into the economics of legal procedure.

Of course, just because I believe there should be more scientific study of the law, and that much of what scientific study has been done, has been done by economists, does not imply that only economists are qualified to study the law in a scientific way. In fact, I would very much favor people from other disciplines examining the law as well. The lawyers themselves are usually quite intelligent people and can, with a little care and retooling, do excellent scientific work. They have indeed done so—for example, the work of Richard Posner and Kenneth Dam. Still, at the moment, most of the people doing work of a scientific nature in the field of law are either economists or people under very strong economics influence. I think this is essentially an accident coming from the personal interests of various economists and a certain number of lawyers. The fact that for many years the University of Chicago Law School always had an economist on its faculty may be important. There is no intrinsic reason why, let us say, physicists should not have become interested in court proceedings by way of a concern with physical evidence and then proceeded to a wider approach. Actually, this has not happened, but I hope it will happen in the future.

The basic structure of the book, then, is theoretical; and we will follow the usual procedure in theoretical works, starting with very simple models and gradually complicating them to make them more realistic. I have already mentioned that we will begin by assuming that in our lawsuits, the only problem is one of fact and only turn to problems of legal interpretation later. Thus, we shall start with a set of extremely simple models, in which the court is called on only to determine what actually happened. We will then complicate these models, making them more realistic, and consider, on the basis of these models, various conceivable court structures and various possible improvements in procedure. When we have completed the discussion of determination of the facts, we will turn to the problem of interpretation and of supplementing the law where it is vague or even completely absent. Then we will turn to an area which is important mainly, but not exclusively, in American jurisprudence. This is the situation in which the court decides it does not like the law and changes it.

There is, of course, no strong reason why the writing and changing of laws should be allocated to the legislature rather than to the courts, and, historically, we can find about as many cases in which law has been changed by courts as by legislatures. Historically, of course, the common case is that the law is written by the absolute despot with advice of judicial officials. However, if we turn to democratic systems, the judges, the executive, and the legislature all can be involved in the matter.

It is an interesting fact that a number of legal systems have been developed by essentially private citizens. Roman law was largely developed by the *juris consults*, who were not government employees. They gave advice on specific cases, but, rather more importantly, wrote books and essays which shaped the law. An even more extreme example is Muslim law, where the law itself is essentially a development from the Koran and the Haddith and was developed by theologians. Many of the theologians concerned did become *kadi* (judges), but their effect on the law was largely through their writings and teachings and not their actual decisions. Further, many of the most influential jurists in this tradition were not in fact members of a court.

A somewhat similar phenomenon occurred in New England, where the religious theocracies which governed the early colonies attempted to apply the Mosaic law, which was, in essence, an effort to use the Bible as the basic legal text, with theologically trained ministers acting as the principal source of legal knowledge.

Our last topic will be constitutional law; i.e., the role of the court in interpreting and enforcing the Constitution. We will also deal with the role which the court seems to have in changing the Constitution; and, last but not least, we will discuss a subject rather rarely dealt with—protecting the Constitution from the courts.

But all of these matters are dealt with at greater length elsewhere. Meanwhile, let me finish this introductory chapter by citing any imaginary case, which can be used to illustrate the points made above. The National Widget Company, a company which (as its title implies) manufactures widgets, has entered into a contract with Associated Builders, a contracting firm, for the construction of a factory. The factory has now been completed, but there is a dispute between National Widget and Associated Builders. National Widget maintains that the factory does not meet the agreed-upon specifications, and therefore they do not wish to accept delivery and pay for it. Associated Builders is suing. The court then has the factual problem of whether or not the factory is indeed up to the specifications for which provision was made in the contract.

It could be that the factory is up to specifications, but National Widget is unwilling to take delivery because business conditions have changed and they do not need the factory, or it could be that the factory indeed is not up to specifications and Associated Builders is making a false claim. The court must investigate the characteristics of the completed factory, and this may not be easy. For example, suppose that National Widget alleges that the foundations under the factory have cracked. The cracks, if any, are now covered by a heavy structure. National Widget introduces as evidence the testimony of a former employee of Associated Builders who alleges that he saw the cracks and was ordered by his supervisor to cover them over so that they would not be visible. Associated Builders maintains that the employee was fired for drunkenness on the job, and his supervisor denies the entire tale.

The cost of cutting into the existing structure in order to find out by physical means whether he is speaking the truth is high and, indeed, might damage the foundations severely enough so that the building would not be usable. Clearly, the problem is a difficult one, and it is not likely that the court will reach a correct solution every time cases of this difficulty arise. Nevertheless, what we are interested in is the method for dealing with such problems, and we will be able to demonstrate that there are theoretical arguments which would indicate that some types of procedure are better than others.

Note, once again, that the importance of this kind of decision lies not only in the individual case itself but also in its effect on people who are deciding whether or not to enter into contracts. There clearly are very considerable savings if a manufacturing company can enter into a contract with a builder to build a building for it, rather than attempting to find an existing building, put up on speculation, which would more or less fit the company's needs. The more certain the parties are that the contract in fact will be carried out as written, the more willing they are to enter into such a contract. Thus, the more efficient the courts in enforcing contracts, the larger the net saving to society from the implementation of sensible contracts. Still, in this book, we are mainly going to talk about the procedure, and are mainly interested in whether or not it reaches a correct decision at relatively low cost in a given case. The reason we are interested in this is because good enforcement of the law means that the law is rarely broken; but that is a distant, and not an immediate, objective for our investigations.

Chapter 2

The Simplest Model

I have promised that we would begin with very simple models and proceed from there. Let us begin with the simplest of all models: assume that God steps down from on high and provides a correct solution to all law cases at zero cost to the parties. By "correct" I mean that decision which would be made by an all-wise, all-knowing God, who would, of course, know everything that had happened, and would make all the correct legal deductions. Clearly, we are not going to get anything which remotely approximates such a procedure in the real world, but we can learn a little bit by investigating this simple system. Later, we will complicate it by assuming costs and errors in the determination of cases. In this model, then, a voluntary breach of contract or voluntary commission of a crime would occur only through miscalculation by the perpetrator,[1] or because the penalty inflicted on the person who broke the contract or committed the crime was, in his view, less than the advantage.

This, then, raises the question of the optimal penalty for whatever has occurred—breach of contract, tort, or a crime. There are two different basic rules for determining this penalty. The first is simply that the victim of whatever misconduct is alleged should be made whole, i.e., be repaid in full for whatever damages suffered. In the case of murder, this is a little difficult; but for other crimes, it is at least conceptually possible.

The second possibility is that the penalty should be so designed as to make the crime, breach of contract, or tort unwise ex ante—it should be larger than the gain the violater would expect from his violation.[2] With our perfect court, the two make relatively little difference. If the penalty is large enough to prevent the violation, then there is no need to make the victim whole; hence, we should not concern ourselves with whether the damage the victim would have suffered if he *had* been subject to the crime (or breach of contract) would be greater than the amount which is taken from the perpetrator. Once again, the problem would not be so easy in the case of a murder,[3] but basically there would be no contract violation, crime, etc., except possibly through miscalculation on the part of the perpetrator. Hence, this problem would be either nonexistent or very minor.

The other possible relationship—i.e., when the injury to the victim of the contract breach, crime, etc., is *less* than the benefit to the perpetrator—is different. In this case, the crime, contract breach, or tort is actually a socially desirable act. Suppose, for example, that National Widget refuses to accept delivery of the factory because, due to a fall in the market for widgets, the cost to National Widget of taking delivery will be something on the order of $100,000. As a matter of fact, Associated Builders has another customer who would be willing to take the building at only $25,000 less than the price National Widget has contracted to pay. Under these circumstances, an agreement between Associated Builders and National Widget, under which National Widget pays Associated Builders somewhere between $25,000 and $100,000 to be relieved of the contract, is clearly in the interests of both parties. Thus, imposing upon National Widget a $100,000 damage payment, because that is the amount necessary to deter them from violating their contract, would be undesirable because the contract should be violated.

In all of these cases in which the amount necessary to deter the action is greater than the damage suffered by the victim, a bargain between the two parties is at least theoretically feasible, and a court policy imposing a sufficient penalty to deter the tort-feasor, criminal, contract breacher, etc., from his act would simply change the terms of the bargain. Thus, granted we had access to a perfect decision-making procedure, presumably we would select making the plaintiff whole as our measure of penalty exacted rather than a sum sufficient to deter the act. In those cases where this sum will be higher than the deterrence payment, the act will not occur anyway, and therefore the amount will make no difference; in those cases where it is lower, this is a more efficient solution.

But now let us complicate our model a little bit by assuming that there is some cost. God requires that His services in any case be rewarded by a sacrifice. To be realistic, let us assume that the cost of this sacrifice is about 75 percent of whatever is at issue. This 75 percent is only realistic for American judicial proceedings; with the European procedure, it would be lower.

Briefly, I might explain how I obtain the 75 percent. I have been assured by practicing lawyers that, as a rule of thumb, each party to a lawsuit will pay about one-third of the amount in question in legal fees, etc. This gives us 66.66 percent, and since the state in fact pays many costs connected with legal proceedings, I have rounded up to 75 percent. This is probably a reasonable estimate of the cost of legal proceedings in the United States, but it is not precise. Here, as in almost every other area of the investigation of the law, we have an absence of high-quality empirical data.

To discuss the impact of these costs, we have to decide how they are allocated. Note that if the whole thing were paid for by the state, then—from the standpoint of the parties—the procedure would be cost-less. Their tax bill would be increased as a result of a proceeding, but in most cases the increase for one case will be imperceptibly small to the parties. With the state paying the cost, then—from the standpoint of the parties—it is identical to our zero-cost case. Let us therefore turn to those cases in which the cost is borne by the parties directly.

There are basically two ways to allocate the cost. One of them is used in the United States—where the parties each bear their own costs—and the other in England—where the loser must pay not only his own costs but "reasonable costs" for the winner.[4] Let us begin with the American system. Assume, then, that the factory has been properly constructed, but National Widget refuses to accept delivery or pay for it, alleging that there is some technical defect in its construction. Associated Builders now has the problem of whether or not they should sue. If they do sue, they will net $62,500 after they have collected damages (and remember that the court procedure in this case is divinely accurate) and paid their share of the costs of the sacrifice.[5]

If they bring suit, National Widget will have to pay out a net of $137,500, consisting of the damage payment of $100,000 (which they will make to Associated Builders) plus their expenses for the very expensive ceremony that is necessary to entice God to make a perfect decision. Clearly, both parties would be benefited by an out-of-court settlement between $62,500 and $137,500. We cannot quarrel with any bargain number which is achieved over this range.

Further, the situation is a little asymmetric. National Widget does not actually have to pay any amount more than $100,000, since they can always decide at the last minute to pay the $100,000 rather than going to court. Thus, the real bargaining range is the distance between $62,500 as payment and $100,000. In other words, Associated Builders is apt to (although not certain to) end up with less than the $100,000 damages which they suffered.

Suppose, then, that the two parties reach an agreement under which National Widget pays Associated Builders $80,000. Is this not a socially optimal outcome? The answer, unfortunately, is emphatically No. Clearly the two parties presented with the situation we have described are better off with this settlement than they would be going to court, so we cannot blame them for reaching this agreement. Further, it is clear that National Widget has saved $20,000 by its refusal to accept delivery of the factory, and so it is hard to argue that it has behaved in an irrational way.[6] Thus, the parties are behaving quite sensibly when they take the actions which lead to the outcome we have described.

Looked at from the standpoint of society as a whole—and indeed from that of the two parties themselves ex ante—this is an inefficient outcome. The fact that at the time the two parties drafted the contract they knew that this could happen surely means that the contract itself would not be as well designed from the standpoint of maximizing total savings as it would have been in our previous circumstance in which the enforcement was costless. Further, no doubt the fact that a certain number of contracts will end in this kind of settlement means that some marginal contracts will not be entered into because the present discounted possibility of this kind of thing occurring makes them unprofitable.

This, however, does not exhaust the social costs inflicted by the possibility of this kind of out-of-court settlement. The settlement is not in itself a costless activity. The strategic maneuvering between the two parties over what is really quite a large sum of money (the $37,500 which is the effective bargaining range) can be very costly. The man who does the negotiating for National Widget, for example, must devote a lot of time and energy to convincing the representative of Associated Builders that he in fact is going to go to court. The Associated Builders representative, on the other hand, must be good at seeing through this kind of thing and in predicting the occasions upon which court proceedings actually will occur.

Further, it should be pointed out that in many cases the court proceedings will occur in spite of being negative-sum. From the standpoint of both parties to this particular negotiation, establishing credibility of threats for possible future negotiations can be quite important and can completely outweigh the costs and benefits of this particuar litigation.

If National Widget can establish a general reputation that it normally *does* go to court, whether its case is just or unjust, it will have many more favorable out-of-court settlements. Of course counterbalancing this—from the standpoint of National Widget—is the fact that it may be harder for it to enter into contracts.

Similarly, from the standpoint of Associated Builders, going to court, even though it is going to cost a great deal of money, may be desirable from the standpoint of impressing future opponents in this kind of bargaining that it *will* fight to the last spasm, and therefore they had better pay up. Nevertheless, the net effect of this strategic maneuvering is likely to be a significant social cost and an eventual settlement which is less than the amount properly due to Associated Builders.

What we see here is that the payment which will be extracted by the court proceedings may be sufficient to deter violation of the contract, torts, and crimes, but the cost of entering into the court proceedings may be great enough to deter the potential plaintiff, complainant, etc., from going to court. If this is so, the law is not enforced. The plaintiff fails to bring the action or settles out of court for less than is rightly due to him, because that is the best thing from his standpoint, and the tort-feasor, contract breacher, or criminal commits his illegal acts because he can predict in advance that the plantiff will behave that way.[7]

What we need is a system of deterring violations of the law, and this system requires a method of rewarding people for taking action to punish the person who has violated the law, simply because that is the only way to get people to undertake the action. The English system, in which people who produce evidence of criminal activity are frequently paid, is an obvious step in this direction.

Here, however, we are going to confine ourselves to a simpler procedure, once again drawn from England, in which instead of the cost being split between the two parties, as it is in the United States, the loser of the lawsuit pays the entire "reasonable" cost. It should be emphasized that this rule seems a great deal better when the court always reaches the right decision through Divine wisdom than it would with the real court;

but, nevertheless, it has advantages, even assuming a sizable error term in court proceedings.

Let us consider briefly how it would work in our present, divinely ordained, and perfect court. Assume that National Widget does not wish to accept the factory and makes false statements about its not being up to specifications. Associated Builders brings an action, and National Widget now has the choice of paying $100,000 (which they justly owe) right now, or paying $100,000 plus $75,000 in costs after legal action. Obviously, they will pay the $100,000. There will be no bargaining costs because there is no motive for Associated Builders to accept any amount less than $100,000; the only threat available to National Widget is to proceed with lawsuits which will cost Associated Builders nothing and will mean that National Widget has to pay $175,000. Thus, the problems we have discussed above are eliminated by this rather simple reform.

Unfortunately, as we go through our analysis, we will discover that the matter is not nearly as simple as it appears here. First, the mere fact that courts are not perfectly accurate raises at least some doubts. If Malefactor brings a false suit against Poor-But-Honest and wins, we are particularly offended if Poor-But-Honest not only has to pay an unjust judgment but also has to pay Malefactor's legal fees. Second, and rather more important, for the system to work effectively, we have to have some measure of "reasonable" legal expenditures, and, as we will see below, this is not an easy task. Nevertheless, it does seem likely that the rule that the loser pays the winner's legal fees would work better than splitting the legal fees between the two parties. More of this later—indeed, much later.

There are two other problems. First, the rule that the loser must pay the winner's legal costs has little or no effect on the behavior of a person whose total assets are not large enough to pay these costs.[8] Thus, in the above example, if National Widget were on the verge of bankruptcy and its management felt confident that it would not be able to pay the $75,000, the threat of exacting this money would be a pointless one.

The problem is probably quite important in those cases in which an impecunious plaintiff sues a large and wealthy corporation. In the United States, he could probably get a young lawyer, whose time is not worth a great deal, to take the case and, thus, inflict great costs on the corporation. This would continue to be true, even under the "English" payment system, unless the payment were interpreted as something other than cash; for example, the bringer of a false suit, or the defender of a correct suit who lost and could not pay the full cost of the suit, would be jailed for an appropriate period. However, this would be a radical change.

As a second point to be made here, we should note that it is not strictly necessary that the loser of the suit pay the full legal costs of the case. We need two things: first, that the party who is right has motives to hold fast and therefore take his part in enforcing the law; and, second, that the party who is in the wrong faces costs which are higher than those which he would pay if he simply carries out the law. There are many institutions which may lead to this combination. For example, the entire cost of the proceeding could be borne by the taxpayers, and the loser be fined, in addition to whatever damages he pays under the proceedings, the sum of $1,000. The reader can no doubt think of half-a-dozen other sets of payments, fines, and subsidies which would lead to the same outcome.

So far we have been assuming that the court, although costly, is perfect. Let us now reverse field and assume that God no longer requires an elaborate ceremony but, rather capriciously, has decided to add an element of randomness to His decisions. Thus, legal costs vanish but the proceedings are not perfectly accurate. Specifically, He first makes up His mind as to which side is right and then throws an eight-sided die. If this die shows up "1," He announces His decision as being directly opposite to His decision as to who is in the right; and if the die shows any other number, He announces His decision as whatever He had decided was the right decision. We need not concern ourselves with why God has chosen this method; after all, His mental processes are not fully comprehensible to mere human minds.

This would mean that in one-eighth of the cases, the decision would be wrong. The one-eighth is partially arbitrary and partially an effort to duplicate conditions in the United States. Once again, there are very little and very poor empirical data on the accuracy of our court system, and what there is in this area will be discussed in the next chapter. To anticipate the discussion, however, these rather poor data do suggest that our courts go wrong about one time in eight. Although the data are poor, we can use one-eighth for illustrative purposes.

Once again, assume that National Widget is refusing to accept delivery improperly. Under these circumstances, if Associated Builders sues, the present discounted value of their claim is $87,500. A settlement at that level would be desirable from the standpoint of both parties and from the standpoint of risk minimization. Reversing the problem, assuming that the Associated Builders claim lacks merit, it nevertheless has an ex ante value of $12,500.

To anticipate briefly the discussion of the next chapter, actual error in the courts is quite complex and our very simple model here only approximates it rather vaguely. Nevertheless, we can get some information from considering this type of error rather than the more complex error form, which, as we shall soon see, characterizes actual court proceedings.

It would appear that this inaccuracy of the Divine judgment could be easily taken care of by simply adjusting the size of the judgments. For example, if Associated Builders won, they would receive a sum which properly discounted the fact that they were only going to win seven times in eight when they are in the right. Unfortunately, this would mean that if they lost, they would have to pay a similar sum, and this sum would have to be calculated to deter people from bringing an action which is known to be false with the intent of winning one time in eight. The losing party would have to pay the winning party $16,667 in addition to either making a $100,000 payment if the winner is the plaintiff, or making this payment without receiving anything in return if the winner is the defendant.

This seems fairly moderate, but note that it does provide a bargaining range. thus, negotiations could take place, and the social costs would be present here, too. Further, in this case, also, the bargaining range is perverse. The person who is in the wrong, whether it is the defendant wrongfully refusing to pay damages or a plaintiff wrongfully making a claim, can terminate the proceedings by either paying up or dropping his claim just before the court proceedings; hence, he is able to control whether or not the two parties are put into a situation of risk. If the party in the right is risk averse, he probably would be willing to pay at least something to avoid that problem. Nevertheless, although there are difficulties here, adding these additional payments to take into account the error of the process improves its efficiency.

So far as I know, there are no cases in the real world in which this is done. The only thing that resembles it is the plea-bargaining process in criminal action. It may be (although I would hate to argue that this is so) that the sentence which would be given to a man who "copped" a plea is the socially correct sentence under conditions of certainty, and that the higher sentence which would be given to him if he takes the chance of going to trial is designed to discount the possible inaccuracy of the trial process. Once again, although this is possible, I would hate to be quoted as saying it is certain.

Let us now combine our two models. Let us suppose that God not only engages in dice throwing but also requires the ceremony. Let us also retain the assumption that the entire cost of the ceremony falls upon whoever loses the case. Then, if National Widget refuses delivery erroneously and is sued, it has seven chances in eight of having to pay $175,000 and a one in eight chance of paying nothing. The present discounted value of this combination is $153,125, which certainly seems worse than paying out the $100,000. On the other hand, the present discounted value to Associated Builders of bringing suit is equal to seven-eighths of $100,000 plus a one in eight chance of actually having to pay out $75,000. The ex ante discounted value of this combination is $78,125.

Clearly, it is to the benefit of both parties to settle at any price between these limits, and, once again, the asymmetry produced by the fact that the person who is in the wrong can always choose at the last minute not actually to go through with the case provides him with some bargaining advantage. The bargaining advantage can perhaps be seen more clearly if we assume that it is a false claim. The false claimant would have a seven in eight chance of having to pay out $75,000 and a one in eight chance of receiving $100,000, or a net cost in discounted terms of $53,125. The discounted cost of this to the defendant in this case is $21,000, that being a seven in eight chance of getting nothing and a one in eight chance of having to pay out $175,000.

Note in all of these cases that, assuming your opponent fights, there is never any motive to bring a false claim or failing to pay a good claim. This is because we are placing the cost of the proceeding on the loser. If we split the cost evenly between the two parties, which is the American procedure, our numbers work out quite differently. Assume, for example, that Associated Builders is contemplating a false suit against National Widget for $100,000. They have a seven in eight chance of paying out $37,500 and a one in eight chance of receiving $62,500, or a net present discounted value of −$25,000. National Widget, on the other hand, has a seven in eight chance of paying out $37,500 plus a one in eight chance of paying out $137,500, or a net present discounted value of the suit of

−$49,375. A settlement in which the false claimant does reasonably well would seem to be not impossible, and certainly a good deal of resource waste in bargaining and unnecessary lawsuits might be expected.

Of course, it is possible to calculate a sum of money which could be paid to allow for the inaccuracy of the system and the cost, a number equivalent to that mentioned when we were discussing the costless but inaccurate model, and which has the same characteristics as the number we computed there. In our present case, this would mean that the payment made by the defendant if he lost the suit would be $204,166, and the payment made by the plaintiff if he lost would be $29,166. These two numbers both work out, so that, assuming that the loser pays the full cost, there is no point in bring a false claim or resisting a correct claim if the parties are risk neutral.

As in the other case, however, the fact that the parties presumably have at least some risk aversion means that some bargaining would be possible. Further, so far as I know, there are no legal systems which overtly attempt to correct for their own inaccuracy by raising the damage payment in this way.

It should be noted that the correction for error in our particular case is rather small, because error is rather infrequent—only one time in eight. If we assume that errors are commoner, then the payments become higher and higher. At an accuracy level of 0.5, the necessary payments to compensate for the inaccuracy of the process go to infinity.

The point is of some interest because a number of economists—Gary Becker comes immediately to mind—have suggested that it might be possible to economize on criminal enforcement costs by lowering the expense of the apparatus which detects crimes and compensate by raising the punishment when the crimes are detected. Since by our measure— how often they are right and how often they are wrong over the entire enforcement procedure—all existing criminal punishments are already less accurate than 0.5, this recommendation might seem to be inconsistent with our calculations.

As a matter of fact, it is not. The Becker proposal implicitly assumes that there is no compensation to the accused when the prosecution fails to establish its case, and certainly no compensation when the police simply fail to catch him. These would be failures in our more complete view of the process. Secondly, Becker more or less assumes that all of the errors are errors of failure to convict, and that punishment of innocent people is either nonexistent or very rare. With these two assumptions, the proposal makes some sense, although in my opinion it is not optimal. In general, however, his proposal is based on a severe bias of the error term. It is assumed that almost all of the errors take the form of failing to detect a criminal or failing to convict him, and only very rarely—if at all—does it take the form of convicting an innocent man. The reduction in the resources used in enforcement in Becker's discussion does not increase the proportion of innocent convictions among total convictions; it simply lowers the total of convictions.

To take roughly realistic figures, suppose that today the police make an arrest for every fortieth burglary, one in five of those arrested are convicted, and one-eighth of those convicted are in fact innocent.[9] Suppose that, under these circumstances, a one-year punishment is thought suitable. If we halved our police investment and, as a result, the police arrested one person for every eighty burglaries, with once again one in five of these being convicted—of whom one in eight were innocent— something on the order of a two-year prison sentence would seem to be called for. This might work out as an economical change in our present procedures, since the saving on police would not be offset by any countervailing cost.[10]

If, however, the reduction in resources took the form of reducing the accuracy of the courts by lowering the resource investment there, or by reducing the accuracy of the police in the sense that they arrested a higher proportion of innocent men, then the above calculations would not apply. Becker has implicitly assumed, and in his particular case it is not a totally unrealistic assumption, that the reduction in resources would only increase the errors on one side—i.e., lack of detection and punishment for crime—and it would not increase the errors on the other side—punishment of people who are in fact innocent. This greatly simplifies the problem, and it makes his simple solution correct. If we are talking about the accuracy of a court system as a whole, with errors possible in *both* directions, then lowering accuracy raises much more difficult problems and does lead to the kind of results discussed in this chapter.

Chapter 3

More on Errors

I began the discussion of the effect of cost and judicial errors on procedure with an extremely unrealistic model. In this chapter, I will attempt to develop a more realistic, albeit still abstract, model of judicial (or jury) errors. Remember that, at the moment, I am talking solely about errors in determining what are the facts, and the decision as to what the law is (or, indeed, whether the law should be changed) is deferred until the latter part of the book.

Here, and throughout the bulk of the book, I will keep a simplifying assumption which is clearly reasonable in the models of chapter 2 but might be thought unduly strict for more general discussion. I will assume that there are only two outcomes of the trial, decision for the plaintiff or decision for the defendant, or in criminal cases, conviction or acquittal. In practice, of course, there are a number of compromise positions available between these two extremes. In regard to the compromises, the assumption follows much the same road as the "only two states of the world" assumption in the Fisherian discussion of risk. It makes life easier but does not change the net effect.

There are some cases in which all possible outcomes cannot be placed on a single dimension between the two extremes. In these cases, a more elaborate mathematical apparatus would be necessary, but since it would not change my basic results, I will not complicate the book by discussing it.

The Fisherian risk assumption is, of course, also a simplification introduced to make the presentation easier. Although it is quite complex to make a general model which deals with continua of outcomes instead of only two, if we turn to any particular case it is generally quite simple to generalize our two-outcome model to the continuous model. Thus, in effect, I am recommending that instead of complicating the model at the very beginning, we use a simple model and only introduce the complications when they are necessary to deal with a real problem. This will greatly ease both the writing and the reading of this book.

I do not suppose that anyone will claim that courts never make errors, or that the evidence is never misleading. Nevertheless, there does not seem to be much theoretical discussion of factual errors in the literature, and therefore it is necessary for me to begin with some rather elementary remarks.

The problem of determining what actually happened is one of the court's duties and the only one we are discussing now.[1] A historic reconstruction, which is what we are now talking about, is a difficult task for a variety of reasons. One is that witnesses lie; and in lawsuits, there usually are at least some witnesses who have a strong motive to lie. They may also simply be mistaken. Another reason is that many things which happen that are of interest to the court leave no physical traces and, indeed, may leave no traces on the minds of the parties. The obvious example of this would be the victim's account of what happened during a murder. The court has no access to this. Further, as a general rule, it has no access to the truthful memory of the accused unless the accused is innocent. Since the court is trying to determine whether the accused is innocent, it should not assume that the accused's testimony is necessarily his correct memory of the event.

There may be physical evidence with respect to the crime, but it is not necessarily easy to interpret. Fingerprints on the gun are a traditional example, although as any reader of murder mysteries knows, they are not 100 percent incontrovertible evidence. There are many other examples. Is the glass of the broken window found inside the house or outside? Is the knife found in the defendant's kitchen the right size and shape to have inflicted the wound found in the body? Are the scrapings taken by the technician from around the base of the blade actually contaminated with human blood and, in particular (although this may be impossible to determine), is that blood the right blood group?

All of these are problems which come up in court; but it should be pointed out that the more difficult case is the one where they do not come up. We are much better off if a knife is found in the kitchen of the defendant and the doctor says it was the type which caused the fatal wound. It is even better if the technician says that the scrapings he took from around the base of the blade contained type O human blood. In many cases, nothing like this is available. Although there is a knife wound in the body, the knife has not been discovered. Even worse, there may be a large number of knives which would fit the wound—and, indeed, this is the normal case—and one of them is found in the possession of the defendant. The defendant testifies that he accidentally cut himself on the knife some time ago, and hence the existence of some human blood in the scrapings is not surprising. In these cases, an effort to reconstruct the past is necessarily subject to considerable uncertainty.

The fact that the most intensively investigated murder cases of which I am aware—the death of Abraham Lincoln and the death of John F. Kennedy—are still subject to a great deal of dispute, indicates how difficult it is to get the actual facts with certainty. As it happens, I have no doubt that John Wilkes Booth killed Lincoln and that Lee Harvey Oswald killed Kennedy; but in neither case is this point of view unanimously held.

Let us, then, concede that different cases have different amounts of evidence of varying quality available, and that this evidence leads us to varying probabilities of reaching the correct decision, as shown on figure 3.1. In this figure, all of the cases are arranged from left to right, from those at the far left, where the evidence is strongest on the side of the truth, to those where it is less strong on the side of the truth and, finally, as line P drops below the 50 percent level, where the evidence is positively misleading. Line P shows the probability—the likelihood—that a court confronted with that particular amount and quality of evidence will reach the correct conclusion. Note here, that when I refer to the correct decision, I do not mean the best decision on the evidence actually presented in court, but the decision that would be reached if the court were all-knowing.

Note that for the cases to the left of X, the court does better than flipping a coin, but for the cases to the right of X, flipping a coin (which would give a 50 percent probability of accuracy) would be better than the court. Unfortunately, the decision as to whether a given case is to the right or left of X is one that we cannot make on the basis of the evidence. In order to decide, we would have to have additional evidence; and, if we had additional evidence, the case would be moved by that additional evidence to some other location on our line. The fact that the court proceeding in some cases is worse than consulting the auspices, or examining the entrails of a dead chicken, is depressing but inevitable. To have a better

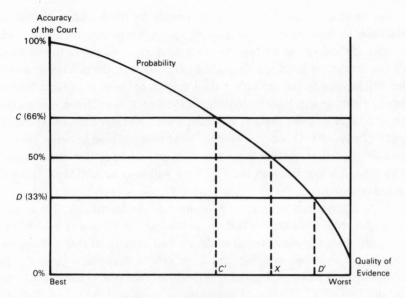

Figure 3.1
Probabilities of Reaching a Correct Decision.

than 50–50 chance for cases to the left of X, it is essential that we take a chance of less than 50–50 odds to the right of X. We hope that line P is fairly high and to the right, although our present empirical evidence does not permit us to say that this is so.

The fact that we have no way to ascertain the probability that the case will be decided correctly does *not* mean that the two parties cannot make probability estimates of the outcome. Thus, assume that some party has a false claim against someone, and the evidence in favor of the false claim is such that he would place it at point C', i.e., he has a 1 in 3 chance of winning the false claim. Both the skilled attorney for the plaintiff and the equally skilled attorney for the defendant may be in agreement as to the odds for the plaintiff's success.

Under these circumstances, if the expected cost of bringing legal proceeding is less than one-third of the likely collections, it is sensible for the plaintiff to sue. Above, I used a rough estimate that American costs are about one-third of the amount in question from each side, and hence those cases which lie to the right of C' (i.e., below C, which is the 66.66 percent line) are those cases in which it would be sensible for a plaintiff to bring suit.

For cases between C' and D', it is sensible for the defendant to defend the case. In these cases, his chances of success are greater than 1 in 3 and he should therefore be willing to put up legal costs equivalent to one-third of the amount at issue. To the right of D', however, the defendant would be well advised to pay up rather than defend, because, even though he is in the right, he will have to pay legal expenses of one-third of the cost of the damages and, for that, he buys *less* than a one-third chance of avoidance of payment. Of course, he may want to settle even between lines C' and D'. All cases outside those two lines should be settled out of court, but a good many between the two lines will also be settled in order to avoid court costs.

Note that we can do this the opposite way. A plaintiff who has a valid claim but who finds the evidence is to the right of D' is well advised not to bring the case, because the odds are bad enough so that the present discounted value of bringing suit is negative. Between D' and C', he would bring the case and anticipate that the other side would defend; and to the left of C', he would threaten to bring suit and find that the defendant paid up without going to court.

The cases brought to court, then, would be those between C' and D'; and we would anticipate that, taking the interval as a whole, the court would go wrong a little less than half the time. The exact proportion of right and wrong times would depend on the curvature of the P line. In cases close to C', it would go wrong *less* than half the time; in cases close to D', it would go wrong *more* than half the time. In the cases to the right of D', it would go wrong more than two-thirds of the time.

In figure 3.2, I have drawn in the P curve for a much more efficient court. In this case, I assume that, one way or another, we have increased the efficiency of the court and that, therefore, it is more accurate in dealing with the cases. It is still true, however, that it is not perfectly accurate and that, in some cases, it faces evidence in which even the superior acuity of this court finds a better than 50–50 chance of going wrong. Once again, assuming that the costs are about one-third of the total at issue, one would anticipate that only cases between C' and D' would be brought before the court. Once again, a little less than half of the cases in this interval would be decided incorrectly.

This result is paradoxical. Increasing the "accuracy" of the court does not significantly change the percentage of the cases it decides correctly. What improving the accuracy of the court does is reduce the number of

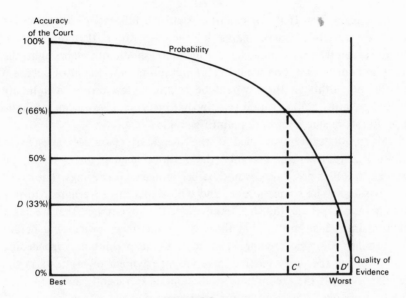

Figure 3.2
Probability of Correct Decision with More Efficient Court.

cases where parties go to court even when they are in the wrong. The movement of C' and D' to the right is the principal payoff. The net effect of switching from a probability line such as that shown in figure 3.1 to that shown in figure 3.2 is that society is better off because the law, contract, etc., is better enforced; but the parties to actual litigation are little affected. Of course, the names of the parties to litigation are changed. If we switched from the court shown in figure 3.1 to the court shown in figure 3.2, a number of people who would have chosen to litigate false claims will drop them, and a number of people who would have chosen to pay, even though they were in the right, will choose to litigate; in the extreme case, if C' in figure 3.2 is to the right of D' in figure 3.1, they will find themselves not even bothered by the false claim.

Note that this argument provides fairly strong support for the appropriate use of public funds to improve accuracy. The principal beneficiaries of the improvement of accuracy are not the parties who actually litigate but the parties who are spared litigation by the improvement in accuracy. They should, therefore, be willing to support some of the cost.

But to say that public funds should be used to support accuracy in litigation is radically different from saying that the government should pay people's legal fees. If it, for example, paid the full cost of litigation for any plaintiff with a charge against a large corporation, then there would be no reason why any claim, false or genuine, should not be brought; the total amount of litigation would be immense—even in the most accurate court, and, although there would be relatively few errors in a highly accurate court, the fact would remain that bringing false claims would be a profitable business for both plaintiffs and lawyers.

This result can be avoided if the increased resources invested in improving accuracy do not take the form of paying the costs of the parties. Another possibility would be preliminary proceedings. The party who wishes to sue someone else, and who wants the government to pay his lawyer's expenses, first has to convince the government that he has a valid claim, which means that there is a preliminary proceeding before the regular court proceeding. The cost of the preliminary proceeding would fall on the party seeking government payment of his costs in the regular court. If the preliminary proceeding is sufficiently accurate, then the total amount of bad litigation is reduced. On the whole, however, it seems silly to have two litigation procedures, the first of which involves attracting the attention of the government-provided fee-paying service and convincing them that you have a good case, and then taking the good case to court. Presumably, people would bring cases to the subsidy agency up to the point where the present discounted value of bringing such cases is equivalent to the probability that they will be subsidized *times* the probability that it will be successful *times* the probable gains or loss-avoidance.

In practice, most of the institutions under which someone pays the fees of plaintiff or defendant involve a preliminary proceeding, in which the plaintiff or defendant does not use a lawyer to plead his case. Thus, there is reduction in the amount of resources invested in such a case. Further, there is usually a good deal of sitting on hard chairs, waiting, being polite to lawyers, secretaries, and office boys, etc., which eliminates a large number of possible claimants. The result of this may be that the total resources invested in these cases is not as great as if individual parties were free to use their resources in the most efficient way to obtain legal subsidies. Since we could apply the same rule in court proceedings, however, it is hard to see why this is an advantage. Indeed, historically, many court systems (the Chinese immediately come to mind) have prohibited the parties from investing very much in the way of resources into the proceedings by prohibiting them from having attorneys.

The reader has doubtless wondered for the last few paragraphs why we are concentrating upon litigation, when so many cases are settled out of court. Settlement out of court involves a decision by both parties that they would rather not go through with the proceeding. To a very large extent, the exact terms of the out-of-court settlement depend on how the costs of the proceeding are allocated and how great they are. Since the costs of the proceedings are to be dealt with in the next chapter, we would like to defer a discussion of out-of-court settlement until then.

I would like now to turn to the problem of measurement of court error. I have earlier offered my estimate that the error term in American courts is somewhere around one-eighth and have emphasized the general poverty of data in this area. I would like now to discuss what data there are. Note that I am not endorsing the research which I report here. I think it is, on the whole, quite inadequate, granted the importance of the matter dealt with. Nevertheless, it is, so far as I can see, the only research in the area which is of any value at all, and I congratulate the researchers for their courage in dealing with a subject which most scholars have shunned.

Many people seem to think that it is in principle impossible to measure the accuracy of the courts, because "you can't tell when they are wrong because there is no way of determining the actual truth except to look at the decision." There are, in fact, a number of possible research designs for testing the accuracy of courts. The first and obvious one would be to rerun the case with a larger commitment of resources, and hence a higher probability of achieving the truth, and to see if this better proceeding reaches the same conclusion as the regular court. In practice, we do just that with respect to points of law: potential errors are referred to a higher court, where they are subject to much larger resource investigation than in the lower court.

The higher courts find that the lower courts are wrong in something like one-fifth of all appeals. One could transfer this 20 percent error term to problems of fact, but there are a number of difficulties. Sometimes appeals, particularly under the European system, are made on facts rather than law, and this would provide a way of checking accuracy of the first court. No one, as far as I know, has collected any statistics along these lines, and there would be very great difficulties—both practical and conceptual in nature—in doing so. Nevertheless, I feel that research of this sort should be undertaken.

A second method for measuring the error term of courts is to arrange that the same case be judged by two different decision-making individuals or bodies. If the two bodies disagree about a given case, one of them must be wrong. If they are in agreement, it is of course possible that both are wrong. If, however, we have statistics showing the number of times that they disagree and we assume that their errors are uncorrelated, it is possible to work out total proportion of errors, including those errors in which both of the decision makers are wrong and hence they agree. If the errors are correlated, as they probably are, then we need to know the degree of correlation to carry out this calculation. Fortunately for the investigator, however, the percentage of errors for a given percentage of disagreements will always be higher if there is correlation between the errors made by the two decision makers than if there is not. The assumption that there is no such correlation then provides a minimum limit on proportion of errors.

For a simple example: a research group in Oxford, England, arranged, in twenty-eight cases, to have a regular jury impaneled and then a second jury of twelve men drawn from the regular jury list to sit in the front row of the spectator's section and listen to the cases. Afterward, both juries went off to deliberate and vote.[2] Of course, only the regular jury's vote was counted in determining the punishment or acquittal of the defendant, and this may have led the other twelve "jurymen" to deliberate a little less seriously.

In any event, in seven of the twenty-eight cases, the two juries disagreed. When we apply our calculation method, it turns out that in a minimum of slightly more than one-eighth of decisions, the jury was in error.[3]

In an earlier study, the University of Chicago jury project tested differences of opinion between judge and jury with respect to the same case. They circulated a questionnaire to judges in which they were asked to mark down the decision of the jury in cases which they had heard and their own decision.[4] They received replies to their questionnaire on about 3,500 cases, surely a large enough sample. Once again, calculations indicate that the difference between judges and juries in evaluating a case can be explained by assuming that about one-eighth of the decisions are in error. Note that there is no way of telling from this data whether it is the judge or the jury which is in error, a problem which seemed to bother Kalven and Zeisel. This is, however, not a matter of very great importance. Many cases in the United States are decided by juries and another large group are decided by judges sitting alone. There is no reason to believe that the judges are more likely to be accurate when sitting alone than when presiding over a jury trial, so presumably their errors are the same in the two groups of trials. Thus the one-eighth, although not a good figure, is still fairly sensible.

The University of Chicago jury project also made up tapes of two law cases. These were genuine cases, but the tapes were put together using professional actors. These tapes were then played for a number of experimental juries under various conditions. The juries disagreed with each other frequently enough so that error terms between one-third and one-half would be needed to explain the difference. I believe that the cases used on the tapes were harder than the normal case. Further, the test juries may not have had the same motivation as regular juries.[5]

Recently a number of investigators in England have examined the accuracy of juries there. The best and most recent of these studies is *Jury Trials* by John Baldwin and Michael McConville.[6] It reports an important piece of research in which the authors compared the decisions of juries with the view (normally expressed before the jury has brought in its decision) of other qualified observers such as, for example, the judge. They also very carefully reviewed the previous work including the work of the University of Chicago Jury Project. The general conclusion is consistent with my one-out-of-eight error estimate, although I believe that they would probably argue for a higher level of error.

These experiments are, as far as I can discover, substantially all of the work that has ever been done to measure empirically error of the courts. I have not concealed my view that they are not perfect, and that the data obtained from them are inherently poor. Nevertheless, I congratulate the University of Chicago jury project (and its imitators in England) for having dared to enter an area thick with taboos. Still, we obviously should have much more research in this area. Indeed, the absence of better data here is evidence of the extremely low scientific level with which study of the courts and of legal procedure has been carried on in the past. I hope that this will change.

It might be thought that although court errors are no doubt deplorable, they do not require any change in the substantive rules of law. The errors could be random and tend to cancel out. Unfortunately, this is not true. The substantive law which would be optimal in the presence of a perfect court system may be suboptimal if there are errors.

To investigate the effect of potential court error on substantive rules, I should like to discuss a particular rule in tort law which has frequently been acclaimed as economically efficient. Janusz A. Ordover, for example, demonstrated that with perfect knowledge (and, in one area, perfect knowledge comes very near to being supernaturally perfect knowledge) the system would indeed be efficient.[7] The rule is that the person who injures another must pay damages if he has taken insufficient precautions to prevent the accident unless the person injured has also taken insufficient precautions.

A number of economists have argued that this rule provides the optimal investment of resources in accident prevention. Although the economists, in general, have done more elaborate mathematical work in the area, the idea is actually a fairly old one in the law. I was taught it in tort law in the 1930s. The lawyers were less mathematical, but no less precise in presenting the argument. I propose to demonstrate that, with errors, the efficiency characteristics vanish. Since errors of calculation either by the parties who are involved in an accident or by the judge and jury will obviously not be zero, the current rules, then, instead of being efficient are inefficient, and we should at least look for some other set of substantive rules which work better in the presence of errors.

Scientific discussion of tort law normally assumes a simple straightforward situation, which is clearly an abstraction from the complexities of the real world. We will follow this custom. It is assumed that there are two parties to a given accident, one of whom is the potential tortfeasor—i.e., the person who caused the accident—and one of whom is the victim, who may or may not also be contributorily negligent. In practice, of course, it may be very difficult to determine which of the two parties "caused" the accident, and there may be more than two parties involved.

For economic analysis, it is assumed that the parties can reduce the probability of accidents by investing resources in accident avoidance. For purposes of analysis, we do not inquire how they invest these resources, we simply assume that they do so efficiently. Since the efficient investment of resources by one party depends to a large extent on exactly what the other party has done, and since many accidents occur between strangers who have never seen each other before, this is a particularly strong assumption. But for the purposes of our current analysis, we can accept it. Note that all these strong assumptions have been made by proponents of the present system. If I can demonstrate that, even on the basis of these strong assumptions, it does not work efficiently in the presence of error or miscalculation, then there is certainly no proof that it would work if we weakened these assumptions.

What then is the current rule in its scientifically sophisticated form? It is really very simple. There is some optimal investment of resources by both parties. This optimal investment minimizes the total costs of the sum of accidents and of accident-prevention activities. For example, if the potential victim invests more resources than the optimum amount, there will be fewer accidents, but the reduction in expected accident cost would be less than the cost of the additional resources. If he invests less than the optimum, the increase in expected accidents would be greater than the saving in resources. Figure 3.3 shows what courts have in mind. The point $V'-T'_F$ is the social optimum, and, in fact, the situation shown on this diagram, in which the potential tort-feasor makes more resource investments, is probably typical.

The calculating problem for the courts is not easy. A good deal of technological knowledge is needed, and proper solution would require

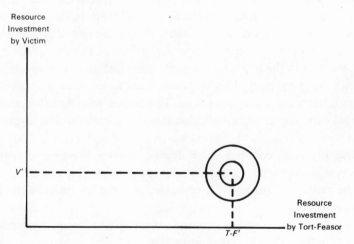

Figure 3.3
Optimal Investment of Resources by Tort-Feasor and Victim.

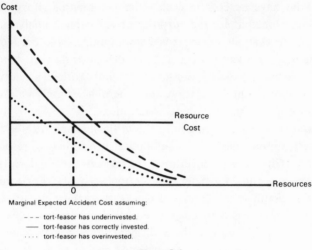

Figure 3.4
Victim's Calculation of Resource Investment.

considerable mathematical knowledge. Granted the complexity of the problem, I suppose that no one familiar with Anglo-Saxon law would be surprised to discover that it is referred to the jury, a group of more or less average people, who generally have difficulty with complex technical problems. For the time being, however, we will assume that they are expected to solve the problem correctly, and will turn to the situation facing the parties. In figure 3.4, we show the calculations that the victim must make. Cost is shown on the vertical axis. The line for resource cost shows the cost to the individual of each additional unit of resources as he increases his investment. This is shown in dollar terms in the traditional way and, hence, is a horizontal line. The curved solid line indicates the marginal expected accident cost associated with each level of investment by the victim in accident prevention. As we would expect, it shows a declining marginal cost but not a decline to zero. We assume that the tort-feasor has invested the optimal amount of resources, and if this is so, then the victim should invest 0 resources in order to optimize the total social investment.

It is, of course, possible that the potential tort-feasor has underinvested. If he has, then the accident production function, assuming perfect calculation by the victim, would become the dashed line, which moves his optimal resource investment to the right of 0. Similarly if the tort-feasor had overinvested in resources and lowered the probability of accidents, the accident production function would become the dotted line, which crosses the cost line to the left of 0.

The current rule, however, deals only with the optimum as correctly calculated by the victim on the assumption that the tort-feasor has invested an appropriate amount of resources. The same calculations for the tort-feasor, or potential tort-feasor, are shown in figure 3.5. The solid horizontal line shows the cost, and the curved line R shows the marginal return to various investments in accident prevention, on the assumption that the victim has made the optimum investment.

We now come to a definition which is, in part, a necessary simplification for the analysis; but, in part, simply a statement of how the law works: the victim is the person most seriously harmed. For example, suppose a person walks around the back of a parked truck and steps into the street in front of my car without looking. I am unable to stop and injure him badly enough to hospitalize him. Even if there were a television crew taking a picture of the event, making it easy to prove exactly what happened, the most I would hope for is that I do not (or, more precisely, my insurance company does not) have to pay his hospital expenses. I may be totally faultless, and he may have been extremely careless, but the pros-

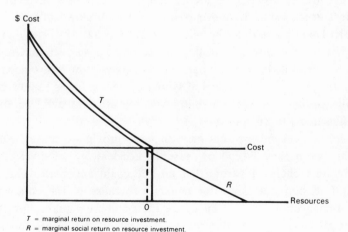

T = marginal return on resource investment.
R = marginal social return on resource investment.

Figure 3.5
Tort-Feasor's Calculation of Resource Investment.

pect that a jury will require him to pay for the damage which his body inflicted on the front of my automobile is nil.

We are now in a situation to consider the actual rule, i.e., that the tort-feasor must pay the victim's cost if the tort-feasor has invested less than the optimum amount in accident prevention, and the victim has invested at least the optimum amount. We shall begin by assuming that everybody calculates perfectly and look at the decision procedure of first the tort-feasor and then the victim. We shall see that the calculation of the social-resource investment requires information which is normally not available. Thus, the best calculation that can be made leads to a suboptimal situation.

Consider then, the situation of the potential tort-feasor shown in figure 3.5. In addition to the curving line R showing social marginal return on resources invested in preventing accidents, I have drawn another line, T, which coincides with it for a considerable part of its length and then drops vertically at 0. Under these circumstances, if the court is perfect, the tort-feasor pays the full cost of the accident out to point 0. Accidents which occur beyond point 0, however, are not his responsibility. Damage in this case remains where it falls—on the victim.

Here, I am making an assumption which is, I believe, good law, but which very likely does not fit the actual practice of the courts. Suppose that the tort-feasor has, in fact, underinvested, in the sense that, let us say, his brakes are not in good condition. He is now involved in an accident which would have occurred even if his brakes had been perfect. In strict law, he would not be held liable for this accident, and that is the law that we are currently testing. In practice, I suspect that in many cases he would be held liable, particularly if the victim was somebody for whom the jury felt a good deal of sympathy, but as far as I know, no one has alleged that this type of liability would be efficient, and I am discussing efficient arrangements.

There is a second problem here, that of "proximate cause." Suppose that his bad brakes did indeed cause the accident, by some very lengthy and indirect chain of events that no one could anticipate. The courts might find him not liable for damages, because of the complex and distant connection between his carelessness and the actual accident. It is not at all clear whether this rule is efficient or inefficient, and I shall simply leave it aside.

It can be seen that out to point 0, if the victim has invested an appro-priate amount of resources in accident prevention, then the tort-feasor has the appropriate incentives. If his investment is less than 0, and it causes an accident, the full cost of that accident will fall on him; and left of 0, the expected costs of the accidents are higher than the cost of their prevention. Similarly he will not go to the right of 0, because beyond that point he has no liability.

Now let us reconsider the situation of the potential victim. If the potential tort-feasor has invested the right amount, then the victim, so the conventional argument goes, has a motive for investing the socially optimal quantity. The argument is simple. If he invests less than that amount, then he will have to pay the full cost of the accident, because he is guilty of contributory negligence and, hence, cannot force the tort-feasor to bear the cost of the accident. Since the expected cost-of-accidents curve to the left of point 0 lies above his resource cost of invest-ment, he will be well advised to invest that amount.

If, on the other hand, both parties have invested the appropriate amount, the victim is not so well off. There will still be accidents—those which lie to the right of point 0 on both figure 3.4 and figure 3.5, or above and to the right of the point $V'-T'_F$ in figure 3.3. The full cost of these accidents will be borne by the victim. Although this is nasty for the victim, it is socially efficient, since the cost of eliminating these accidents would be greater than the benefit. Those who feel sorry for the victim should remember that compensating him in this area will lead him to invest less than the optimal amount of resources in accident prevention by the conventional argument.

So far, the contributory negligence rule has stood up very well. But that is because we have been assuming that both the potential tort-feasor and the court have superhuman knowledge. The cost to the victim of the accident is, to a very considerable extent, pain and suffering, and only he knows how much value he places upon it. Indeed most of his costs are subjective. He may be very risk averse or a risk lover. He might have a very high discount rate, with the result that he is quite willing to under-invest in things which will affect his future, or a very low discount rate, which would mean that he would tend to overinvest.

There is surely no way the potential tort-feasor can know these subjec-tive evaluations of a man whom he has never met. Further, even retrospectively, the court probably cannot properly evaluate them. Under the circumstances, the law must, of necessity, act not on the individual's true cost but on some general idea of average cost. When this is realized, however, the optimality of the procedure vanishes. The victim, instead of selecting 0 will select some other point—either to the right or left of that—because that is optimum for him. After all, if the tort-feasor has put in an appropriate amount of resources, then the victim is not going to collect damages anyway.

Suppose, for purposes of illustration, that the victim happens to be particularly sensitive to pain and hence puts a high negative evaluation on pain and suffering. From his standpoint, the cost of the accident will be the dashed line rather than the solid line in figure 3.4. He would, from the standpoint of the tort-feasor and the judge, be overinvesting. This would, of course, not affect the outcome of the lawsuit but suppose that the reverse were true. Suppose that the potential victim happened to have a greater than normal ability to stand pain, or a very high discount rate, or was a risk lover, and hence considered the cost to himself as the dotted line. Under these circumstances, he would underinvest, and when the matter came to court, the judge would think him contributorially negligent.

There is, of course, no way in which the potential tort-feasor can predict in advance what the individual victim will do, but he can make a not bad guess as to the likely range of probability he faces. Some of the people whom he might injure will have overinvested and some will have underinvested. With those who have overinvested, this overinvestment in essence lowers the cost to the potential tort-feasor of achieving a given level of expected accident prevention, but this is presumably a fairly small factor.

Those who underinvest produce a radically different result. In these cases, the tort-feasor will not have to pay damages even if he underinvests himself, because the victims will be contributorially negligent.

If we assume that the social level of due care calculated by the court is the middle of the range of individual-victim optima, then in about half of all cases, the potential victim will have "Underinvested"; in other words, the potential tort-feasor will only have to pay damages in about half the cases. This is shown in figure 3.6. As before, line R represents the return on accident prevention by the potential tort-feasor. If there is a 50/50 chance, however, that the victim was contributorially negligent, then the

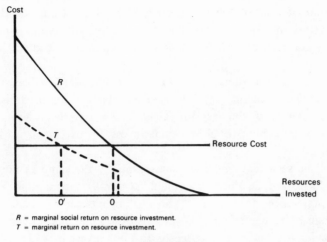

R = marginal social return on resource investment.
T = marginal return on resource investment.

Figure 3.6
Underinvestment by Tort-Feasor.

tort-feasor's anticipated payments follow not line *R* but line *T*. He will have to pay for only half of the accidents which occur left of point 0, because, in half of the cases, the victim will be denied recovery due to contributory negligence. Instead of investing 0, the tort-feasor will invest 0'.

If, however, the potential tort-feasor will invest only 0' in figure 3.6, then it is to the interest of the potential victim to invest 0 in figure 3.4 resources. This amount will not be the individual's own subjective calculation of his costs but what he thinks the court will require. If he so invests, then it is to the interest of the potential tort-feasor also to invest 0, which, in turn, deprives the potential victim of any motive for investing the optimal amount. It will be seen that we have here a situation related to the paradox of the liar. There is no logically coherent solution to the problem unless we assume that the court and tort-feasor can both make their calculations on the basis of a perfect knowledge of the preference function of the victim. This is, of course, absurd.

So much for the situation with perfect knowledge. Do we do better with partial or imperfect knowledge? The answer is Yes, but unfortunately, although we do better, we do not achieve the optimum which is so often claimed for the rule.[8] In discussing the outcome with less than perfect knowledge, I am going to consider the matter from the standpoint of each of the two parties, under the assumption that they regard either the court or the other party, or perhaps both, as not being perfectly accurate, and make the best calculations they can on this foundation.

Let us begin by assuming that we are the potential tort-feasor and we think that the judge and jury will make a perfectly accurate decision, but that the potential victim may miscalculate. For simplicity, let us assume that we expect him to either underinvest or overinvest with equal probability.

It will be seen that this case is substantially the same as the one we already discussed, in which we pointed out that the victim might have different preferences than that of the median citizen. The consequences which can be read off figure 3.6 are also the same and, in general, it is sensible for the potential tort-feasor to underinvest in accident prevention.

Now let us turn to the situation of the victim and consider how he should respond to the probability that the potential tort-feasor may make mistakes. For this purpose, I wish to define the "correct" investment in resources the way it is defined in the conventional literature, not the way implied by the above reasoning. In other words, the "correct" decision for the potential tort-feasor is to put in the socially optimal amount of resources. He may make an error in the sense that he overinvests, or in the sense that he underinvests.

The situation is a little complicated. In figure 3.7, the horizontal line again presents the resource cost of antiaccident activity for the victim. Line V shows the expected cost of the accidents prevented by each increment of investment by the victim if the potential tort-feasor has invested the socially optimal amount. We are assuming, however, that the tort-feasor may invest either more or less than that with equal probability. If the tort-feasor invests more than is the socially optimal amount, then the function which shows a number of accidents to be expected with each investment of resource by the victim would be below the solid line, and hence the victim for those particular accidents would be engaging in a small overinvestment if he invested the quantity 0.

But for half of the potential accidents, the potential tort-feasor can be expected to underinvest in accident prevention, which produces a probability of accident for each investment resource by the potential victim as shown by the dashed line V'. One might think that these two

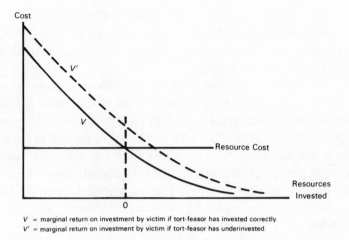

V = marginal return on investment by victim if tort-feasor has invested correctly.
V' = marginal return on investment by victim if tort-feasor has underinvested.

Figure 3.7
Victim's Response to Mistakes of Tort-Feasor.

lines would tend to be about the same distance from line V, and hence the best accident reduction assumption for the victim would be line V. This is not true, however, because of the assymmetry of the legal arrangements.

If the tort-feasor has underinvested, then there will in fact be more accidents with any given investment resources by the potential victim. The expected cost of these additional accidents are shown by the distance between the dashed line V' and line V. The cost of these accidents will be borne entirely by the victim if his resource commitment to accident prevention is less than 0, because he will be guilty of contributory negligence. If it is 0 or better, however, the cost of these accidents will be shifted to the defendant in the action, i.e., the tort-feasor.

This means that the actual return to the victim on accident-preventing activity has a sharp spike at point 0. Left of point 0, every dollar he puts into accident prevention reduces the number of accidents, and that is all that happens. The same is true of the points to the right of 0. At 0 itself, however, the investment of the final marginal increment which eliminates contributory negligence, there is another effect. For a great many potential accidents, he can collect damages, i.e., it shifts the cost of these accidents from him to the tort-feasor.

It is not clear how large this factor is, but my assumption would be that is indeed quite large. Thus, there would be fairly strong incentive for the potential victim to invest that amount of resources regarded as socially optimum, even if his own aversion to an accident is less than normal, and hence the value to him of each investment in accident prevention is less than the average.

In a way, the return to him on resources invested in accidents crosses the cost line three times. A person who is, let us say, relatively immune to pain would find the return to him of resource investment in accident prevention cutting the cost line well to the left of point 0 and then continuing under the cost line to point 0. At that point, the court would suddenly begin giving him damages for all the accidents caused by the tortfeasor's negligence. Hence the payoff to this marginal increment could be very high. The question would be, of course, whether the loss he suffered in extending his investment out to point 0 beyond the point where his expected cost of accidents first cut the resource cost line was more than paid for by this increased probability of collecting damages. I can think of no simple empirical tests of this matter, but my own guess would be that, at least in many cases, this would turn out to be true. The sharp rise at point 0, of course, would be followed by a fall back to his cost line.

So far, we have been considering only errors by the parties and assuming a perfect court. Now let us assume that the court makes errors, while the parties calculate perfectly. Let me now assume that the judge and jury make errors, and instead of assuming a simple probability of 50 percent of an error above or below the optimum—which in any event is a little hard to define in this case—let us assume that their error is normally distributed. Returning to figure 3.3, one notes that around the optimum I have drawn a series of more or less concentric circles. These are intended to be probability lines, indicating that the court cannot determine the optimal point with exact accuracy and hence may place it anywhere in the general vicinity of that optimum, with the probability falling in the usual bell-shaped distribution.

Not only will I assume here that the judicial decision maker—whether it is the judge or the jury—makes this kind of random error, I shall for the time being assume that the parties both make perfect calculations and expect the other party to be aiming at the social-optimum investment. This assumption is for simplicity only. The assumption that the other parties were also making random errors would add a number of unnecessary complications.

Figure 3.8 shows the potential tort-feasor's situation in our usual way. Again, the cost of prevention is shown, and the marginal return on his behavior is shown by the line T. The line T', forming an ess curve between the objective return-on-accident-prevention line and the coordinate, shows what happens if the court is not perfectly accurate and is, in fact, imposing a random error. As he approaches the social optima, the probability that the court will make a mistake and assume that he has already reached the social optima, i.e., the probability that they will place the social optima to the left of their actual location, means that his actual cost of accident, i.e., the cost of being found guilty and having to pay damages, is less than the objective amount that it should be. This error lowers his actual cost to the point where he pays for only 50 percent of total accidents at the social optima. The probability that he will be found guilty and compelled to pay remains positive well to the right of the social optimum. This is because the court may mistakenly exaggerate the amount of resources which he should invest.

The effect of this on him, however, is fairly unambiguous. He should underinvest; that is, put in resources out only to the point where the line which shows the cost to him—i.e., the objective cost of the accident as modified by court error—crosses the cost of prevention of $0'$.

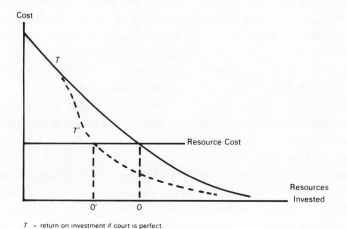

T = return on investment if court is perfect.
T' = return on investment if court is imperfect

Figure 3.8
Underinvestment by Tort-Feasor.

The situation in respect to the victim is somewhat odd. Once again, in figure 3.9, we show our familiar cost-curve diagram, but note the existence of figure 3.9b with a hump on it, and then the fact that I have added that hump on top of the objective reduction-in-accident curve in figure 3.9a. The line in figure 3.9b shows a return that the potential victim gets from resource investment which is not a reduction in accidents, but an increase in the probability that he will receive compensation. As he approaches the optimum point, there is increasing probability that the court will find that he has in fact provided the optimal social amount of resources, and hence that he has at least some chance—depending, of course, on the behavior of the other party—of getting damages. The benefit to him of this chance is shown in figure 3.9b, and, of course, reaches its peak at the social optima and falls afterward. The exact size is unknown, but it could easily be quite large.

The result of this is simple and unambiguous. The potential victim will invest more than the social-optimum quantity of resources in preventing accidents, or 0′.

So far, we have assumed that the two parties are each making their calculations on the assumption that the behavior of the other party is randomly distributed around the "correct" calculation. Suppose, however, that each party not only takes into account this random variance but is aware of the other party's tendency to do the same thing, and hence assumes that the courts random error varies around a point which is calculated by the other party with the random variance in mind.

The first thing to be said about this is that it is not clear that there would be a convergence on any fixed solution. The outcome could be explosive. It would, of course, be easy to assume parameters which would lead to convergence, but there does not seem to be any strong reason to believe that these parameters are any better than those which would lead to explosion.

The exact point of convergence also would depend on the assumed parameters. There does not, however, seem to be any reason to believe that, if the series converges, it will converge at the theoretical social optimum. A priori, we would rather assume that it would converge with the potential tort-feasor underinvesting and the potential victim overinvesting. In any event, the elegant demonstrations that the standard-liability rules lead to optimum investment of resource in accident prevention fails in the presence of error.

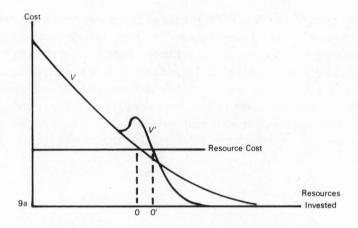

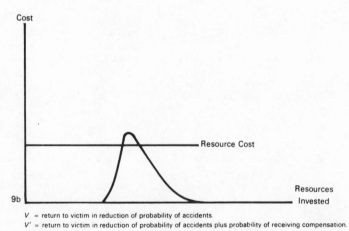

V = return to victim in reduction of probability of accidents.
V' = return to victim in reduction of probability of accidents plus probability of receiving compensation.

Figure 3.9
Returns to Victim.

Since all human institutions are error prone, the rules should be revised to take error into account. I offered one such set of revisions in The Logic of the Law.[9] This is, of course, only one possibility. But this is clearly an area where rules which are optimal on the assumption that no one makes any errors are not optimal if we take a more realistic view of the performance of the courts. There are probably many other such areas.

The object of this discussion of liability law is simply to point out the importance of errors. I have not used the tort example because I think the errors are particularly important here, although, as a matter of fact, determining what happened in an accident, in which everything really happened too fast to be remembered, is an empirically difficult problem. The point, however, is simply that rules designed on the assumption the courts would behave perfectly may have not only inaccurate, but positively perverse, results when we recognize that courts behave inaccurately.

Chapter 4

More on Costs

In chapter 3, when dealing with accuracy and inaccuracy of the courts, it was necessary to talk about the costs of the proceedings. In this chapter, which is mainly concerned with problems of cost, it will also be necessary to talk about accuracy or inaccuracy. To simplify the discussion, I will assume that we are always dealing with a case in which the amount at issue is $100,000 and the plaintiff is in the right, i.e., an all-knowing God would decide in his favor. Thus, the defendant, in fact, owes the plaintiff $100,000; however, he may choose to contest the claim in court. The reader should have no difficulty in generalizing from this single case to all cases.

Figure 4.1 shows the situation. The line P is the probability of success, but I have expressed it not as a percentage, but in terms of the present discounted value of the plaintiff's claim against the defendant, with varying qualities of evidence available. As is usual, the cases in which the evidence is highly convincing and accurate are at the left side of the diagram and those where it is poor and misleading at the right. The actual slope of P, as drawn here, has been selected mainly to make it convenient for me to draw the diagram, rather than as an effort to duplicate the real world. Readers who do not like this particular shape are free to redraw the figure in some other shape that impresses them as better.

If we assume a costless court,[1] the present value of the claim to the plaintiff with any particular quantity and quality of evidence is shown by simple geometric construction. We proceed along the horizontal axis to the point where the evidence is of the appropriate quality—in this case, E—and erect a perpendicular. The probability of the plaintiff winning is shown by the intersection of the perpendicular with line P. The projection of that point on the left axis is the value of the case to the plaintiff—in

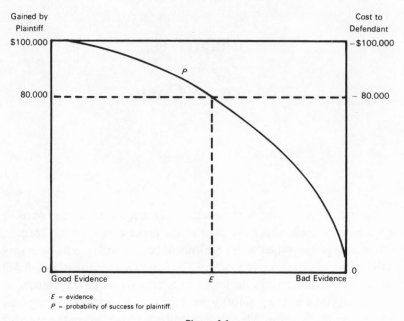

Figure 4.1
Probability of Success for Plaintiff.

this case, $80,000—and on the right axis to the defendant—in this case, −$80,000.

In the costless case, the only motive for out-of-court settlement would be risk aversion. If we assume that the plaintiff and defendant are both risk averse, we would anticipate that the plaintiff's justified claim for $100,000 would in fact be settled for something like $80,000. If we assume that they are not risk averse, then they would go to court; and there would be a 4 in 5 chance of judgment for the plaintiff. Over a long series of similar cases, the results would work out the same as if they settled each one out of court. In other words, it would always be wise for the defendant, even though he is in the wrong, to refuse payment of the full amount and either go to court or make a settlement.

It might be that one of the parties is risk averse and the other is not, or that one is more risk averse than the other. In that event, the settlement would be, in money terms, to the advantage of the less risk averse of the two parties but, in utility terms, would be mutually beneficial. It might also be that the parties would calculate the probabilities differently. If the defendant calculated that the probability of judgment for the plaintiff was higher than the plaintiff thought, then settlement would be highly probable and there would be a bargaining range. If, on the other hand, the plaintiff thought that the probability of his success was higher than the defendant calculated, presumably they would go to trial. Note that the outcome of this particular case would not tell which of them was right, since their disagreement was on the odds and a single observation cannot tell us what the odds are.

As a matter of fact, lawyers are quite good at this kind of probability estimate, and there is less dispersion in lawyers' estimates of total damages collected in injury cases, for example, than there is in jury awards. The narrowly dispersed set of lawyers' estimates of a good settlement price tends to be about the median value of the much more widely dispersed jury decision, which would indicate that the lawyers are making an estimate of the center of a distribution of probability and are doing it quite well.

In lawsuits in the real world, of course, there are significant costs. I begin my discussion of these costs by assuming that we are following the American system, in which most of the costs are paid by the two parties, and each party pays its own costs; we will then proceed to a discussion of the English system, in which the loser normally pays the total "reasonable" costs.

On figure 4.2, I have drawn in another line, DC, which shows the defendant's costs—the costs to the defendant of actually going through the litigation. This is his present discounted value of the outcome plus the legal costs that he will have to pay. I have also drawn in line PC, which is the plaintiff's gain—the present discounted value of the outcome of the case minus his legal costs.

With these predictable large costs of litigation, there is obvious room for out-of-court settlement. It is no longer just a matter of risk aversion. Left of D', which is the point where the line DC crosses the $100,000 level, the plaintiff might reasonably assume that the defendant will settle, regardless of what his attorney says, and therefore insist on proceeding with the case. Note that this would not be certain. The defendant might be willing to take a gamble with a negative present value in an effort to develop a reputation for toughness in future cases. Still, on the whole, cases to the left of D' are not likely to be brought, and in those areas the defendant will probably pay up.

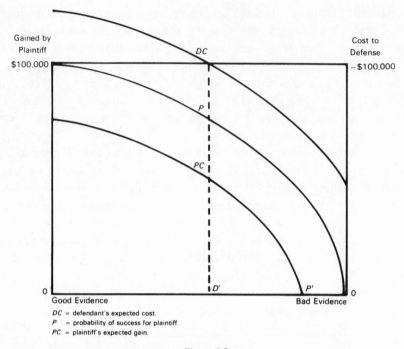

DC = defendant's expected cost.
P   = probability of success for plaintiff.
PC = plaintiff's expected gain.

Figure 4.2
Expected Net Returns from Litigation.

The same line of reasoning applies to cases to the right of P', the point where the present discounted value to the plaintiff (who, you will recall, is in the right) minus his court costs becomes negative. The defendant can probably assume that the plaintiff will not press cases to the right of that point. Although, once again, he might do so to establish credibility in future negotiations. Basically, however, the cases brought and the cases in which there are very serious negotiations for out-of-court settlements will lie between D' and P'.

Even in this range, risk aversion, together with the very real costs of taking the case to court, often leads to out-of-court settlement. Let us therefore turn now to a discussion of the bargaining negotiations for an out-of-court settlement.

The problem of bargaining is one of the most important in economics, and so far it has resisted formal analysis. Beginning with the classic *A Theory of Games and Economic Behavior*,[2] game theorists have devoted great attention to the problem and have contributed greatly to a clarification of the issues. This discussion, while it will not use the formal models they have developed, will nevertheless owe its general approach to them. The game theorists, in addition to developing formal techniques, also produced a philosophy of bargaining, and it is this philosophy of bargaining which underlies our approach. I will, however, leave aside "the part of bargaining that consists of exploring for mutually profitable adjustments, and that might be called the 'efficiency' aspect of bargaining. Instead we shall be concerned with what might be called the 'distributional' aspect of bargaining: the situations in which a better bargain for one means less for the other."[3]

Instead of trying to deal with both parties to the pretrial bargaining process simultaneously, I will begin by looking at the matter from the standpoint of one of them. My procedure will be to trace a bargain through, using only the information available to one of the parties. When I have completed this analysis, I will discuss both parties.

Using the individualistic procedure, figure 4.3 shows the situation from the standpoint of the plaintiff. The horizontal axis is the money settlement dimension and the vertical measures investments of resources in bargaining. For the time being, I will not inquire as to what sort of bargaining costs are involved but just accept it as true that there are such costs. For the next few pages, I will rule out one particular bargaining technique; plaintiff will not make a take-it-or-leave-it offer.[4] Since such offers have played a major role in the theoretical investigation of bargaining—indeed, much more of a role than they play in real-life bargaining—this may seem a radical departure, but the reader may be assured that it is only a temporary omission.

The plaintiff has a maximum amount of resources that he is willing to expend to get a settlement. This would be his estimate of the ex ante value of his suit minus an amount to cover his risk aversion. He would, of course, like to get more. The top of his preference mountain—getting the $100,000 with no expenditures for bargaining—is at the origin of our diagram. His indifference curves would be lines like *I-I*. It might be argued that they should be straight lines, the individual being indifferent between the investment of resources in bargaining or on cuts in the settlement. I have assumed that the plaintiff is not completely indifferent between the two types of resource expenditures, hence the lines have some curvature; but this assumption is not crucial to the argument.

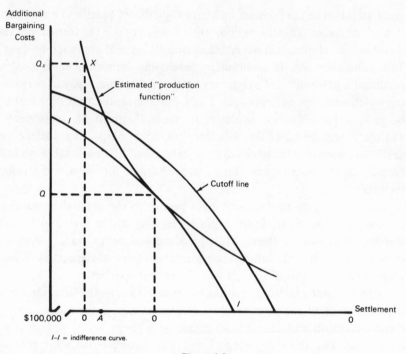

Figure 4.3
Plaintiff's View of Instants in the Bargaining Process: The Beginning.

Among the plaintiff's indifference curves, there will be one which indicates the maximum resource commitment he would be willing to put into getting a settlement rather than suing. I have labeled this indifference curve the "cutoff line" and its intersection with the settlement line is the minimum settlement he would be willing to accept if he anticipated no bargaining costs. Rather than accept any smaller amount he would sue. Similarly, a point such as X would involve so much in bargaining cost that he would rather not go into the negotiations, though the settlement taken by itself would be quite acceptable.

The bargaining costs, however, are things which are not themselves the subject of bargaining or mutual agreement.[5] Further, once resources have been put into some bargaining maneuver, they are sunk costs and should have no influence on further investments. Thus bargaining costs in this model are ex ante estimates rather than actual expenditures. Point X would be an ex ante guess that the investment of Q_x resources in bargaining would lead to settlement at O_x. In deciding whether or not to bargain, the plaintiff must make this sort of estimate, explicitly or implicitly, and lay his plans accordingly.

The estimate of the likely payoff of bargaining is, in fact, an estimate of the response of the other party to the bargain—the defendant—to the plaintiff's maneuvers. This is a sort of "production function" (as I have labeled it), which shows the settlement that the plaintiff expects to obtain with various amounts of resources invested in bargaining. I have assumed that resources invested in bargaining are subject to declining returns which gives a curve of the general shape shown. If this estimated production function for investment in bargaining lies entirely outside the cutoff line, the plaintiff will simply sue. If part of it lies inside the cutoff line, the plaintiff will plan to invest enough resources in bargaining to put him on the highest possible indifference curve, which is $I–I$, in figure 4.3. This means that he enters the bargaining process with an intention of investing

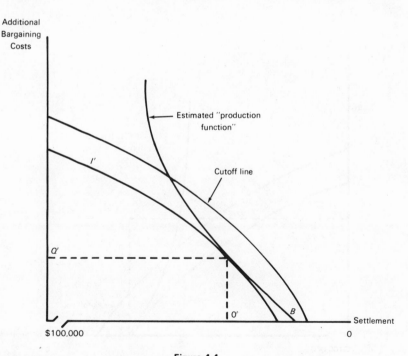

Figure 4.4
Plaintiff's View of Instants in the Bargaining Process: Settlement Situation as Seen After Some Negotiation.

Q units in bargaining and getting, eventually, settlement O.[6] Note that he does not typically make an immediate offer of O, but a higher price. All of this, of course, is ex ante, and he should not be surprised if things do not work out according to plan.

In figure 4.4, I show a situation which might develop after some negotiation. Some resources have now been invested in negotiation, and the plaintiff is now considering his future plans. The resources already invested in bargaining are sunk costs and should not influence his future decisions. Similarly, there is no particular reason why the process of negotiation should have shifted either his cutoff line or his other indifference curves in any predictable way. What the negotiation has done is improve his state of information. The new estimated "production function" is more steeply tilted than before, partly because the defendant has made him a definite offer at B, hence he can get this with no bargaining cost, and partly because in this particular case the process of negotiation

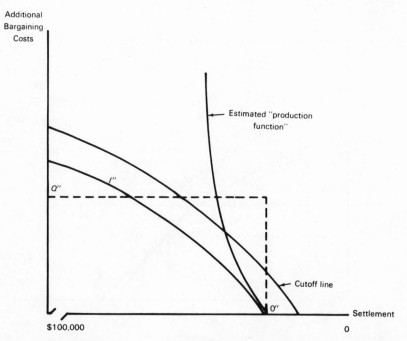

Figure 4.5
Plaintiff's View of Instants in the Bargaining Process: Situation at Settlement.

has led him to feel that the original estimate was too optimistic in general.

The plaintiff will only continue the negotiations if, as is the case in figure 4.4, the estimated production function still has a segment lying under the cutoff line. If such negotiations are continued, and eventually reach a successful outcome, the situation at the time of agreement between the two parties will be as shown in figure 4.5. Because of the overoptimistic original estimate of the production function in this example, the individual has (probably) invested more in bargaining than he originally intended and ended up with a poorer settlement. The estimated production function does not show actual expenditures on bargaining, but only prospective estimates. It is thus perfectly possible for the individual to be in a position where he would be well-advised to settle at O'', but still to have been made worse off by the whole course of the bargaining. Assume that he expended Q'' resources in the bargaining process. If he had known ex ante that he would need that expenditure to obtain O'', he would have sued.

The reader, particularly if a practicing lawyer, may have been disturbed by my treatment of the suit and settlement negotiations as alternatives. In actual practice, at any given point in time, the parties are normally both preparing to bring the case to trial *and* negotiating for a settlement. In fact, the preparations for the trial in the way of collecting evidence, examining authorities, etc., are also part of the bargaining process. First, they improve the probability of victory and, second, they are a threat actually to go to trial. Further, by lowering the cost of proceeding to trial, they move in the cutoff line. If you've already spent half the total cost of the trial in making preparations, that is sunk cost, and only the remaining half is still an expected cost of trial.

Nevertheless, conceptually the two processes can be separated and, of course, there are some activities—such as the literal negotiation between the two attorneys—which clearly are part of the bargaining process rather than preparation for the trial. The only effect of this expenditure, then, is to improve the settlement. Ex post, we can tell whether the expenditures had the effect of making the settlement more favorable or making it more likely that the plaintiff would win at the trial.

Figures 4.3, 4.4, and 4.5 represent but three instants in the bargaining process. Presumably, the plaintiff is continually not only actively bargaining, but also making estimates of the future outcome. Thus, I

draw in figure 4.6 the course through time of his estimate of the future of
the bargaining process. Line C represents roughly the particular bargaining process I have so far used as an illustration, and the other three lines
are representative of other patterns which might show up. Line C
represents the likely course of negotiations (as seen by plaintiff) if he
began with a mildly overoptimistic estimate of the situation. Line D
shows his likely expectation path if his original estimate is overpessimistic. Lines A and B show outcomes of seriously overoptimistic estimates, but in these cases the improvement of information as the bargaining proceeds moves the plaintiff beyond the cutoff line with the result
that he drops the negotiations.

From this model, we can fairly easily deduce one conclusion which has
played little role in previous theoretical investigations of the bargaining
process. The plaintiff knows that the defendant also is going through the
same process, although he has no detailed knowledge of the defendant's

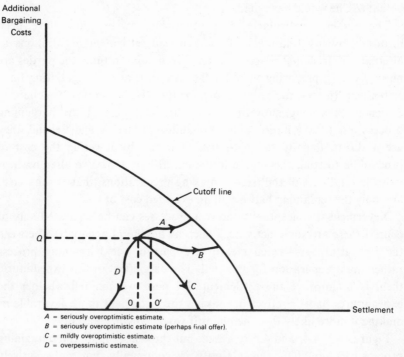

A = seriously overoptimistic estimate.
B = seriously overoptimistic estimate (perhaps final offer).
C = mildly overoptimistic estimate.
D = overpessimistic estimate.

Figure 4.6
Plaintiff's Estimates of the Bargaining Process.

expectations. He realizes that unless he keeps the defendant below his cutoff line, the defendant will terminate the negotiations. Not only must the plaintiff try to plan his negotiations in order to get as good a settlement as possible, he must also try to assure the defendant of a potentially profitable deal.

Traditional bargaining theory has put great emphasis on the problem of getting the best deal, and this would normally lead to the negotiators playing down the importance of the deal to themselves. Unfortunately, this is exactly the pattern of behavior which is most likely to convince the other party that nothing is to be gained from further negotiations. The plaintiff, if he wants to continue the negotiations, must offer inducements to the defendant and, at the same time, avoid showing so much enthusiasm that he gets a bad settlement. Observationally this fits what people engaged in bargaining actually do. The plaintiff's policy must be informed by a continual appraisal of the current psychological state of the other party. Altogether, bargaining is a most difficult process, both for the analyst and for the bargainer.

At the beginning of this discussion, I temporarily ruled out the use of the "take-it-or-leave-it" offer as a bargaining technique. We still do not have enough analytical tools to fully discuss this maneuver, but there is a special case which can profitably be considered here. Suppose that the plaintiff finds himself following line *B* on figure 4.6 and is almost at the cutoff line. Under these circumstances, a "final offer" to settle at price *A* might well be sensible. Since the plaintiff is on the verge of breaking off negotiations anyway, he has little to lose, and there is a possibility that the offer will be accepted, with corresponding gains. It seems likely that a good many genuine final offers are of this sort. Not all are, however, and we need to go further with the analysis before we can treat the others.

So far I have discussed bargaining in a radically individualistic manner. My figures have shown an individual and his estimates of the outcome. The other party to the negotiations has been relevant only as his behavior may affect the plaintiff's estimated production function. This is realistic, since individual bargainers really do not have any definite knowledge about the true intentions of the other party. Nevertheless, I can put two of these individual figures—one to represent the plaintiff, the other the defendant—on the same set of axes. In figure 4.7 I show a situation in which each of the parties to the bargain had made estimates which were overoptimistic, but in which the process of bargaining

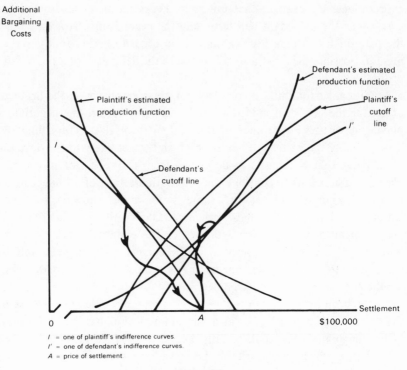

Figure 4.7
Settlements with Over optimistic Estimates.

eventually led to settlement at price *A*. In figure 4.8 I show a bargaining process in which the two parties began with overpessimistic estimates and ended up with a settlement at point *A*, which was probably highly satisfactory to both of them. If the bargaining had not led to a settlement, then the lines indicating the time progress of the two individuals' ex ante estimates of the situation would have moved out to their cutoff lines and negotiations would have terminated.

There is no reason for the two parties' estimates to have any very close relationship to each other. The plaintiff, for example, makes an offer. This should affect the defendant's estimates, but there is no reason why the plaintiff should change his estimates until he receives a communication from the defendant.[7] If the bargain is to be made, then the two parties must end up at the same point on the horizontal axis, but they may reach it by widely different routes. The plaintiff, for example, makes an offer of $90,000. He does not expect it to be accepted; in fact, he expects a price of $80,000 after considerable further bargaining. The defendant, however, sees himself at point P'' on figure 4.5 and accepts. This introduces a sort of discontinuity in the plaintiff's time curve as he immediately moves to the same point.[8]

In figure 4.9 we show a possible segment of a bargaining process in which the parties have a difference of opinion about the bargaining process itself. When the stage indicated by the end of the time lines is reached, the plaintiff will drop the negotiations. The defendant, however, would try to get the negotiations going again. His efforts would either lead the plaintiff to reappraise the situation so that he moves down from the cutoff line, or, just as likely, move the defendant up to his cutoff line as he sees how little result his offers have.

We are now at a stage where we can discuss the "take-it-or-leave-it" offer or "locking oneself in" technique which has played such an

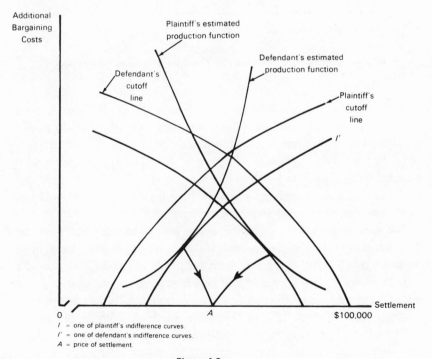

I = one of plaintiff's indifference curves.
I' = one of defendant's indifference curves.
A = price of settlement.

Figure 4.8
Settlement with Over pessimistic Estimates.

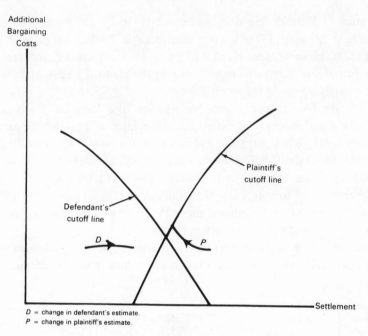

Figure 4.9
Bargaining with Differences in Opinion About the Bargaining Process Itself.

important role in the development of bargaining theory. In figure 4.10 we show the plaintiff's cutoff line (C). Let us assume that the plaintiff makes an offer of A, and makes it clear that the defendant must either accept it or go to trial. The objective of the plaintiff is to face the defendant with an estimated production function like the one shown, with the result that the offer will be accepted and the plaintiff will get a settlement which is nearly the highest possible under the circumstances.[9]

The reason this course of action is not always adopted is, of course, that bargainers seldom have accurate knowledge of their bargaining partner's cutoff point. If the defendant's cutoff line is actually C', and if a settlement lower than A' would still be better from the standpoint of the plaintiff, presentation of the take-it-or-leave-it offer kills the possibility of a favorable settlement. If, on the other hand, the cutoff line of the defendant is C'', then there is a possibility that by engaging in ordinary bargaining, the plaintiff would improve his information and obtain a better price than A, perhaps even A''. These risks are, of course, a cost which the person contemplating making a take-it-or-leave-it offer must consider. The other method of bargaining also has its risks, but they are less concentrated. The estimated production function we have been using for ordinary bargaining contains some elements which are the properly discounted values of the risk run. If take-it-or-leave-it bargaining is resorted to, however, the costs are almost entirely discounted risk.[10]

In figure 4.11, we show ex ante "production functions" for these two types of bargaining. Line $E–E$ is our familiar function for ordinary bargaining. Line $E'–E'$ shows the discounted value of the risks associated with take-it-or-leave-it offers of different settlements. Their particular relationship is not intended to be general, but merely as representing one possibility. In this case, the highest indifference curve tangent to either of the lines is $I–I$, and it is tangent to the ordinary bargaining line, not

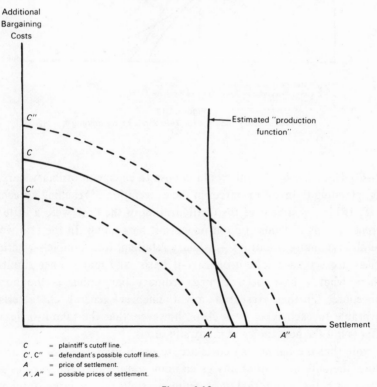

C = plaintiff's cutoff line.
C', C'' = defendant's possible cutoff lines.
A = price of settlement.
A', A'' = possible prices of settlement.

Figure 4.10
A Take-It-or-Leave-It Offer.

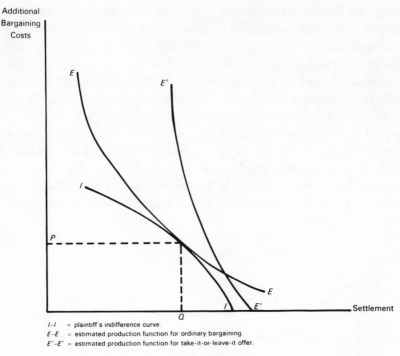

I–I   = plaintiff's indifference curve.
E–E   = estimated production function for ordinary bargaining.
E'–E'   = estimated production function for take-it-or-leave-it offer.

Figure 4.11
Production Functions for Two Kinds of Bargaining.

E'–E'. Thus, the defendant would choose to engage in ordinary bargaining, planning to invest resources in the expectation of reaching agreement at P. If his investment of the configuration of the lines were a little different, he might choose take-it-or-leave-it bargaining. In the real world, we observe many situations—ordinary retailing, for example—where the prices are set on a take-it-or-leave-it basis, and many other situations where what I have been calling ordinary bargaining is the normal procedure. Further, research might uncover general characteristics favorable to each type. It is clear, however, that the take-it-or-leave-it offer is not the best choice in many situations.

Note that the bargaining costs are, to put it mildly, nonzero. Furthermore, the bulk of them at any given point in time take the form of sunk costs, with the result that it is quite possible that a large amount of bargaining expenditures will be undertaken and the case will still go to court.

It seems likely, however, that the out-of-court settlements do normally involve fewer resources than the actual court proceeding. When I was in law school, one-third was suggested as the lawyer's bill for winning a damage suit, whereas in an out-of-court settlement, he should charge only one-quarter. Using that as an estimate and assuming that the same costs apply not only for the plaintiff but also for the defendant, we could return to figure 4.2 and draw in another pair of lines, one just below DC and the other just above PC, which would show the costs of settlement out of court.

Let us now turn to the English system in which the loser pays the "reasonable" costs of the winner. The situation is shown in figure 4.12. Here, as before, P shows the present discounted value of the $100,000 as we move from left to right—from cases in which the evidence is best to those where it is poorest and then positively misleading. However, this is not the present discounted value of the case from the standpoint of the two parties. These are shown by line P_L and line D_L. P_L shows the present discounted value of the case to the plaintiff, granting that if he loses, he will have to pay $66,000 in legal fees—his own and his opponent's. Similarly, line D shows the present discounted value for the defendant who, if he loses, may have to pay $166,000 instead of simply $100,000.

Line D_L cuts the $100,000 line at point D_L'. This means that if the evidence puts the case to the left of point D_L', the value to the defendant of going to trial instead of simply coughing up the $100,000 is less than the expenditure of $100,000. We would anticipate, then, that in cases to the left of this point the defendant would rather pay than be sued.

With respect to the plaintiff, the value of the suit drops to zero at point P_L', and hence they would not bring suits to the right of that point. Note that there is a gap between D_L' and P_L'. With this particular conformation of the lines, there would be few actual lawsuits. There might be a good deal of threat behavior in the interval $P_L'-D_L'$, with each party threatening to take the matter to court. Success or failure in this threat would be a matter of considerable real importance; but in most cases there should be a settlement without a trial. Indeed, the only reason for both parties deciding to go to trial over that particular interval would be

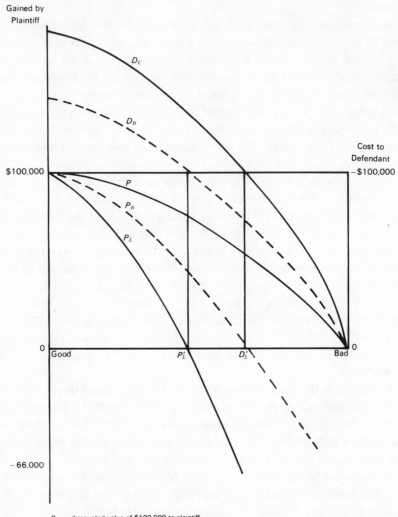

Gained by
Plaintiff

D_L

D_H

Cost to
Defendant
$-$100,000

$100,000

P

P_H

P_L

0

Good P'_L D'_L Bad   0

$-$66,000

P = discounted value of $100,000 to plaintiff.
P_L = discounted value of $100,000 to plaintiff considering risk of having to pay legal fees.
D_L = discount value to defendant considering risk of having to pay legal fees.
P_H = discounted gain to plaintiff using British costs.
D_H = estimated cost to defendant using British costs.

Figure 4.12
The English System of Loser Paying Costs of Winner.

to improve their bargaining position in future transactions, since the present discounted value of the trial is negative for both parties.

But note that this result comes simply because we are assuming that the British system involves legal fees and other legal expenses as great as they are in the United States. There are a number of techniques for restricting the amount that parties spend on their lawyers and other legal maneuvering in England. First, the compensation obtained from the loser is only the reasonable legal fee, as determined by a specially appointed taxing master. It seems likely in most cases that this is not actually the total expenditure; but, in any event, this custom does put a limit on the total amount that is transferred in the lawsuit. Further, there are some controls on the total expenditure which can be put into legal services in the British courts.

It is not clear whether these controls are intentional or accidental by-products of long-standing customs; but, in any event, the British legal system is markedly cheaper than ours. If we assume that as a result of these reduced costs—together with the fact that not all costs are, in fact, payable by the loser—we can draw in lines D_B as the British costs of the defendant and P_B as the British costs of the plaintiff. Since we do not have any actual numbers on these costs, I have simplified my drafting by drawing these lines in such a way that D_B crosses the $100,000 line at P_L' and P_B crosses the zero line at D_L'. With these costs we have a range between P_L' and D_L' where it is rational for both parties to go to trial, because each of them faces an ex ante profit from that course of action rather than either abandoning the claim, on the part of the plaintiff, or paying up without going to trial, on the part of the defendant. Naturally, we would expect a great many out-of-court settlements in England as in the United States, but this would be the basic interval in which significant out-of-court settlements or actual court trials occurred. Since the risk is greater in England, risk aversion would probably lead to more cases being settled out of court than in the United States.

There is a third technique for assessing the costs of legal proceedings which is beginning to pop up occasionally in American courts. This is a procedure in which one of the parties must pay the other's legal expenses if that party loses but the other party is not compelled to pay the legal expenses of the first party if the second party loses. Indeed, there have been a few cases recently in which the winner has been ordered to pay the

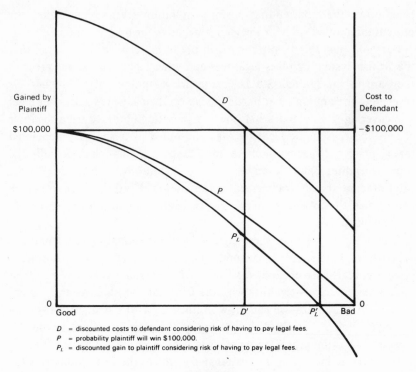

D = discounted costs to defendant considering risk of having to pay legal fees.
P = probability plaintiff will win $100,000.
P_L = discounted gain to plaintiff considering risk of having to pay legal fees.

Figure 4.13
Payment of Costs by Defendant If Plaintiff Wins.

expenses of the loser, and one, in fact, in which a third party was ordered to pay the expenses of the losing party in the suit.[11]

This particular procedure is largely an invention of the courts, but in antitrust law, and in a few other areas, Congress is in the process of enacting laws providing something like it. For example, the plaintiff in an antitrust action may collect his legal expenses from the defendant if the plaintiff wins; but if the plaintiff fails, the defendant cannot collect legal expenses from the plaintiff.

This particular set of institutions makes it more likely that lawsuits will be brought. Further, they make it more likely that settlements in favor of the subsidized party will be made out of court. Consider, for example, the situation in which there is some possibility of suing a company for violation of the antitrust act. There is in this case triple damages, and let us assume that the triple damage payment would come to $100,000 if the suit was successful, so that we can use our basic figures.

The defendant, under these circumstances, faces a curve like line D in figure 4.13, which discounts, first, the probability of losing with the various states of evidence as shown by line P; together with the fact that if he loses, he will have to pay the other person's legal fees; but, even if he wins, he will have to pay his own. The plaintiff, on the other hand, faces a curve like P_L, reflecting the fact that he has to pay his own legal expenses only if he loses. The range $D'-P_L'$ has shifted to the right, compared to either the British system of payment or the American system, in which each party pays his own expenses. The defendant would be advised to settle cases where the evidence against him is not good enough to make it worthwhile under either of the other systems, and the plaintiff will be well advised to push cases which would not be sensible to push with other cost allocations.

You might favor this kind of thing if you thought that on the whole it was desirable that a lot of cases be brought. So far as I know, this particular technique is used nowhere in the world except, very recently for special cases, in the United States, but perhaps legal scholars with wider knowledge can point to other examples.

Chapter 5

Optimal Procedure

So far I have developed only a very primitive idea of the objectives toward which courts should aim. Instead of beginning by setting down some function the courts are designed to maximize and then discussing how well or how badly the courts do, I have discussed court efficiency in terms of two very simple criteria—cost and accuracy. There has been an assumption that we want to lower cost and raise accuracy, but little or nothing has been said about how these two characteristics should be traded off against each other, or whether or not there are other things we want from the courts.

This somewhat unusual approach was chosen, quite simply, because I could hardly talk intelligibly about what the courts' objectives should be—the success indicator for a good court system—until I had covered the material in the previous four chapters. Efficiency in the courts involves understanding certain things which the average person would find paradoxical on first glance, and therefore I thought it desirable to discuss cost and errors before I began discussing true optimization.

I will now repair the omission and discuss the characteristics of a desirable court and the trade-offs between the various desirable characteristics. Of course, accuracy and low cost are among these characteristics and, indeed, by a wide margin the most important, but the social value of these two characteristics is rather indirect and its measurement not exactly simple.

Let us begin by assuming that the substantive law is socially desirable, or that the contract which is to be enforced is in fact desirable from the standpoint of the parties to the contract and with no negative externalities. In both cases, of course, these considerations are ex ante. By the time the matter comes to court, there most certainly is at least one person who would rather the law not be enforced.

These assumptions may be a little strong. All of us know at least some laws which are not in the social interest—indeed, they may be positively perverse—and foolish contracts are sometimes drawn up. Still, the point of procedure is to carry out policy decisions made in other areas, whether these other areas are the legislature or the salesroom in which an installment contract is made, not to *create* these laws or contracts. Thus, I will leave aside the investigation of perverse laws and foolish contracts for some other time and place.

As pointed out in chapter 3, however, the defects of the court proceedings necessarily *do* have some effect on what is an optimal substantive law. Further, they clearly have an effect on which contracts should be made and the clauses thereof. The contract must be drawn up with knowledge of the efficiency or inefficiency of the procedure which will be used to enforce it, and some provisions will differ from those which would be chosen in a nirvana of perfect enforcement.

But this matter can be left for another book. An improvement in the efficiency of the court in general means that the law can be made substantively better and that contracts can be drawn up which lead to greater net gain to the two parties. We can simply regard these changes in the law and in the contracts as supplementary gains to the improvement in the efficiency of the courts.

Let us begin by considering, once again, the diagram used in the preceding chapters. As usual, in figure 5.1, line P shows the probability of judgment for the plaintiff, who in this particular case is in the right. Once again, the assumption that the plaintiff is in the right is only a convenience for purposes of exposition. Also, line P has been drawn not on the basis of empirical knowledge but on the basis of drafting convenience. We badly need good empirical research on the accuracy of the courts but, with the present ignorance in the area, it seems sensible to try to draw diagrams so that they are readable.

As is usual, the costs are shown by lines P_c and D_c. I am assuming for this diagram that each party pays his own legal costs, simply because that approximates the way we normally do it in the United States. Anyone who wishes can fairly easily adjust the diagram to show some other way to handle the costs. Thus the line D_c shows the expected cost for the defendant and the line P_c shows the expected gain for the plaintiff.

The defendant, who is in the wrong, is apt to simply pay up if he is to

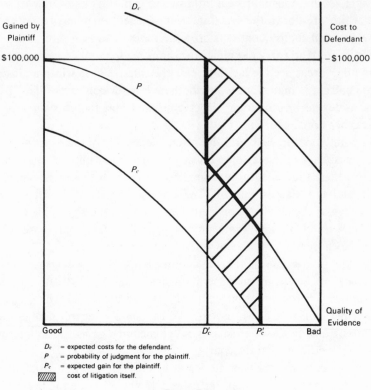

Figure 5.1
Social Cost of Litigation.

the left of line D'_c. In that area, the legal system justifies its existence by bringing about a correct result. On the other hand, to the right of line P'_c, where the present discounted value of collection minus the litigation costs is less than zero, the plaintiff will not bring suit; therefore, in this case the legal system not only does *not* justify its existence, it will be positively perverse.[1] In the area between P'_c and D'_c, which is the area in which most litigation occurs, we only have a probabilistic idea of whether the court will promote or hinder justice.

Fortunately, the probability line permits us to get an idea of the total number of cases which are carried out correctly. Specifically, the area below P and between D'_c and P'_c is the ex ante value of the correct decisions reached by the court, and the area above that line is the ex ante value of the cases in which the system goes wrong. Thus, below and to the left of the thickened line, we reach the right result; above and to the right of that line, the court is wrong. To repeat what I have said before, these lines are drawn for drafting convenience; I would not like to be on my oath that the comparative sizes of the areas to the left and below the thickened line and those to the right and above *in fact* represent the error propensity of our courts. As an offhand guess, I would think that the errors would be less prominent than shown in the diagram, but, in the absence of empirical evidence, this is merely a guess.

The benefit we receive from the court proceedings, then, is the area below and to the left of the thickened line. There are two costs. First are those costs in which the system goes wrong—those above and to the right of the thickened line. Note that there may not be any net social cost as a direct result of the court's decision. The defendant's success means that the defendant is wealthier and the plaintiff less wealthy, which, no doubt, is regarded as a cost by the plaintiff, but, from the social standpoint, the two cancel out. Inaccuracy of the court, in this case, simply means that opportunities in the form of possible bargains, which could have been made if the court were more effective, or laws could have been socially adjusted, are missed. On the other hand, there are cases in which the decision itself imposes positive costs on society: for example, suppose that the defendant had the duty to undertake some action which had a social benefit, and the court erroneously fails to compel him to do so.

The second cost is the cost of litigation itself, shown in figure 5.1 by the shaded area. Thus, the total opportunity cost is the sum of the area above and to the right of the thickened line *plus* the shaded area. This means that in the point where these two overlap, as they do above the thickened line and left of P_c', there is a double cost, i.e., there are the errors of the court *and* the costs of the lawyers who talk them into making the errors.

I suppose it is obvious that an improvement in accuracy will lower the total costs. Figure 5.2 is identical to figure 5.1, except that we assume that the court is more accurate, i.e., that it is less likely to be misled by deceptive evidence, etc., and therefore it achieves a higher P line. The area above and to the right of the thickened line is smaller, and the area below and to the left of it is larger. Thus, one element of cost is reduced.

The element of cost involved in the actual court proceedings themselves can be larger or smaller, depending essentially on the slant of

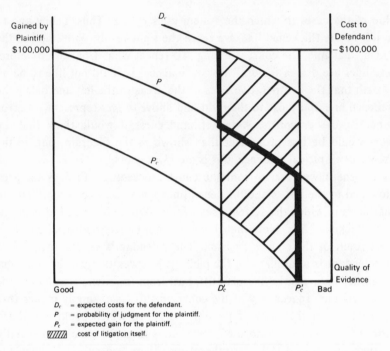

D_c = expected costs for the defendant.
P = probability of judgment for the plaintiff.
P_c = expected gain for the plaintiff.
▨ cost of litigation itself.

Figure 5.2
Social Cost of Litigation with More Efficient Court.

line P in the range between D_c' and P_c'. In the diagrams 5.1 and 5.2, it is roughly the same size, but, as an offhand guess, it would tend to be smaller with the more accurate court. There would be less litigation, even though the cost of each case were the same as before. Thus, improving the accuracy of the court leads to an unambiguous gain. Further, a large part of this gain accrues to people who do not participate in the litigation. All those cases which lay to the right of line D_c' in figure 5.1 and to the left of D_c' in figure 5.2 have been shifted from litigated cases to nonlitigated cases by the improvement in accuracy of the court. The shrinkage of the number of cases in which there is no litigation because it is predicted by both parties that the court will go wrong is also an important variable here.

It could be argued that my cost structure here is too simple. Many cases are settled out of court. Further, those cases which are never actually carried to the point of litigation—ones lying left of D_c' or right of P_c'—may in fact involve high legal costs as the parties inform themselves of the actual legal situation and perhaps engage in preliminary legal sparring. Thus, the real cost would not be my lozenge but a canoe-shaped structure along the P line. I do not think there is any great damage in using my approximation, but any reader who disagrees with me is free to draw in the canoes and use them instead of my lozenges.

While improvements in accuracy clearly lead to social gain, it is obvious that reduction in cost of litigation with *no* change in accuracy can also reduce social cost. Unfortunately, although this is true, the reduction in cost has to be handled carefully in order to avoid imposing indirect costs on society. The point is shown in figure 5.3, where I have used the same accuracy curve as in figure 5.1, but assume that there has been a very sharp reduction in costs, so that the costs to the defendant in refusing to pay the just claims of the plaintiff are only D_c', and the plaintiff's costs in suing are only P_c'. As a result, the number of cases where it is sensible for the defendant to refuse to pay is greatly increased, and the number of cases in which the plaintiff also should refuse to drop his claim, because the evidence is perverse, is reduced; consequently, there is very much more litigation. In this particular diagram, there are actually more total legal expenses when the cost of litigation per suit has been lowered, than there were in the higher-cost conditions of figure 5.1. This is an artifact of the drawing, but it does not seem to be a particularly improbable event.

The increase (if there is one) in total legal expenses, however, is not the major problem here. It is clear that the area above and to the right of the thickened line has been greatly increased by this reduction in cost. The number of correct decisions by the system has been lowered and the number of incorrect decisions raised.

Obviously, this is not an inevitable result of lowering court costs. It comes not from the reduction of the court costs but from the way in which the saving from the cost reduction was allocated. Suppose, for example, that the real resource cost of court proceedings was reduced as much as the reduction shown between figures 5.1 and 5.3, but there was a tax placed on the two parties so that their cost remained the same. Under these circumstances, we would have an unambiguous social gain, because there would be no change in outcome or costs for the parties and the government would obtain a revenue. I do not, of course, argue that such a tax would be socially optimal.

This obviously brings me to an important characteristic of lawsuits.

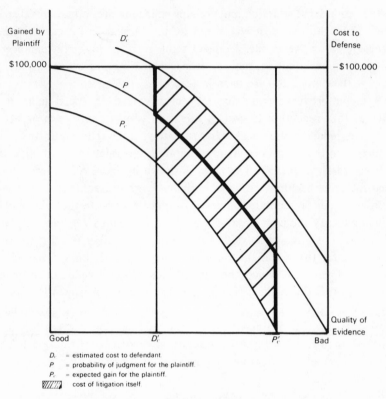

Figure 5.3
Social Cost of Litigation with Cheap But Inaccurate Court.

The cost of the lawsuits is not only a direct cost but it is also a factor in deciding which suits will be brought. Granted the court does make errors, the decision as to which cases will be brought also affects the efficiency of the system. Suppose, and I realize this is an unrealistic assumption, that a tax was imposed on legal proceedings, carefully calculated so that in all cases in which the probability of success to the plaintiff is more than 50 percent he could anticipate a positive return, ex ante, on his investment, but he would lose if he brought a case where the probability of success were less than 50 percent. Assume the converse set of institutions for the defendant. Under these circumstances, the only cases brought would be those in which the probability of success to both parties was exactly 50 percent (which would be a very small number of cases), the thickened line of figures 5.1, 5.2, and 5.3 would become vertical, and we would minimize social costs for a given level of court accuracy.

Obviously, no one feels that lawyers' judgments on probable outcomes are accurate enough so that this kind of institution would be sensible. Still, when we discuss changing court costs, we must always keep in mind that this will change the number of cases that are brought, as well as changing the costs of those cases which actually do get to court. Both effects are socially significant. Further, cases may be settled out of court at their ex ante value. For these cases, this 50 percent rule would lead to a rather bad disposition, with the plaintiff receiving only half of what is actually due him minus his costs. Further, for those cases to the right of the 50 percent line, a guaranteed perverse result would occur. Altogether, this institution could reduce the efficiency of the basic law or contract, and that, too, would have costs.

The problem is particularly severe if we have a program for reducing the costs of the actual parties by subsidizing their legal expenses. If we subsidize both sides' legal expenses, then the results can be extremely perverse. For example, suppose the real legal expenses are as shown on figure 5.1 but subsidies reduce the legal expenses to the parties to those shown on figure 5.3. Under these circumstances, we not only get the reduction in the social payoff to the law-enforcement scheme shown by the shift of the thickened line, but we also pay a resource cost in the form of lawyer's time, etc., which is about three times as high as it was in figure 5.1.

Another "reform" that is frequently recommended is subsidization of the legal expenses for only *one* side. The arguments for doing this may be arguments for bias, and discussion of this will be delayed for a few pages. For example, if we want the courts to be biased in favor of the accused, then paying the accused's legal expenses may be one way to acquire that particular bias. In making such a decision, we should realize that it will mean that the accused is much more likely to go to trial, even if the evidence is against him, than if we do not subsidize his defense. Once again, this will be discussed later.

The other situation, in which we subsidize both sides (the poverty-program lawyers, for example, representing both parties in a divorce case), is perverse *unless* there is some kind of preselection of the cases. If there is preselection, then the actual total legal procedure must include the preparation for, and activity in, the preselection process. In essence, as I have said before, we have two proceedings—the first of which is entered into for the purpose of obtaining government payment of one's legal fees, and then, once one has convinced the government that he is eligible for subsidization, a regular trial.

In sum, then, the benefit derived from court proceedings is the enforcement of the law or the contract, and a very large part of that benefit is derived from cases where the law or the contract is simply carried out without ever going to court. Of course, in many cases, it would be carried out even *without* the threat of legal proceedings, and if we had data, we could eliminate those cases. The costs are (a) the actual cost of the procedure itself, and (b) those cases in which the court goes wrong, in the specific sense that the parties are ordered to do something which they normally would *not* do and which imposes social costs. Thus, for example, an innocent man is imprisoned, or specific performance of a contract is erroneously ordered.

There is another element of opportunity costs. If the law were better enforced, then many contracts that are now considered undesirable could be undertaken. Further, the substantive law could be adjusted in such a way as to obtain greater benefits. These are opportunities for gain which we could hope to obtain if we improved the efficiency of the law, but it is hard to argue that they are positive costs for court errors. After all, if the court did not exist at all, these lost opportunities would be greater than they are now. Still, we should keep in mind that the efficiency of the court affects both the efficiency with which the contract-negotiation process is carried on (because the parties will have in mind the probable efficiency of the court enforcement of the contract) and the efficiency with which the substantive law can be drafted, for the same reason.

Actual measurement of the cost and benefit of a court system would be difficult, even at the conceptual level. Still, generally speaking, we can recognize improvement when we see it. Improvement in accuracy is an unambiguous gain, and reduction in costs is also an unambiguous gain, unless the savings are allocated among the parties in such a way as to perversely change the pattern of litigation. Such a perverse change must, of course, be large enough to offset the reduction in costs.

So far, I have not said anything at all about the problem of bias. Almost all discussions of judicial matters strongly urge that the procedures should be biased in some way. Normally, the bias in criminal actions is supposed to be in favor of the accused. For example, in Anglo-

Saxon countries, the accused is not to be convicted unless he is "guilty beyond reasonable doubt." In Continental countries, the slogan is, "If there is doubt, acquit." Lenin thought that in cases where people were accused of opposing his government, the bias should be in the other direction.

Our procedure in some cases imposes fairly strong biases against the "accused." To pick an empirically important example, the so-called Dohaney Amendment provides that drugs, additives, and a variety of other things must be removed from the marketplace if there is any significant evidence pointing in the direction of their being a carcinogen.[2]

Application of this amendment led to the abolition of the cyclamates industry (in the United States only; cyclamate is still readily available in Europe) on the basis of what now appears to be erroneous—and what even at the time, must have seemed very inadequate—evidence. Obviously this is not a criminal penalty, but the costs imposed can be extremely high. In a cyclamate case, the cost imposed on various chemical companies appears to have been in excess of $100 million. This is a clear-cut legal case of very strong bias against the company or individual producing the product alleged to be a carcinogen.

Somewhat the same procedure is apparently used by the Food and Drug Administration in the certification of new drugs. There are two parties at interest—the manufacturers and the potential customers. So far as I know, no studies have been made of the effect of the Dohaney Amendment on consumers, but the studies on the FDA seem to indicate that the withholding of drugs from the market by the FDA kills far, far more people than it protects. The delays in the introduction of new drugs, although such delays certainly make it less likely that defective drugs will come on the market, also lead to people dying because the new and successful drug is not available; it would appear that the excess deaths from the delay are more numerous than the lives saved by keeping defective drugs off the market.

It is not very obvious, however, that magic phrases like "beyond reasonable doubt" have any great effect on the behavior of judges and juries. The only empirical evidence on the subject of which I am aware is contained in two articles, one by Rita James Simon and one by her and Linda Mahan.[3]

In the Simon and Mahan article, various groups of people, including jurors and judges, were asked to translate "beyond reasonable doubt" into a percentage probability statement. The translations were extremely various, running from 50 percent to 100 percent but, roughly speaking, the mean was 85 percent. Interestingly, in the same study, the standard rule for civil proceedings—"a fair preponderance of the evidence"—was also translated by the respondents, and the mean result here was about 75 percent. Thus, it would appear that in actual practice, judges and juries probably use a very similar, but not quite as stringent, rule in determining transfer of funds from the defendant to the plaintiff in a civil suit as they do in determining whether to imprison someone for a crime. In both cases, it would appear that the plaintiff bears a substantial burden of proof if we believe that this, the sole empirical investigation of the subject of which I am aware, is in fact correct.

Once again, the fact that this is the sole and only investigation of which I am aware, and the fact that it contains many defects,[4] is, I believe, a very serious criticism of the present state of both the social sciences and the legal system. We should have a great deal more empirical evidence upon which to make decisions than we now do. The immense number of people engaged in "legal research" have produced almost nothing that is of any real value in determining whether our procedure is good or bad. In general, they have simply elaborated on court decisions or argued, usually on the basis of rather cloudy ethical ideas, that previous court decisions should be changed. There are almost no properly controlled studies of the actual impact of different types of procedure.

But let us consider this problem of bias a little more formally. For this purpose, I should like to turn to a diagram which I introduced in the *Logic of the Law*.[5] In figure 5.4, on the vertical axis is shown the likelihood that people in a given category of evidence are, in fact, guilty. On the horizontal axis, then, the cases are arranged in accord with the weight of evidence. Line E shows the percentage of persons in each evidence category who are, in fact, guilty. The shape of the line carries with it an assumption that the evidence is normally distributed, which seems a good null hypothesis, although once again, I would like empirical evidence.

Note that there are some guilty people at the far left, even though in this case there is practically no evidence against them. Similarly, there are some innocent people at the far right, even though the evidence is very strong against them. Both are cases where the evidence is perverse. On the other hand, the individuals who are at the far right, and are in

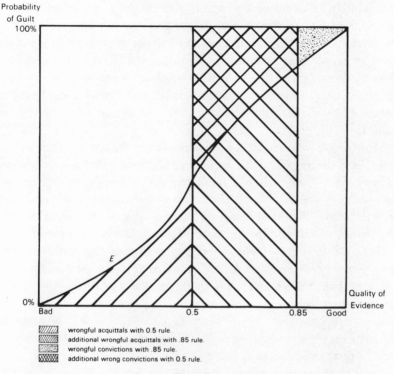

Figure 5.4
Bias in Favor of the Accused.

fact guilty, are examples of the evidence being strong and correct, and those at the left who are innocent benefit from strong evidence.

There seem to be two obvious ways to decide on the weight of the evidence needed to convict. The first would be simply to try to choose that required weight of evidence which minimizes total errors. As a general rule, this means that weight which gives about as many erroneous convictions as erroneous acquittals, which in our particular shape of the curve is 0.5.[6] Using this 0.5 weight of evidence, we would acquit in all cases to the left of line 0.5. Cases at the left of 0.5 and above line E–E are correctly decided, and those which are to the left and below (those that are ruled slanting downward to the left) are in error. Similarly, those to the right of 0.5 are convicted and all those which lie below line E–E are cases where this is correct. Those cases in the cross-hatched area and the dotted area are errors.

Suppose we bias the proceedings by moving the weight of evidence line to 0.85, which is about the mean of the one and only empirical study of the matter. This lowers the number of improper convictions to the dotted area but it increases a number of improper acquittals by the area ruled slanting downward to the right. Clearly there are more total errors. Is this increase in total errors compensated (or overcompensated) for by the reduction in the particular errors in which the defendant is unjustly held guilty?

Most people who have been indoctrinated in the conventional wisdom will regard the answer to the question as so obvious that it is foolish even to raise it. In fact, it is not at all obvious, although the conventional wisdom may well be correct. If we wish to use the threat of punishment to deter crime, then the present discounted value of the crime, including the chance of punishment, must be negative. If we bias proceedings in favor of the defendant, then, of necessity, we reduce the number of guilty persons who are convicted. It will be noted that the area on figure 5.4 which is shaded down and to the right (i.e., the area where guilty people are acquitted because of the change in the weight of evidence) is much larger than the area which is cross-hatched (which represents the *innocent* people who are acquitted). The minimum punishment which will deter is therefore necessarily increased.

Look at the matter entirely from the standpoint of innocent persons. The decision to bias the proceedings in favor of the defendant reduces the likelihood that he will be convicted, but it increases the penalty that he will suffer if he is convicted. It is not immediately obvious that innocent parties are benefited by this change.

Suppose there is a movement from 0.5 to 0.75 in the weight of evidence required to convict. Let us assume that this reduces the likelihood of conviction of a randomly selected innocent person by one-half. Suppose, also, that the reduction in frequency of conviction of guilty persons which was caused by this increase in the burden of proof on the prosecution required that sentences be doubled in order to retain the same deterrent effect. The increase of the sentence for the guilty people is sensible, and the fact that it cancels all of the gain to the innocent is unfortunate.

The real issue here would be whether increasing the burden of proof does or does not reduce the likelihood that innocent persons will be convicted *more* than it reduces the likelihood that guilty persons will be convicted. Assume that movement from 0.5 to 0.75 halved the probability that guilty persons would be convicted but cut the probability that innocent persons would be convicted by 0.75. Doubling the penalty would leave the deterrent effect of the court and punishment system unchanged.[7] On the other hand, the innocent person who previously would have faced, let us say, a 0.5 chance of one year in jail now faces a 0.125 chance of two years. Clearly, he has benefited.

The real issue, of course, is the relative reduction in the likelihood of punishment of guilt and innocence as we raise the burden of proof. Once again, that is an empirical issue upon which, so far as I know, nothing has been done. It does not seem particularly improbable, however, that innocent persons do gain from increasing the burden on the prosecution. Note, however, that the gain would be lower than it first appears, since the increase in the sentence certainly eliminates a good part of the expected gain and may (once again, our empirical knowledge is scanty here) more than cancel it.

I began this discussion by saying it was by no means obvious that we should bias proceedings in favor of the accused, and that seems to me a correct statement. The very common and very strong statements that this is a desirable policy, I think have to be put down to the fact that, before I wrote *The Logic of the Law*, no one had noticed the implication of biasing proceedings for the length of sentence. For reasons which will be discussed below, judges and juries are in fact apt to act in this way—giving the benefit of the doubt to the accused or the defendant—but the rationalizations which have been used for this activity are erroneous. However, further investigation may well lead to the conclusion that it was a correct policy, even if it had been reached by corrupt reasoning methods.

Before turning to why we observe this type of behavior on the part of the judges and juries, let us discuss briefly the situation in civil cases. As I have said, the only empirical study we have seems to indicate that the behavior of judges and juries in civil cases is not very much different from that in criminal cases. "A fair preponderance of the evidence" is translated as being 0.75 probability, whereas "beyond reasonable doubt" is translated as 0.85. Clearly, these are not very different.

In my opinion, juries, in general, are not willing to bring in large damage cases against ordinary citizens unless the weight of the evidence is considerably better than 0.5000001. This is of course an example of bias for the defendant. On the other hand, there are cases in which the jury may be biased in the favor of the plaintiff. If the defendant is a large corporation[8] or the government, then the jury may exhibit prejudice against the defendant. Note that it is also apparently true that corporate or government plaintiffs have trouble under similar circumstances. Needless to say, this is only a *large* corporation or government. A small corporation—let us say, a local grocery store—does not seem to suffer from this particular kind of difficulty.

The result of this bias against plaintiffs is clearly perverse. Assume, for example, that we are talking about a contract which is allegedly breached and for which large damages are claimed by the plaintiff. If the judge and jury use the rule under which there must be a 0.75 probability of being correct before a damage claim can be brought in, this means that many more just claims will be rejected than with a 0.5 rule. However, in this case there is no increase in the penalty to offset this reduction. Thus, the application of this rule means that the present discounted value of a claim is almost always less than the actual damage caused. Out-of-court settlements, then, tend to go against the plaintiff much more strongly than one would anticipate.[9]

The result is that many otherwise profitable contracts will not be negotiated, which surely imposes considerable social cost, and that many laws will either be enforced in a rather ineffective way or must be drafted with the idea that this type of bias exists. They are therefore less efficient than they could be if the courts maximized their performance by using the 0.5 rule.

The only attempt in our law to offset this kind of thing is the occasional use of triple damages in civil suits. This is an unusual expedient and, as far as I can see, the particular cases in which it is used are frequently badly chosen. For example, it is frequently possible to sue for triple damages in monopoly and Sherman Act cases. In these cases, the jury and judge are almost certainly biased against the defendant to begin with. Thus the triple-damage claim, instead of offsetting the bias in the proceedings, actually magnifies its effect.

Why do we observe a general bias against the prosecution in criminal cases? In spite of Lenin, it does seem to be very widespread in almost all legal systems. The standard arguments for it ignore the effect of the rule on the necessary punishment. Thus, the first assumption would be that this type of bias involves intellectual error.

I think, however, it is not quite that simple, although intellectual error is surely there. The real problem here is analogous to public goods in economics. Suppose I am making a decision as to whether or not a particular accused shall go to prison for twenty years. The decision to send him to prison is a clear-cut, straightforward imposition of specific, very great harm on a person I see before me. The contrary decision raises the total crime rate in the community by some small amount. The effect is highly dispersed, since it amounts to a slight reduction in the average well-being of the rest of the population as a whole, and it is hard to see. Under the circumstances, it is fairly easy for any individual to pay careful attention to the concentrated effect and very little attention to the highly dispersed effect.

This same line of reasoning would apply both to civil cases and to criminal cases. My decision that the defendant in this case shall pay $100,000 in damages, which will mean that he will lose both his business and his house (to say nothing of his car), inflict a very definite harm on him. The social benefit obtained by a contrary decision is much less clear and direct; therefore, it is easy to overlook.

In civil suits between two individuals this affect is not as clear. It is still true, however, that the defendant is likely to be badly harmed by a decision against him, while the plaintiff simply suffers an opportunity cost—i.e., he does not gain as much as he otherwise would—in a decision against him. If the plaintiff has already been very badly injured in an automobile accident, perhaps bias might go the other way; but, in practice, such cases normally involve an insurance company as the defendant.[10]

The bias against large corporations and the government can be explained in a similar manner. The cost of a large judgment against a corporation, or the failure by a corporation to collect, is actually widely dispersed in very small units to the stockholders of that corporation. Further, many citizens would think that really the cost does not get passed on to the stockholders anyway, because they do not understand how corporations work. Much the same can be said about the government, which is also subject to bias of this type.

Thus, if what I have said above is correct, the basic explanation for the "beyond reasonable doubt" rule in the criminal law and the effective, although not properly rationalized, bias in civil law is not a carefully thought-out line of reasoning but a fairly natural and normal way of thinking on the part of judges and juries. They are wrong in the sense that the social optimum is not achieved in the civil case, but it is possible that the rule is correct in the criminal case.

Finally, I should like to deal with one set of cases in which the bias is in the other direction—the bias is very heavily in favor of the prosecution and against the defendant. This is a collection of minor cases, mainly traffic violations, in which the cost to the defendant of conviction is usually quite small. The proceedings in this area are very heavily biased against the defendant. It is nearly impossible for the defendant to win the case, unless the officer who gave him the ticket admits that he has done something which is clearly improper. Note that in this case, although the cost to the defendant is usually very small, it can be very high—he may lose his driver's license. The loss of a driver's license to a cabdriver in Washington, D.C., is really a serious penalty.

Once again, I think this can be explained in terms of the dispersed and concentrated effect. In most cases, the cost of a traffic violation is very modest for the person convicted. The possibility of serious damage from auto accidents is clear to everyone, and hence this particular bias is not terribly hard to understand. It is notable that in most cases, the actual deprivation of the individual's driver's license is not done by the court. Courts are very reluctant to convict people of traffic offenses if it will lead to the revocation of their driver's licenses. The actual severe penalty that is then imposed on people, usually as a result of repeated convictions, is done by a completely anonymous agency, before which the individual has no right to a hearing. The outcome, I think, would be held unconstitutional by the Supreme Court were it not for the fact that Supreme Court justices can be killed by a careless driver, too. They are, therefore, less tender than with defendants accused of murder or robbery, crimes to which high-level jurists are very rarely subject.

Chapter 6

Technology: The Anglo-Saxons versus the Rest of the World

Turning to the technology of courts, we see that among Western countries there are two basic procedural systems.[1] One, which descends from the Roman law, is used by most Continental countries; and the other, which mostly descends from medieval precedents, is used in the Anglo-Saxon countries. There are a number of differences between these two methods, but only one will be discussed in this chapter. The Anglo-Saxon procedure is called the adversary system, because the proceeding is dominated by the two parties to the litigation with, in most criminal cases, one of the parties being a prosecuting attorney. It descends in part from trial by battle, in which the government official present at the trial simply refereed the contest. Under modern circumstances, the evidence and arguments are presented by the two sides and a judge, board of judges, or a group of conscripted private citizens (called jurors), decides which one has won.

The other system, used on the Continent, is usually called the inquisitorial system. In this system, the judges or judge are, in essence, carrying on an independent investigation of the case, and the parties play a much more minor role. I should warn the reader that I argue that the Roman jurists were right and the medieval feudal lords were wrong. The line of reasoning used will not rigorously prove this proposition.[2] Further empirical research will be necessary to prove that the inquisitorial system is superior to the adversary system. I shall merely establish a theoretical structure for the analysis of the two systems and present a strong argument that the inquisitorial system is better.

In practice, of course, the inquisitorial system of necessity has some adversary elements, since the parties are given some role in court; and

the adversary system has some inquisitorial elements, because the judge
(and, in some rare cases, the jury) also engage in some direct investigation of the case. The judge, for example, may occasionally ask questions
of the witness.

Consider the situation of a party in the adversary-type proceedings. He
can invest various amounts of resources in hiring lawyers, investigating
the facts, testifying himself—either truthfully or falsely, etc. Since he
knows a good deal about the facts of the case and can make an estimate
of the resources the other party will invest in his case, he should have an
idea of the likely probability of success for various investments of
resources. On the basis of this estimate, figure 6.1, line P_1, shows for one
party, Mr. Right, the probability of success for various resource commitments in a particular litigation.

We assume that there are two parties, Mr. Right and Mr. Wrong, and
that, as their names suggest, Mr. Right is the one who (if we had divine

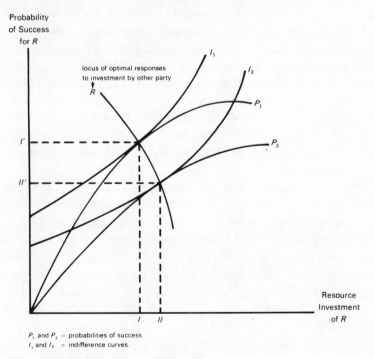

P_1 and P_2 = probabilities of success
I_1 and I_2 = indifference curves

Figure 6.1
Resource Adjustment of One Party.

justice) would win. Line P_1 then shows the probability of success that he can purchase by each investment of resources. The investment exhibits the usual declining marginal productivity. R's tastes are depicted by a set of indifference curves, I_1, I_2, and his bliss point is in the upper left-hand corner, with certain success at a zero resource investment. He chooses the resource commitment where his highest possible indifference curve is tangent to the production function line, with the result that he invests I resources and obtains a probability of success at I', as shown on the diagram.

If we consider the evidence available for the case, there are two meanings to the term. First, there is whatever still remains in the world which might have bearing on the case. This is more or less unchanging. Second, however, there is the evidence that is actually dredged up and presented in court. This is a function of the resources put into the case, and there should be better evidence actually presented to the court if more resources are invested. Suppose that Mr. Right thought Mr. Wrong would put in more resources, and hence that there was a lower probability of success with each investment by Mr. Right. This would produce curve P_2. Mr. Right is forced to be satisfied with the lower indifference curve I_2. Under these circumstances, he would invest II resources and obtain II' possibility of success.

In this case an increase in resources invested by Wrong leads Right to both increase his resources and reduce his likelihood of success, but this is not general. In cases in which the resource commitment or evidence is very one-sided, an increase in resources by the party in the stronger position may lead the other side to reduce his resource commitments and take the corresponding increased probability of losing the suit (see figure 6.3). It depends on the payoff to the marginal dollar of resources invested and, where it is less than $1, there is a motive for reducing instead of increasing expenditures.

If we consider all possible resource commitments by Mr. Wrong, each would be accompanied by a risk-production function, like P_1 or P_2, for Mr. Right, and Mr. Right would have an indifference curve tangent to it at some point. A line can be drawn connecting all such points. A segment of such a line is shown as R in figure 6.1. It is the reaction curve of Mr. Right to various possible investments of resources by Mr. Wrong. In figure 6.2, reaction curves for both of the parties are shown. On the vertical axis are the resources invested by R and on the horizontal are

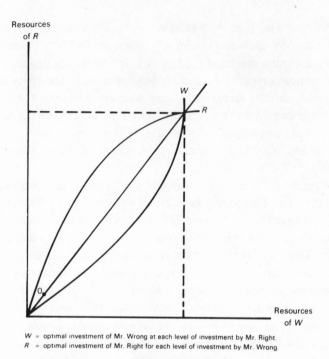

W = optimal investment of Mr. Wrong at each level of investment by Mr. Right.
R = optimal investment of Mr. Right for each level of investment by Mr. Wrong.

Figure 6.2
Resource Investments by Two Parties.

those invested by *W*. The probability of success in this diagram is a fan of rays from the origin. The straight line running through point 0, for example, shows those pairs of resource investments which all give the same probability of success for Mr. Right. Granting declining marginal returns and that the evidence is reasonably close to equal, the two curves will have the shape shown and will intersect as shown in the figure. The point of intersection is the equilibrium of the model, which would occur with Mr. Right investing R resources and Mr. Wrong investing *W*.

In figure 6.3, I have shown by line P the situation in which the evidence happens to be very strong for Mr. Right, and hence that he can purchase a high probability of success with a relatively modest investment of resources. Line P_1 goes up very steeply and is, of course, tangent to a very high indifference curve with a relatively low resource investment and a high probability of success. It might be, however, that the evidence is positively misleading, and hence that Mr. Right would have a low marginal return on resources invested in raising his probability. Line P_2 shows these circumstances, and the indifference curve tangent to it, I_2, which is a low one, shows the best that Mr. Right could do under these circumstances. It will be observed that Mr. Right would choose to put fewer resources into his suit in the unfavorable case than in the very favorable cases; but this is simply an artifact of the particular lines I have drawn. The reaction curves for the later case are shown on figure 6.4, and the equilibrium point is, of course, very near to the horizontal axis.

Looked at from the economic point of view, it is immediately obvious from figure 6.2 that the outcome is not ideal. I have drawn an equiprobability line from the equilibrium point to the origin and put a point 0 on it. Point 0 has the same probability of success for the two parties, but with a much lower investment of resources. Clearly, it dominates the equilibrium solution. This is also true of point 0 on figure

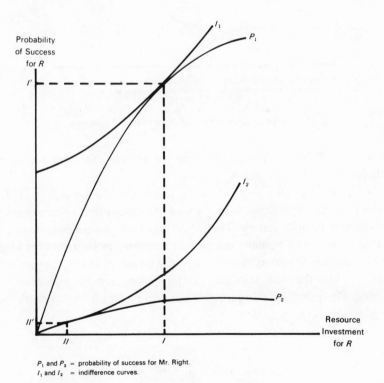

P_1 and P_2 = probability of success for Mr. Right.
I_1 and I_2 = indifference curves.

Figure 6.3
Response of Mr. Right at Different Levels of Evidence.

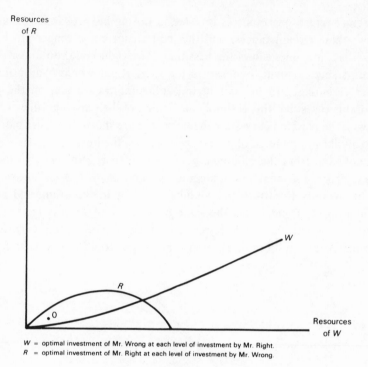

W = optimal investment of Mr. Wrong at each level of investment by Mr. Right.
R = optimal investment of Mr. Right at each level of investment by Mr. Wrong.

Figure 6.4
Response of Mr. Right at Different Levels of Evidence.

6.4. The only question is whether an institutional structure can be designed which will reach 0.

I should now like to introduce a game which is helpful in analyzing court proceedings. Suppose that a sum of money is put up as a prize for a particular form of lottery. The lottery has only two contestants and each of them may buy as many tickets for the lottery as he wishes for $1 each. One ticket is drawn at random, and the owner of the ticket receives the prize. Note that the payments for the tickets are not added on to the prize. The payoff to this game for our two parties is shown on the set of equations (6.1).

$$V_R = D \cdot \frac{R}{R + W} - R$$

$$V_W = D \cdot \frac{W}{R + W} - W$$

(6.1)

The ex ante value for Right, for example, is the prize (D) times the probability that the ticket purchased by Right will be drawn [$R/(R + W)$], minus the amount of money put in by Right (R). Wrong's value is symmetric. It is obvious that we could solve this equation set, although in the real world we might want to add in risk aversion.[3]

This set of equations, of course, would generate a set of lines of the same nature as those drawn in figure 6.1 and a set of reaction functions similar to those shown in figure 6.2. The probability of success is a function both of resources invested by the player and those invested by the other party, and exhibits declining marginal returns.

This game can be changed so that it maps many different types of trial institutions. Temporarily we are interested only in one particular type here. The equations as given are egalitarian, i.e., they indicate that two parties, in the nature of things, have the same inherent likelihood of winning. In the real world, the physical evidence available in a case is rarely evenly balanced. This can be easily dealt with by adjusting the equation.

For example, we might alter the rules of the game so that Mr. Right can purchase two lottery tickets for \$1, whereas Mr. Wrong must still pay \$1 for each one. This would increase the value for Mr. Right. Indeed, there are many complications of this sort that can easily be put into the game; but since we do not know a great deal about the real-world parameters, there is no great reason for us to be extremely complex in our discussion of the matter. No doubt the payoff to various conditions which may make the trial less than completely equal—such as evidence in favor of one side—is quite complex; but, for the moment, let us use a very simple function. A variant of the game, in which the number of tickets Mr. Right can buy for \$1 is R times some function (f) of the evidence (E), is shown in equation set (6.2).

$$V_R = D \cdot \frac{f(E)R}{f(E)R + W} - R$$

$$V_W = D \cdot \frac{W}{f(E)R + W} - W \tag{6.2}$$

To make it easier to deal with some matters to which we will turn shortly, I should like to further simplify these equations and change them from statements as to the payoff of the game to the probability of success. This permits me to drop part of the equation as in equation set (6.3).

$$P_R = \frac{f(E)R}{f(E)R + W} \qquad P_W = \frac{W}{f(E)R + W} \qquad (6.3)$$

Note that the reason I have attached the evidence function to R instead of to both R and W is simply that they would be different functions and, without any knowledge of their exact shape, it seems a waste of time to make the matter more complicated than is necessary.

In this form, the equation shows in a particularly pure form the externality associated with adversary proceedings. If I increase the likelihood that I will win by 1 percent, I automatically reduce the likelihood that you will win by 1 percent. Under the circumstances, the likelihood that I will choose the resource investment which is socially optimal is, to put the matter mildly, slight.

So far, we have discussed almost exclusively the adversary proceeding rather than the inquisitorial, and hence I have not fulfilled my promise that the two will be compared. To make a comparison, I would like to introduce another set of equations, set (6.4).

$$P_R = \frac{f(E)R}{f(E)R + W} + g(F) \qquad g(F) > 0$$

$$P_W = \frac{W}{f(E)R + W} - g(F) \qquad g(F) < 0 \qquad (6.4)$$

This is, of course, the same as set (6.3), except that another term has been added on at the right. This term shows the investment of resources in the actual judging process, something which, up to now, we have not considered. This function is assumed to improve Mr. Right's chances as the resources invested in judging (F) are increased simply because he is right.

With this modification, we can now deal somewhat more generally with the problem. It is clear that increasing the skill or diligence of decision makers will increase the likelihood of accuracy, and this is not subject to the kind of externality we were discussing earlier. The difference can perhaps best be seen from considering a rather unusual way of investing resources in a trial. Suppose that instead of permitting the parties to decide how much they were going to spend on legal fees for their own attorneys, we let them decide how much they would like to put in to hire a judge. Each one could contribute whatever he wished, and then the authorities would purchase for this trial the best judge that could be obtained for the sum of the two contributions. Of course, the judge would not be told which of the two parties put up the most money.

Unless we assume that, in making selection of judges, we are random or, perhaps, systematically perverse, surely a better judge would be hired if there were more resources available.[4] If, then, with larger amounts of money we get a decision maker who is better qualified and more likely to reach the right conclusion, it will be contrary to the interests of Mr. Wrong to have a very good judge and he would tend to put no money at all into the pot.[5] Mr. Right, on the other hand, would want a good judge and would be willing to make a suitable payment. Presumably, the amount he would be willing to pay would be less if the case looked to him to be an easy one and, hence, suitable for a rather poorly qualified judge.

The interesting feature of this little *Gedankenexperiment*, however, is not Mr. Right's investment but Mr. Wrong's. Mr. Wrong would have no motive to try to improve the quality of the judiciary, because the better the judiciary, the worse off he is going to be. Whereas he might have very strong motives to hire excellent attorneys and put a lot of money into his legal defense under the adversary system, under this system he would have no motive for investment at all. A good judge in essence changes the production function of the initial parties, as shown on figure 6.1, in the sense that he raises the production function for Mr. Right and lowers the production function for Mr. Wrong. Thus, each improvement in the quality of the judge tends to move cases in the proper direction.

The point of this chapter has been to compare the European-type procedure (inquisitorial) with that used in Anglo-Saxon countries (adversary). It can be seen that the basic difference between these two is the amount of resources put on the two parts of our set of equations. The adversary proceeding puts almost all of its resources on R and W in (6.4); and the inquisitorial proceeding puts almost all of them on F. I have, so far, been simplifying the situation when I talk about the adversary proceedings by assuming that $g(F)$ is zero, and I could take the complementary simplification and assume that, in Europe, R and W are zero.

An American attorney who read this section accused me of setting up a straw man. He claimed that the system is not anywhere near as pure as the model would indicate. Judicial-supervision control of the process is already significant and growing more important. There are, in fact, now rules that penalize a party for the cost caused to an adversary who is forced to prove a fact that should have been admitted.

The lawyer's comments are both correct and incorrect. It is certainly true that judicial control is somewhat greater than zero. It is also true that just at the moment it is growing. The history of law in the United States shows phases in which judicial control grows and phases in which it is reduced. We are in one of the growth phases right now. A point the lawyer did not mention is that in England judicial control on the proceeding is very much stronger than the United States.

Nevertheless, the difference between the system in the United States, or even in England, and Continental procedure is still very, very large. We can say that there are elements of inquisitorial proceeding in American procedure and much stronger elements in England, but, nevertheless, they are still basically adversary. It is, of course, also true that there are elements of the adversary approach in Continental courts, but these are relatively minor compared to the strength of the adversary procedure in Anglo-Saxon law.

The basic difference between the two, as will be seen, is the W which appears in all of the equations. In the adversary proceedings, a great deal of the resources are put in by someone who is attempting to mislead. Assume, for example, that in the average American court case, 45 percent of the total resources are invested by each side and 10 percent by the government in providing the actual decision-making apparatus. This would mean that 55 percent of the resources used in the court are aimed at achieving the correct result, and 45 percent at reaching an incorrect result. Under the inquisitorial system, assume that 90 percent of the resources are put up by the government which hires a competent board of judges (who then carry on an essentially independent investigation) and only 5 percent by each of the parties. Under these circumstances, 95 percent of the resources are contributed by people who are attempting to reach the correct conclusion, and only 5 percent by the saboteur. Normally, we would anticipate a higher degree of accuracy with the second type than with the first.

This line of reasoning is so simple that I always find it difficult to understand why the Anglo-Saxon court system has persisted. Its origins, from trial by battle, are obvious enough and, at a time when the law quite literally was the will of the stronger, it was indeed quite rational. Its persistence can perhaps be explained in terms of the inertia of established custom, but customs do change.

There is, of course, an immensely powerful interest group favoring the preservation of the present situation in Anglo-Saxon courts. The number of lawyers per capita in Anglo-Saxon countries (and, in particular, the United States) is a high multiple of the number in systems using the inquisitorial system. We also probably have more judges per capita than such countries as Switzerland and Sweden, in spite of the greater emphasis put on judicial decision-making in those countries. The higher inherent accuracy of their court system means that there are fewer cases brought before the courts; and, once the case is brought, the judge makes the decisions as to how much time will be spent on it, rather than the parties, with the result that cases are frequently disposed of quite quickly with good accuracy.

A change from our system to the Continental system would eliminate a sizable part of the demand for lawyers. This statement is not, of course, made under the assumption that our lawyers spend all of their time in court; indeed, they spend relatively little of their time in court. The advice they give, however, is very heavily affected by the type of judicial proceeding they anticipate if a court case does arise. Further, they spend much time negotiating cases and preparing cases. All of this is less expensive in Europe.

A sharp fall in the demand for lawyers would, of course, impoverish the present profession. Many lawyers would become vacuum-cleaner salesmen, law schools would be compelled to close, immense bodies of accumulated personal capital would cease to be of any relevance, and, altogether, the legal profession would suffer a major disaster.[6] Under the circumstances, the opposition of the lawyers to the type of legal system used on the Continent is understandable.

Lawyers defending our current system do offer some arguments for it. The first I usually encounter in talking to the average American lawyer is an expression of incredulity that any other system exists. They will then tell me a few myths about European procedure, such as, that the defendant is compelled to prove his innocence rather than the prosecution being compelled to prove his guilt; but, once one has penetrated through this smoke screen, there is an intellectually possible defense of our system.

The point of this defense is that the judge may be undermotivated, and hence will not work hard enough. The two sides, whatever else may be said about them, are strongly motivated; hence, they can be expected to put a great deal of resources into influencing the decision. The judge has nothing personal riding on it and may not put much effort into his decision, according to this argument.[7] This matter will be discussed in considerable detail in chapter 8.

One of the problems in research of this type is, of course, that the courts have the power to prevent themselves from being investigated. In general, we take the view that people who try to avoid investigation do so because the investigation would turn up things that are not to their credit; but it must be admitted that courts may have a valid reason for not wanting to be investigated. It is possible to argue that the judicial system works better if it is surrounded by myths and magic than if everyone concerned knows that the court regularly makes mistakes.

Regardless of this, I now turn to a second issue, which is how hard judges and juries work. It seems fairly certain that judges and juries are not particularly highly motivated in law cases, and hence there is something to be said for the view that leaving everything to them would be undesirable. It should be pointed out that there are various methods used in Europe to provide stronger motives for judges than are provided under the Anglo-Saxon system. The judicial career is organized with promotion, regular transfers, etc. This would normally motivate judges under this system more strongly than the judge under the Anglo-Saxon system. Certainly the jurors, who are conscripted amateurs, have practically no motives to work hard.

In fact, there is no reason to believe that judges and juries under either system are optimally motivated. Research should be undertaken for the purpose of developing institutions which will give them a better motivation. But the undermotivation is more extreme with respect to the jury and the Anglo-Saxon judge than with respect to the European judge. In Anglo-Saxon adversary proceedings, the parties have every motive to put great resources into presenting their case; but this case is to be presented before a group of people who, in the case of the jury, are amateurs, of average intelligence, and are not strongly motivated to hard intellectual labor to understand the case. As a result, the parties' arguments are unlikely to be designed in such a way as to put great strain on the minds of the listeners, even if the situation is such that truth can only be obtained with such great strain.

Still, the weak motivation for the public officials concerned is a defect in both court systems. It is not obvious that it is less of a defect for the Anglo-Saxon than for the European system, but it is clear that public officials play a larger role in the European system. Thus, it is at least conceivable that the undermotivation of the judges more than counterbalances the overinvestment of resources by the parties, with which this chapter has been mainly concerned.

It will not have escaped the reader that, personally, I favor the European system. It seems to me the theoretical arguments in its favor are much stronger than those against it. But I cannot be sure. The whole field of legal research has been dominated by essentially unscientific techniques. This has been particularly true of the comparison of these methods of reaching decisions in lawsuits. This chapter has been an effort to set the matter on a sound theoretical basis. Without further research, particularly empirical research, it is not possible to be certain that the Continental system is better than the Anglo-Saxon, but the presumption is surely in that direction.

Appendix

A Digression on Arbitral Geography

When a portion of this chapter appeared in *Kyklos*, my argument that the European system was basically better than ours apparently upset a great number of people and, in particular, there were two comments on it, one by McChesney and one by Ordover and Weitzman.[8]

Frankly, I did not think that either comment made much of a dent in my basic reasoning. This may, of course, simply represent the usual author's vanity but, in any event, my reply to them was rather brief.[9]

In general, the arguments offered by these three critics seem to have had very little impact. One particular argument by McChesney, however, has since been repeated by other scholars. In my opinion, once again, this is a rather weak argument, but granted the support it seems to have, I do not feel I can simply pass over it in silence. On the other hand, I do not see why all of my readers should devote their attention to what I think is basically a fallacious argument. Hence, this Appendix which can be either read or skipped.

Let me begin by quoting McChesney's argument.

Arbitration permits parties to agree beforehand that any disagreement between them in the course of future dealings will be settled, not in court, but in pre-arranged private proceedings whose result is binding on the parties. Most importantly, the parties are able to stipulate the procedures, including those relating to evidence, that will be followed. To quote from one legal source:

"The essence of arbitration is its freedom from the formality of ordinary judicial procedure, and unless it is stipulated that the arbitrators should follow legal rules of procedure, the courts have no jurisdiction to set aside and award for failure of the arbitrator's to follow court rules.... Where *unrestricted by the agreement* or by statute, the arbitrators are allowed much latitude in their procedure, and there is no requirement that they observe technical rules and formalities, so long as the proceedings are honestly and fairly conducted."

"All questions as to the admission or rejection of evidence as well as the credit due to evidence, and the inferences of fact to be drawn from it, are matters for the arbitrators to decide in the exercise of their honest judgement. Formal rules as to the admissibility and the weight and sufficiency of evidence do not bind them . . . unless a statute or the *agreement so directs*."

There are other differences as to rules of evidence that are important: arbitrators may minimize total costs by stipulating the time within which evidence must be produced and refuse to hear that brought in too late. They may limit the number of witnesses to be heard, and need not rely solely on the evidence brought forth in arbitration proceedings but may draw on their own experience or knowledge, and even testify themselves. But the important point is that these provisions are all matters of negotiations between the parties, such that the externalities claimed by Tullock can be internalized.[10]

McChesney then goes on to point out that parties to international contract can frequently contract in such a way as to have the case tried in a selected jurisdiction. He then continues:

In fact, this is no idle theoretical game. It is precisely the sort of contracting that occurs when parties form an international sales agreement. Legal commentator's note:

"The parties to a contract for sale of goods abroad are well advised to provide expressly which legal system they desire to be applied to their contract. . . . The parties may submit their contract to any legal system which they like to elect and, in particular, they are not limited to a legal system with which the circumstances surrounding their contract have an actual connection.

". . . The parties to the contract are permitted, if they so wish, to nominate the law of a particular country as the proper law of the contract. If they do this, their choice is conclusive. . . ."

Given this situation of free contracting, it is of great interest for the controversy at hand that the majority of such international contracts, regardless of the nationality of the parties, specify that litigation is to take place in England. If Anglo-American common law is inferior, its inferiority is not borne out by the behavior of the parties able to select the most efficient jurisdiction for themselves.[11]

Let me begin with a problem of fact. McChesney gives no source for his statement about the courts chosen.[12] On being asked, he said he had been told this by one of his law professors (he was a law student at the time). It seems likely that that law professor's sample of cases from which he made his subjective judgment was drawn in the United States and England. The superiority of the courts of England over those in the United States is, of course, strictly speaking, not relevant. Nevertheless, for reasons I will discuss below, I would not be surprised to discover that international litigation was very commonly carried on in an English-speaking court.

Before turning to these matters, however, I should like to go on to a second rather similar comment contained in an article by Landes and Posner.[13] They say:

> Notwithstanding all the above reservations, the use of arbitration as a benchmark for evaluation of the judicial system may help resolve a recent controversy between Gordon Tullock and others regarding the relative efficiency of the Anglo-American adversarial and Continental inquisitorial procedural system. It appears that most arbitrators are conducted according to English or American arbitration procedure—and, as mentioned, a nation's arbitration procedures tend to follow its judicial procedures. Here then is some, albeit limited, marked evidence of the superiority of the adversary system.[14]

Note that Landes and Posner are not endorsing McChesney's point of view. Indeed, instead of saying most cases take place in England, they say that most arbitration cases follow either English or American arbitration procedures. Once again, however, there is a question of fact. They footnote three sources,[15] none of which contains any statistical evidence. The basic problem with their remark, however, is the phrase about arbitration procedures tending to follow judicial procedures, for which they state no source at all. Indeed, in the next paragraph, they point out a number of rather radical differences between arbitration and standard procedures of Anglo-Saxon law.

The theory underlying the McChesney, and Landes and Posner, argument is that if people are free to choose the type of judicial procedure they will face in enforcing a contract, they will tend to choose the most efficient one. I agree, and indeed took the same point of view in *Logic of the Law*.[16] We might expect technological progress, in the sense that new techniques are discovered which are better than existing ones, and some inertia, in the sense that the parties will not instantly switch to the most efficient method, but on the whole we would expect parties to choose the most efficient course of action if they have a choice available to them. I would argue that the rapid growth of arbitral proceedings in the United States[17] is evidence that we have had here a technological change[18] to which the commercial community is adapting. All this is evidence of the superiority of the arbitral technique over the regular courts. It is, of course, the evidence of the superiority of arbitration over the Anglo-American courts, not over Continental courts. Nevertheless there is, in fact, a good deal of arbitration on the Continent too. This is clear evidence that the Continental procedure is not optimal, even if it is better than the Anglo-Saxon.

To demonstrate from statistics on arbitration that Anglo-Saxon procedure is better (or worse) than Continental, we need fairly good statistics. The total number of arbitrations is of little or no use, because the overwhelming majority of these arbitrations are fairly minor matters, which are handled very quickly and easily by arbitration, and in which the parties have not made any real choice as to what arbitral tribunal they will take. They will simply take the one that is readily and immediately available, because the issue is not of such importance that they make a worldwide search for the best tribunal and then run all across the world to take the case to London or, for that matter, Tokyo.

Most large-scale commercial contracts are in English simply because that is the language of international trade. This would point toward an English-speaking tribunal to interpret them. Further, an arbitral tribunal is not capable of enforcing its decisions and must turn to the regular courts for this purpose. We need, then, an arbitral tribunal located in a country where the courts will enforce its decisions, and where the loser is apt to have enough assets on hand so that the enforcement can proceed even if he objects. This tends to lead toward England, or better yet, the United States, as the place of arbitration. In this connection, it should be said that Anglo-Saxon law puts very few restrictions on what one can contract to do and hence gives greater freedom to the parties. Presumably, a French court in enforcing an arbitral tribunal would only enforce it if the contract itself were legal in France.

Probably as a result of these factors, together with the fact that London used to be the commercial center of the world, and English courts were much kinder to arbitration in the early years than American, the development of a set of external economies for arbitration procedures in London has occurred. It is simply somewhat easier to run arbitration there than almost anywhere else. We should not be particularly surprised then to find many cases in London.

Finally, however, the question arises as to whether the fact that an arbitration procedure is carried on in London is any evidence at all with respect to common law as opposed to Continental procedure. Clearly the procedure is different from the common law or the parties would have no motive to seek arbitration. Indeed, Landes and Posner point out no less than six major differences between the common-law procedure and arbitration.[19] In essence, they are saying that the common-law version of arbitration is superior to the Continental version of arbitration. Whether there is very much difference between the two is not in any way examined empirically. My own impression from scattered reading is that arbitration resembles the Continental procedure for civil suits, although it does not resemble the procedure for criminal actions. This, however, is a mere impression.

It does seem to me that looking into what parties choose when they are given freedom to choose—i.e., the type of arbitral procedure that they select—is a valuable research technique. Further, I would rather anticipate that improvements in legal procedure would be more likely to come out of arbitration procedure than out of the regular government courts. Nevertheless, in order to engage in this kind of research, we actually have to do the research and not simply speculate. I must admit that I have been as casual here as McChesney, Posner, and Landes, but at least I have not claimed any particular conclusions from my lack of research. I simply suggest that we look into this area to find out whether the law can be improved.

Chapter 7

Various Ways of Dealing with the Cost of Litigation

In the last chapter, on the basis of the cost/accuracy trade-off, I argued that the Continental system of procedure is better than that used in Anglo-Saxon countries. I find that this normally shocks lawyers.[1] This chapter will be devoted to the adversary system and an investigation of different methods of paying lawyers' fees. For this purpose, I will use the gambling game which I introduced in chapter 6 as a simple model of court procedure. The reader will recall that I promised a demonstration that the model could be used to investigate other methods of paying for litigation; we will proceed to that task now.

In the models that follow, I will make certain simplifying assumptions. First, the costs of judges, juries, courtrooms, etc., will be ignored. Normally the parties do not pay these expenses; and adding figures into our equations for the minor "court costs" which they *do* pay would be an unnecessary complication. Since these publicly provided resources are not taken into account by the parties, the actual social investment of resources is greater than that shown by our equilibrium points. In arbitration proceedings, of course, the parties *do* pay for the cost of the "judges," and presumably there is a more rational allocation of resources under those circumstances. Arbitration will be dealt with later.

No doubt the most common way of reallocating legal resources in the United States is the "contingent fee." A lawyer takes the plaintiff's case in return for a promise that he will receive some percentage of the proceeds (usually one-third) if he wins and nothing if he loses. It is not very clear in the discussion of this situation in the legal literature whether or not the court is supposed to take this fee into account in fixing the damages. In some cases—for example, some antitrust cases—Congress has provided that the defendant may pay the plaintiff's fees; and in civil rights cases, some courts have recently required a defendant to pay the plaintiff's fee even when the defendant wins. In these cases, the fee is added onto the decision (at least in theory). In most automobile damage suits, it is subtracted from the decision. This may or may not make a difference in the size of the fee and/or the amount actually received by the plaintiff. But leaving this unsolved question unsolved, it is clear that under these circumstances there are three parties at interest—the defendant, the plaintiff, and the plaintiff's attorney. Their interests are shown by equation set (7.1).

$$D_V = \frac{D}{D + P + L} \cdot M - D$$

$$P_V = \frac{P + L}{D + P + L} \cdot \tfrac{2}{3} M - P$$

$$L_c = \frac{P + L}{D + P + L} \cdot \tfrac{1}{3} M - L \qquad (7.1)$$

In this case, D is the defendant, P is the plaintiff, and L is the lawyer.

In practice, L, the resources invested by the lawyer for the plaintiff, are larger by quite a wide margin than P, the resources invested by the plaintiff himself; so the real issue in bringing the system of equations into equilibrium is primarily that D and L each maximize their return (minimize loss in the case of D). The plaintiff (in most cases) does not have enough money so that he could pay the fee of a really first-class attorney under any system other than the contingent-fee system. In a way, the attorney is acting as a banker for the plaintiff. Presumably the reason that the credit market covering plaintiff fees in this case has developed in this way is simply that bankers would have much less knowledge as to the relative likelihood of success in a case than will a skilled attorney. The fact that younger attorneys usually have a lot of spare time—hence, the opportunity cost of taking a case is low—may also be significant.

As a first approximation, I would tend to say that this system leads to underinvestment of resources for the plaintiff. The lawyer will receive only one-third of the damage suits he wins and hence will only invest resources up to the point where it pays, granted that one-third payoff. Under the circumstances, there are fewer resources supplied than would be the case if both of the parties were able to hire an attorney out of their own funds, but there's no reason to believe that the system is unfair to the plaintiffs.

There is, however, something that I have glossed over here. The plaintiff invests relatively little in actual cash and may get a great deal out of it. Under the circumstances, one would anticipate that plaintiffs would make every effort to obtain a leading lawyer. Thus, there is a preliminary decision by the attorney as to whether or not he will take the plaintiff's case. This decision can be decisive. If the plaintiff cannot get an attorney to take his case, he has lost.

I have been unable to find any serious discussion about how attorneys make their decisions in these matters. Certainly there is no formal hearing with both parties represented. The potential defendant would be particularly anxious to be represented if it were permitted. I imagine that the attorneys in fact investigate these cases very carefully, since they do not want to waste their own time on a poor case. One might even hope that they would only take those cases in which they were personally convinced that their client was in the right. Their investigative methods, I am sure, are not adversary but inquisitorial.

Under these circumstances, the potential plaintiff provides any information that the lawyer requests; and the lawyer either investigates—or sends out junior members of his office to investigate—the actual circumstances. The plaintiff does not really have control, although he may devote a good deal of energy in attempting to attract the attention of a lawyer, and indeed may even hire a lawyer for the purpose of making approaches to another more highly qualified lawyer. The resource investment, therefore, is probably much smaller than we see in court. But there is no reason to believe that the decision is any less accurate.

Indeed, the attorney probably makes a much better decision than the judge and the jury, albeit on a different subject. He is going to invest his own resources in this case, and he will lose them if he makes a mistake. This is a totally different situation from that of the judge and jury, who will be out not one single cent if they reach the wrong decision.[2] Thus, the decision by a plaintiff's attorney as to whether the situation in a given case is such that the present discounted value of his fee is greater than his own investment is a matter which he considers much more carefully than the judge and jury will later consider the actual case.

Since a large part of the cost of such a case is in the time of a very skilled man—i.e., the plaintiff's attorney—and his assistants, one would anticipate that the cases would tend to be distributed in such a way that the most skilled of the attorneys took those cases which had the highest probability of large judgments and the less skilled took those which involved smaller judgments and/or smaller probability of success.[3] Of course, this is rational, and it improves the efficiency of the court system if we assume that these lawyers are adept in determining what is a sound case. I see no reason to doubt this, and the fact that they use inquisitorial methods rather than adversary proceedings in order to make that estimate seems to me a point in their favor, rather than a point against them.

In any event, the procedure is fairly straightforward. The plaintiff seeks out a plaintiff's attorney. The plaintiff's attorney then investigates the issue and decides whether he wishes to take the case. This part of the proceeding, which may be very important indeed for the plaintiff (and, for that matter, for the defendant), is not covered by our equations, because they deal with adversary proceeding. If the attorney turns down the plaintiff, the plaintiff is free to seek out another attorney. In part, the shift from attorney to attorney would be merely random with attorneys making different judgments. In the long run, however, the plaintiff is apt to work his way down to less- and less-skilled attorneys. The less-skilled attorneys tend to be less busy and, hence, the opportunity cost to them of taking even a bad case is less. On the other hand, of course, they are less likely to win, and presumably know that.

If the attorney accepts the case, then the matter goes to trial (or negotiation) with the plaintiff's attorney putting up most of the resources and making substantially all of the important decisions. Under the circumstances, the P equation more or less drops out, because P, although he is the principal beneficiary if he wins, puts in few further resources. He has already invested his resources (wisely, we hope) in securing the services of the attorney. That this was relatively inexpensive simply reflects the fact that inquisitorial proceedings are usually more efficient than adversary proceedings. As a reasonable approximation, equation set (7.1) could be solved by omitting the P equation and solving the D and L equations.

Whether this system is an improvement over the system in which the two parties put up the resources is not clear. The usual argument is that it permits impecunious clients to sue. Note, however, that it only assists impecunious *plaintiffs*. Perhaps it is assumed that impecunious persons are not likely to be defendants because they have few assets. It also clearly leads to a situation in which lawyers who happen to have a little free time can bring suits of little merit if they think that the court system is inherently inaccurate. For example, assume that the court system with respect to some particular type of case is apt to go wrong one time in four. A young attorney just starting out in the business would be well advised to try to find a client for whom he could act as a contingency-fee attorney, even if the client's case were poor. Still, as I said before, it is by no means obvious that this is either a poorer or a better system than one in which each party pays his own expenses.

The "crime" of barratry is relevant here. Surely if the court system were both accurate and cheap, the person who instigated lawsuits would be performing a public service for which he should reasonably be paid. Lawyers would be the obvious persons to perform this particular type of service for society. It is only if the legal system is both expensive and inaccurate that this type of activity is socially undesirable.

There is another example of the same problem—suits against judges for bringing in erroneous decisions. If court proceedings were inexpensive and reasonably accurate, such suits would be rare, for judges would rarely bring in erroneous decisions, but this would surely be a sensible institution to have as a way of motivating judges to concentrate on the cases. Indeed, a special court for the specific purpose of imposing this kind of discipline on judges would probably be desirable. If, on the other hand, court proceedings are expensive and uncertain, then it would be almost impossible for judges to perform their duties if this sort of lawsuit were permitted. Suppose, for example, that incorrect suits could hope for success one time in eight. The expected cost to a judge bringing in a decision which inflicted injury on anyone, even a mass murderer, would be high. Thus, the errors of the court system are one of the reasons why the court is protected against suit, although I have never seen any of the judges discuss the matter using this particular argument.

We now turn to a system for paying the costs of adversary proceedings that is in vogue in England. In England, after a decision is made in a civil suit, the legal costs of the winner are usually paid by the loser. A simplified version of this cost structure is shown in equation set (7.2).

$$P_v = \frac{P}{P + D} \cdot M - \frac{D}{P + D} \cdot (P + D)$$

$$D_v = \frac{D}{P + D} \cdot M - \frac{P}{P + D} \cdot (P + D) \tag{7.2}$$

Each party has some chance of winning the prize and an inverse probability of paying both parties' legal fees. In general, one would anticipate that this system would lead to parties being reluctant to bring litigation, because of the greater risk involved, but fighting very hard once litigation has been undertaken.

In practice, however, things are not quite this simple. The winning party does not simply present all of its bills to the defeated party for payment. A "taxing master" is appointed, and this official is usually a lawyer (barrister) and may be generous to other lawyers. In any event, he decides how much should be paid. Exactly how he decides is not clear, but it is clear that he does not necessarily award all expenses. It seems quite probable that he awards expenses in the amount that seems to him reasonable in those areas which are traditional. But this is merely an external estimate; I honestly do not know how taxing masters decide what to allocate. Granted this complication, however, the actual situation faced by the parties is shown by equation set (7.3).

$$P_v = \frac{P}{P + D} \cdot M - \frac{D}{P + D} \cdot (P_R + D_R) - P_E$$

$$D_v = \frac{D}{P + D} \cdot M - \frac{P}{P + D} \cdot (P_R + D_R) - D_E \tag{7.3}$$

In these equations, I have put in P_R and D_R to indicate the reasonable expenditures for P and D, and P_E and D_E to designate any expenditures they chose to make beyond the "reasonable" amount. All of this is, of course, ex ante. The parties must make estimates of how much the taxing master is apt to permit when deciding whether or not to sue and what resources to put into the suit.

Clearly, under these circumstances, the litigants would attempt to game the system. Until we have a better idea of how the taxing masters actually decide the reasonable "expenses" of the parties, I do not see any way to say much more about this problem. There is another complication here. The barrister is required to collect his fee in advance. This may have been intended as another way of reducing the amount of litigation. It certainly meant that impecunious people could not bring actions.

In recent years, the British government has remedied this situation in some cases by providing legal aid for the barrister's fees. This, of course, raises the question of how government decides who will get legal aid. The problem of outsiders paying for all, or part, of the legal expenses is an important one. Let us begin our discussion not with impecunious people but with people whose cases are of such political importance that some outsider or group of outsiders is willing to pay the legal fees.

Both Angela Davis and the Watergate defendants (up to the time of their first trial) had their legal expenses paid by political allies.[4] This system can be analyzed by equation set (7.1a) which is a modification of (7.1), assuming that P_v is the prosecution and D and L represent, respectively, the defendants in the case and the people who are actually putting up the money; L_v represents the satisfaction obtained by the financiers.

$$P_v = \frac{P}{P + D + L} \cdot M - P$$

$$D_v = \frac{D + L}{P + D + L} \cdot M - D$$

$$L_v = \frac{D + L}{P + D + L} \cdot M - L$$

$$(7.3a)$$

Once again, the defendants play a relatively minor role because the bulk of the resources are contributed by other people who thus gain basic control over the case.[5]

All of my equation systems so far are readily solvable for any given case. I have left out the variables dealing with the strength of the evidence and of the commitment of judicial decision-making resources, because they are not the subjects under discussion, but adding them would cause no difficulty. All of the sets so far would lead to the same type of equilibrium as the simple set of two equations introduced in the previous chapter for ordinary adversary proceedings. These proceedings differ from those simple adversary proceedings only in that the amount at issue is greater (in the case of the English system) or that some third party chooses to pay part of the costs of one of the two original parties. No doubt from the standpoint of one of the original parties, the latter is a great advantage—and to the other, a great disadvantage—but looked at from the standpoint of the whole system, it makes little difference. In essence, in these cases there is simply another party interested on one side.

In these cases, however, we have private persons making their contributions to the side they prefer. The use of government money raises somewhat different issues. In general, we do not want the taxpayers to take a partisan role.[6] We would like to have the judicial system, as a whole, reach relatively impartial conclusions. Thus, if we decide to subsidize someone's legal fees, we would prefer that this only be done where it is more likely to lead to a just conclusion than not. It is not at all obvious that any of the existing set of institutions under which the government pays one side's legal fees have this characteristic; but let me take them up one at a time.

Suppose someone comes to one of the new government-financed neighborhood law clinics in a poor district and asks for legal help in getting a divorce. If the divorce is contested, the other party might also want legal help, but let us (for the time being) confine ourselves to cases in which only one side is to be given legal assistance. This is simply so that I can continue to use equation set (7.1). First, the aid is going to the plaintiff rather than the defendant. Hence, it should be $P + L$ instead of P in the first equation, with a similar alteration below. Second, M represents a divorce in this case rather than a pure monetary payment. The divorce, of course, does not accrue to the aiding agency and hence the bottom equation should be dropped off and the two-thirds in the second from the bottom equation should be eliminated.

Success in this particular litigation will, once again, be partially determined by the resources put up by the plaintiff and by the government attorney, on the one hand, and by the defendant on the other. Since I am assuming that the government helps only one side, this means that the defense must pay his entire cost himself.[7]

Once again, the plaintiff is going to use very few of his own resources in court; the bulk of the costs will be borne by the government. The government, however, presumably does not wish to allocate infinite resources to helping people win cases. In practice, these neighborhood law clinics have resources which are distinctly limited, considering the demand, and they must decide which cases they will take, and how much energy they will put into them, in terms of the inability to take other cases or the necessity of skimping on cases.

Obviously the government attorney must undertake some kind of an investigation to determine whether or not to undertake this particular case. The possibility of simply taking cases as they come in and then putting maximum resources behind the first few is too foolish to give any serious consideration. Another possibility is that of appropriating enough money so that all cases anyone wishes to be brought *can* be brought, and maximum resources can be applied to each one. But this is politically implausible.

Thus, there is a restriction on the resources, and some decision must be made as to how these resources are to be used. One hopes that the attorneys look into the matter and select the "best" cases. Since they are using the taxpayers' money, one would indeed hope that they only accept cases in which they feel their client is "in the right." In those cases where they feel doubtful about the rightness of their client's case, their investment of resources may lower accuracy. Thus, in general, they should aid only those cases which they think are right.

This is particularly important, since on my present set of assumptions, the government is not going to pay the other side's attorney's fee, and hence the other side must either face a trial without legal advice (which is costly) or acquire an attorney on his own. Thus, the attorney, in deciding to take a contested divorce case, is not only deciding how some government resources should be allocated,[8] he is also—even before any court proceedings have begun—inflicting heavy costs on a third party. One hopes that he only does this in those cases in which he is confident that he is correct. Indeed, many people accuse the storefront lawyers of selecting cases not in terms of the convenience of the client but in an effort to establish precedents for future cases. This policy is particularly hard on the potential defendants, who are compelled to invest resources not so much to defend themselves as to defend a category of other people— people in their same situation—from the establishment of an unfavorable precedent.

There is another and much more important case in which the state subsidizes one side of the litigation. In this particular case, indeed, the custom is so old that most of my readers may not realize that this is what is happening. The state pays the prosecution in most criminal cases. This developed from an earlier system in which the parties paid the prosecution cost, and the earlier system still does have some legal remnants. Until very recently, private parties were perfectly free to bring actions against people they believed to be criminals in the British courts, and if they were successful, the convicted person would be imprisoned. In the United States, this is not the case; but it is still true that, as a general rule, the police are legal agents of the victim of a crime in making arrests.

But this is merely a brief and inadequate discursion into the history of the law. The resulting situation is that the government does pay the full cost of prosecuting criminals. In most cases, no private party directly benefits from the prosecution; but there are cases in which private individuals will benefit substantially if conviction is obtained. An obvious example of this is in the antitrust cases.

Since, once again, the resources available to the district attorney—and, for that matter, the court—are not infinite, he must make decisions as to which prosecutions he will bring. Looked at overall, these decisions are far more important than the decisions undertaken by the court itself. Of all people charged with crimes by the police, the district attorney characteristically decides not to proceed against about six in seven, who are thus "acquitted." Among those he does decide to prosecute, approximately 95 percent are convicted. Thus, his initial decision as to whether or not to proceed with the matter is, for the average defendant, very nearly decisive of the outcome. It is genuinely decisive if the district attorney decides to drop; and if he decides to proceed, the defendant faces a 95 percent chance of conviction.[9]

This important decision is made entirely in an inquisitorial manner. The district attorney investigates the matter and usually talks to the defendant. Sometimes he has a small detective force attached to his own office, which will investigate the issue and try to unearth evidence which will be of help to him in making this decision (and later in prosecuting the case, if he decides to prosecute it). The defendant has no right to be represented in these decision-making processes (although the prosecuting attorney normally is willing to talk to the defense attorney). In particular, none of the so-called safeguards for the accused in the judicial procedure apply here. They apply in a somewhat indirect way in the sense that the prosecutor will realize that they will affect the trial, but they are not directly controlling. The prosecutor, for example, in deciding whether or not to prosecute should (and normally will) consider any evidence the police have, regardless of whether this evidence can later be presented in court. In trying to make his estimate as to whether there will be an eventual conviction—which is important to him in making his basic decision—he should also consider whether such evidence can be presented in court.[10]

Let us now consider the situation that would occur if the government is asked to subsidize *both* sides. For simplicity, let me return to the case in which someone approaches the legal aid office for a divorce, and assume that the other partner to the marriage also approaches the legal aid office seeking assistance in defending the case. If legal assistance is given, then the outcome will be determined by the set of equations below (7.4).

$$P_v = \frac{P + G_1}{P + G_1 + G_2 + D} \cdot M - P$$

$$G_{1v} = \frac{P + G_1}{P + G_1 + G_2 + D} \cdot M - G_1$$

$$G_{2v} = \frac{D + G_2}{P + G_1 + G_2 + D} \cdot M - G_2$$

$$D_v = \frac{D + G_2}{P + G_1 + G_2 + D} \cdot M - D \tag{7.4}$$

The attorneys on the two sides, both employees of the legal aid office, would each obtain satisfaction from having his side win, but in other respects their situations are identical. The bulk of the resources would come from the legal aid office and not from the two parties; hence, G_1 and G_2 would be fairly large and P and D would be small.

Of course, this assumes that the case is actually litigated. If I were in charge of the legal aid office, or if the people who were in charge of it considered my well-being as a taxpayer, the result of this visit to the office by both parties would be an investigation of the issue, a decision as to the merits of the case, and a suggestion to the two parties that they accept that decision. If either of them refused, then legal assistance should be provided only to the other party. I am not at all convinced, however, that this particular prescription will be that of the reader. In any event, I have never seen it proposed before—so let us look at the alternatives.

To make matters simple, let us assume that the divorce itself is not contested but the custody of a child is at issue. The husband first approaches the legal aid office and requests assistance in obtaining the divorce and custody of the child. Without legal assistance, he would have only a 10 percent chance of getting custody; if the legal aid office decides to assist him, he has a 40 percent chance of getting custody of the child. Now his wife approaches the legal aid office and asks them to represent her. Let us assume here that as a result of their dual representation, the odds for the wife getting custody of the child are 85 percent and for the husband 15 percent.[11]

Under these circumstances, should the legal aid office undertake the representation of the wife, also? The first thing to be said the moment one begins dealing with these problems is that representation is not of zero value. In our previous work dealing with adversary proceedings, the two parties invested resources in litigation out to the point where they reach the equilibrium point of the two reaction lines. In this case, since the parties are investing no resources to speak of, and indeed are unable to invest any resources to speak of, the government must invest the resources for both sides, and clearly each party would like to have an infinite amount of resources on his side. This cannot be provided, and hence the government must make a decision as to how much it should invest on each side. I can see no way to do this without a considerable degree of arbitrariness; but, in any event, let us assume that some kind of decision is made.

If the government decides to provide legal assistance to the wife as well as to the husband, they should increase their legal assistance to the husband. The amount of legal assistance which is appropriate in dealing with someone who will have to handle their own case is considerably less than the amount appropriate in dealing with someone who will be represented by an attorney. Thus, the decision to represent the wife not only involves a direct expenditure, but it also involves an increase in the amount of money spent representing the husband.

So far as I know, there is no way to determine the optimal amount of resources to be introduced into the litigation process under these circumstances. An inquiry into what private parties would do under the same circumstances is not helpful, because the income of private parties is one of the variables in their determination of how much resources they will invest in a divorce action; hence, one would have to decide what income one is going to allot to these impecunious customers of the legal-aid office in making one's calculation.

Let us suppose that it is decided to invest $500 in representing the wife and $750 in representing the husband; this will, as we said before, provide an 85 percent chance that the wife will obtain custody of the child and a 15 percent chance for the husband. It is immediately obvious that we could obtain this 15 percent chance for the husband and the 85 percent chance for the wife in a much more economical way. Assume that if we were supporting the husband only, not the wife, it would only cost $100 to improve his chances from 10 percent to 40 percent. Instead of giving that $100, we could give him, let us say, $25 in legal assistance, thus moving his probability not from 10 to 40 percent but only from 10 to 15 percent. The wife would receive no assistance under this plan. Thus, we would have a net expenditure of $25 to purchase the same present discounted value of the outcome for the two parties as can be obtained with $1,250. Clearly, this is the dominating solution.

Although this is clearly the dominating solution, so far as I know it has never been discussed in the literature before. Indeed, it took me a very long period of thought before it came to me. It is always possible that an idea which has never been discussed has just not been thought of before. It is also possible, however, that there are very good reasons why the idea should not be applied, and the lack of discussion stems from the fact that everyone realizes that there are such good reasons. The only suggestions that I have been able to unearth as to why we might prefer to have the government paying attorneys on both sides to having them get the same probability of outcome by helping only one side are, in my opinion, unconvincing.

First, there is the possibility that we just have some primitive ethical idea involved here. For example, perhaps it is thought that adversary procedure is right in some metaphysical way, regardless of the outcome attained.[12] If this is the explanation, then people who do not happen to have that particular moral set would not agree. People who do have that moral set should at least be willing to consider the costs.

There are two other possible explanations. In a way, they are closely related but not identical. The first is that we might feel that the adversary process, with good representation on both sides,[13] is an efficient way to reach the truth. It might be argued that the more resources we invest on *both* sides, the more likely we are to achieve an accurate outcome. Not everyone seems to argue this way. When discussing matters in which the accuracy was important, I have sometimes been corrected by lawyers who tell me that improving the quality of the legal representation does not increase accuracy. I am somewhat puzzled by this, partly because it seems to me that it should, and partly because it would seem to me that it would be in the interest of the lawyers, or at least the best lawyers, to argue that it does.

It seems likely that we are indeed improving the accuracy of the court procedure when we increase the resources put into the adversary proceeding. Unfortunately, the increase is a very slow one. Doubling the resources of both the man who represents the truth, and the man who represents falsehood, may make it more likely that the court will recognize the truth from the falsehood, but it surely does not double the probability. Indeed, I would anticipate only small improvements in accuracy from quite large increases in resource investment.

The second reason is, in a way, a derivative of the first. We could always, by reducing the resources being invested on one side of the case, obtain the same probability we can obtain by increasing the resources on the other; hence, it is always possible to obtain the same probability of a correct outcome by a cheap method as by an expensive one. It might be difficult, however, for us to predict accurately the result of changing the resources on both sides. In our simple divorce case, if there are no legal representatives, the odds are nine to one in favor of the wife obtaining custody. If both sides are represented, the odds are 85 to 15. Without running the case 100 or so times, it might be difficult to determine what those odds are; hence, it might be difficult to duplicate them by reducing resources for one side only.

I am not at all sure that this is true; what little experimental work has been done seems to indicate that lawyers are quite good at estimating the odds. But if the odds are indeterminate, it is not at all obvious why we would regard one resource investment as better than another unless we had an implicit belief that the adversary proceeding does increase accuraracy as the resources invested in it are increaseed. To repeat what I said before, I am inclined to go along with this assumption, but I think that the accuracy is purchased very expensively.

Chapter 8

The Motivation of Judges

In this chapter, I will reverse field and talk about the decision-making apparatus itself and not the efforts of the parties to influence it. Although I have entitled [it] "The Motivation of Judges," I intend to use the word "judge" in a very broad way. It will include jurors, lay assessors, arbitrators and, for that matter, boards of judges as well as individual judges.

If we look around the world, there is quite a variety of ultimate decision procedures. Perhaps the United States has the widest variance here of any country. We use a board of conscripted citizens or a single judge as our basic decision-making procedure. Most countries in the world tend to use some compromise between these two—either a board of judges or a board composed of judges and lay assessors. The American custom of either the single judge or the jury of conscripted citizens presumably comes from the historical development of law in England, although at the present time in England the jury seems to be in the process of being phased out in favor of a single judge.

The arbitrator is characteristically a judge or a member of a board of judges who is called an "arbitrator" because of historic accident. In most cases, he is selected by the parties rather than appointed by the government, and this probably makes considerable difference in his motivation; some arbitrators are former judges—indeed, a prominent one in the United States is a former Supreme Court justice. Thus, there seems no strong reason to distinguish between arbitrators and judges in our current discussion.

In general, the people who are used to decide court trials fall into two categories, amateurs (who are usually conscripted) and professionals. The American jurymen and the lay assessors in the European courts are amateurs. American judges, judges in European courts, and many arbitrators are professionals. There are advantages to both professionalism and amateurism, but, on the whole, one would think professionalism would work better. After all, the professional does have a good deal of experience, and hence he is less likely to make errors than the amateur. On the other hand, it must be admitted that he is more likely to make systematic errors than is the amateur; for example, if he gets something in his head, he may repeat it again and again. The amateur will not have any opportunity to repeat the same error.

As I turn to the motivation of these decision-making officials, there is another classification scheme which crosses my previous classifications. The member of the board of judges in European courts is motivated, to some extent, by the desire for promotion, which will be obtained by behaving in a manner his superiors think is efficient. (In Germany, officials rather systematically take into account the number of reversals by appellate courts in deciding on promotion.) No doubt he is also interested in finding the truth, serving the public interest, etc., but an altruistic approach is not relied on as the sole drive for obtaining good performance. If we consider, however, American judges (who are rarely, if ever, promoted), lay assessors in Europe, or jurymen in the United States, their income and prospects are little, if at all, affected by their performance in court.[1]

The argument for not rewarding good performance is that any reward system for the judges is apt to lead them to try to do what the people manipulating the reward system want rather than to "seek justice." Of course, if the people who are operating the system are in favor of "justice," then this argument does not apply. It must, therefore, be based on the untested theory that for some obscure reason, one particular set of government officials—the judges—are less "corrupt" than others—the higher officials—who could be higher-ranking judges, as they characteristically are in Europe.

Another explanation for the sole dependence on "virtue" of judges would be a distrust of democracy, and I believe that this motive, at least in part, impelled the founding fathers of the United States. They did not want the judges subject to "political" criteria. Of course, they were not naive and realized that the President and Senate would consider political matters in making the initial appointments; but they felt that by guaranteeing judges lifetime tenure and fixed salaries, they would lead them to gradually move away from their friends and into a position in which political influence would be much less important than the objective nature of the cases. They may very well have been right.

The most political of all decision-making processes, if we are thinking of democratic politics, is the jury. Many people think of the jury as being a random sample of the population. It is not, partly because it is small enough so that the variance of the sample would be great in any event, and partly because the people who compose the jury are by no means a random sample. It is also likely that the jury contains relatively few highly intelligent or very stupid members of the community.

The selection process tends to weed out people who would suffer a significant financial loss from their service on a jury, those who are particularly knowledgeable about anything with which the jury might deal, those who seem to be either a little dumb or peculiar and, last but not least, anyone who does not want to serve on that jury and is bright enough to realize that exhibiting bias will get him out of it.

The people who act as juries in those cases which are expected to be very long, and in particular those cases where the juries are to be sequestered, must be really quite an unusual group of people. In actual practice, no one who does not wish to serve on such a jury has to do so, although some people may not realize that indicating bias will get them off.[2] An interesting empirical study could no doubt be made of these people who have chosen what must be an unpleasant and boring experience. Probably they go into it under the impression that it will be exciting and only later discover how dull legal proceedings are.

In any event, however, the jurymen are motivated entirely by their curiosity as to what actually happens in a case and by their feeling for justice. In this respect they are thus like the professional judge, who can be neither promoted nor fired. On the other hand, they see only a very few cases. This means they lack experience, which has both advantages and disadvantages. The disadvantages, I suppose, are obvious; the advantage is that they are apt to be more interested in the cases simply because they have never seen them before.

There does not seem, however, to be any reason at all to believe that the jurymen devote any great effort to understanding the case. Indeed, trial practice is very largely based on the implicit theory that jurymen are mainly impressed by image and only to a rather modest extent by facts. Convincing the jury that your opponent is a rat is far more useful than convincing them that he actually defaulted on his contract. Once they are convinced he is a rat, they are apt to believe he defaulted; and if they are convinced he is an honest man, they are apt to believe he did not, almost regardless of the objective evidence.

The above point, although generally true, should not be exaggerated. Jurymen, of course, do not totally disregard objective evidence and, indeed, the objective evidence is one of the things which gives them the impression that the defendant is or is not a rat. Still, so far as I know, there is no other walk of life in which we make important decisions by dragging twelve persons off the street and permitting two highly paid people to make arguments in front of them. Normally, we have better ways to reach the truth.

The final type of judge is the professional arbitrator. He receives a fee for each case.[3] It seems likely, however, that his major motivation is not his fee for this particular case, but the fees he hopes to receive for future cases. Thus, he should attempt to carry out his duties in this particular case in such a way as to motivate people to hire him as an arbitrator in the future. In my opinion, this particular motivational system, although a long way from perfect, probably works better than any of the ones I have so far discussed.

But this chapter is about the motivation of judges. Although telling them that they should do right, be virtuous, and industrious surely can do no harm (and might do some good), normally we try to motivate people by giving them rewards for good behavior and penalties for bad behavior. How can we apply this system to judges? The obvious problem is that in any individual case, we have no automatic mechanism for determining who is right and who is wrong. Further, we not only want the judges to make the right decision, we want the right amount of resources invested in the decision. We do not want minor traffic offenses to involve lengthy hearings with the jury sequestered and the Supreme Court eventually involved, even if all of that would mean a higher probability of accuracy. The cost of the proceedings should be offset against the importance of the accuracy which results. Of course, in the Anglo-Saxon system, the judges or jury do not have very much control over the total resource investment; but in other systems (particularly the Continental system), they have a good deal, and we would like our motivational scheme to work there as well.

It will not surprise the reader to discover that, although I think we can do better than we now do, this is not a problem to which I can give (or, indeed, think anyone can give) a highly sophisticated and guaranteed efficient answer. Nevertheless, there are some things we can do. First, it would be sensible to avoid giving perverse incentives. Most judicial systems are rather good on this score, although there are occasional exceptions. A justice of the peace, for example, used to be (and, indeed, still is in some cases) paid only from the fines he collects; hence, he had an incentive to find the defendant guilty. In some cases, judges may find a situation confronting them where a particular decision will greatly reduce their work load; they are likely to move toward the lower work load because their pay is not affected by the number of hours they put in on the job.

But, note, that even these cases are not necessarily perverse. Presumably, the justice-of-the-peace payment institution described above increases the number of convictions, but it is not at all obvious that it increases the number of errors, in the sense of decisions which are different from those which God would have made had we been able to consult Him. Similarly, in the second case, it certainly should reduce the total amount of time that judges devote to legal activities; but, once again, it is not clear that it increases the number of errors. In both of these cases, it presumably leads to errors being distributed differently.

The two examples above are simply special cases of the general problem of conflict of interest. The judge has a personal interest in deciding in one direction—in one case, because it increases his income; and in the other, because it reduces his work load. There are many other cases in which he may have such a motive, and the efforts to reduce "conflict of interest" are efforts to reduce their frequency. The judge may be related to one of the parties, have a direct or indirect financial interest in one side or the other, or merely be personally friendly with one of the parties. In all of these cases, the judge is removable, although in the particular case of federal judges in the United States, he normally decides himself whether he is biased.

This is a particularly bizarre rule, since, presumably, if he is really biased, he either will not notice that fact (since he believes he simply knows the truth) or if he does notice it, he will be strongly motivated to conceal it. Most state judges in the United States are subject to a rule under which the parties suspecting bias can have them removed from the case without the necessity of convincing the judge himself that he is biased.

It should be pointed out that it is by no means obvious that this type of conflict of interest actually leads to any high degree of inaccuracy. Suppose, for example, that Judge Sirica is convinced before the trial begins that the defendants in the Watergate case are guilty and refuses to concede his own bias—he knows that he is right, and hence it is not bias but simple devotion to the truth. He also arranges a jury, the bulk of whom have been watching the Watergate hearings on television, and who were very heavily favorable to McGovern in the election to which Watergate was relevant; then, during the course of the trial, he makes a number of rulings which are clearly beneficial to the prosecution. This does not lead to error if the defendants were guilty (and most people do think they were).

Suppose that a judge believes, as Judge Sirica apparently did, that almost everyone brought before his court was guilty. Suppose, further, that this led to a conviction rate of 90 percent in his court as opposed to the more normal 80 percent rate in a federal court. It does not follow from this that his court makes more errors than the more normal court. It simply means that the distribution of errors is different. It might be, for example, that 95 percent of all defendants brought before both courts were guilty; that the normal court found, of every 100 defendants, 77 guilty persons guilty, 3 innocent persons innocent. They would have gone wrong in 20 of the 100 cases. This is somewhat above what I would regard as a normal error rate; I merely use these numbers for illustrative purposes.

Judge Sirica, on the other hand, might find 86 people who are in fact guilty guilty, 9 people who are guilty innocent, 4 people who are innocent guilty, and 1 person who is innocent innocent. Errors are less frequent in Sirica's court than in the more normal court. The distribution of errors between the innocent and the guilty is different, and if the reader is one of those who believe that the court should be biased in favor of the accused, he would regard the normal court performance as better than Judge Sirica's. Surely, however, it is not more accurate.

The above numerical example illustrates the point that the conflict of interest problem is more complicated than it appears at first glance. This is one of the many areas where what is normally referred to as "fairness" is not necessarily identical to minimization of error. "Fairness" essentially means sticking to a set of rules which are thought to put the two parties on an even footing. In the trials by combat, from which our trials in a way descend, it would have been unfair to give one knight a longer lance than the other. If, however, we assume that the ability to win in combat is unrelated to guilt or innocence, then it is fairly obvious that this would not have led to a more erroneous set of outcomes. Regardless of the length of the lances, the relationship between the outcome of the combat and the "correct" outcome would be random.

The objection to bias or conflict of interest, then, is not as straightforward as it normally appears. In order to object to it, we have to feel that judicial or jury decision-making proceedings are normally accurate enough so that the introduction of what is essentially a random factor (because bias can be on either side) lowers total accuracy. Most of us would feel that this is true, but the effect is probably fairly weak. Nevertheless, we attempt to eliminate conflict of interest because it is a very cheap and easy thing to do. Note that this is, in fact, the way our law operates. In those cases where it would be very difficult to find a court without bias, we simply accept biased courts under a doctrine going back almost five hundred years.

So far, we have been examining possible incentives which might have a perverse effect and have judged them not all that important. But if there are few positive incentives to actually go wrong, there is very little in the way of incentive to go right, except the desire to be virtuous, diligent, and just. As we shall see below, the arbitrator is a partial exception to this, but even in his case, the incentives are hardly simple and straightforward.

If we knew what the truth was in every case, we could provide for differential rewards, depending on whether the judge and jury reached the correct conclusion. We could also save money by omitting them. At a somewhat more mundane level, it is possible to make certain that the judge and jury have paid careful attention to the case by a fairly simple, although radical, change in our present institutions. If, at the end of the trial, the judge and jury were given a short examination on the strictly factual side of the evidence and then rewarded for their knowledge, it is likely that they would concentrate much more on the details of the case than they now do. Note that there would be no particular problem of bias or, for that matter, complexity in the examinations. In any lawsuit, there are a great many uncontroverted facts, such as how old the defendant is, the address where the murder allegedly took place, whether the body had two or three bullet holes in it, etc.

But this is clearly a rather minor reform, the only purpose of which is to make judges and jurymen pay careful attention. Further, in the case of the European-type procedure, where the judges play a major role in investigating the facts, we would want to ask at least some questions aimed at determining whether they had engaged in a sensible investigation rather than simply whether they remembered what they had uncovered.

Still, the fact that they know some of the simple facts of the case does not prove they are reaching the correct conclusion. Another technique which might be used to deal with this problem would be to draw a random sample of cases and rerun them with a much higher investment of resources in the second run. Presumably, this would mean that the second time cases were run through, more accurate determinations were made. A statistical comparison between the behavior of the original judges in these cases and the more accurate decisions would indicate which judges were better, and which judges were worse, in determining what had happened. Their pay could then be varied accordingly. The judicial promotion system in Germany roughly approximates this system.

Unfortunately, only the judges in the first series would be subject to this type of pressure. The judges who were applying greater resources in the second round would not be subject to it.[4] Hence, they might not be motivated to pay careful attention, do a good job, etc. As a result, in practice, the first round could have about as many real resources invested as the second, even though budgetary costs of the checking-up round were much greater.

There is another problem. It might be that the judges in the first round of cases would have some idea of the foibles and special prejudices of the judges who will be checking on them, and therefore they would incorporate these foibles and prejudices into their own decisions. Thus, although this procedure would mean that the judges in the first round were under pressure to behave in the way that the judges in the second round thought they should, it might not reduce the total number of errors. Suppose, for example, that the judges in the first round know that the judges in the second round, who are very senior and therefore elderly judges, do not understand statistics. Under the circumstances, they might disregard statistical evidence because they know that it will be disregarded when their accuracy is evaluated.

The basic problem with this procedure, however, is the one I have mentioned earlier in a note. It might provide a technique for policing the behavior of the judges in the first round, but eventually we would come to a stop—a group of judges who are not being checked by other judges. This would be true even if we did not have a set of levels of judges but simply reassigned an occasional case from any given judge to another judge, at random, to rerun. This would mean that there would not be a first and second level of judge, but it would still be true that the judge taking the second round would know that he would not be supervised and the judge taking the first round would know that he was. Nevertheless, although this system is far from perfect, I would think that it would tend to move the current legal system to a higher standard of accuracy, simply by providing an automatic and completely unpredictable check.

Note that I have talked mainly about judges here and not juries. Presumably the juries would not care very much whether they were found to have been inaccurate after the event, because it would not affect their future income. If they were given an additional payment in the event that their cases were selected for examination, and they were found to have been right, this would provide them with an incentive. Granted the stochastic nature of the process, however, they might treat this mainly as a simple gamble rather than as a motive to be more careful.

When we turn to the arbitrator, the incentive system is quite different. The professional arbitrator is unlike a judge in that his decision in a given case increases or decreases the likelihood of his being employed in the future. Since he wants to be employed in the future—he is making money from his arbitration practice—he will attempt to choose that decision which is most likely to lead to his being selected for arbitration in the future. Where the two parties to any future contract have roughly equal levels of information, I shall argue below that this leads him to choose an economical and accurate procedure if that is possible for him. If, however, one of the parties to future contracts is apt to hold superior information, it may lead to a very strong element of bias on the part of the arbitrator.

This point is, I suppose, fairly obvious; but a little discussion may not be out of place. If the arbitrator, for example, deals exclusively in small-scale consumer complaints, he may feel that most consumers will not know anything at all about the arbitrator and therefore will be willing to accept the arbitrator suggested by the retailer. Under the circumstances, a bias toward the retailer might be the arbitrator's profit-maximizing course of action. It might not, however, because the retailer might be interested in his general reputation and want an arbitrator who was either impartial or, for that matter, actually procustomer.

I have noticed that when I have a complaint in my dealings with retail establishments, their usual reaction is not one of making a fair judicial decision between themselves and me but of giving me every benefit of the doubt. Presumably one reason for this is that careful consideration of the issue would be an expensive process, and the complaints desk would have to be greatly enlarged if they attempted it. Even more important is their feeling that damaging their relations with the customer is a good deal more expensive for them than the cost of replacing some piece of merchandise which the customer claims is defective. They do not accept the customer's position in every single case, but they very decidedly tend to favor him. They might select arbitrators with the same set of biases. On the other hand, the fact that their complaints desk is lenient, and therefore that only cases the complaints desk thought were fake were transferred to the arbitrator, might mean that they would want an arbitrator who normally decided for them. In any event, the arbitrator would not aim at true accuracy but at whatever outcomes were favored by the retailer. The customer might or might not benefit from that.

Most cases where arbitrators are now used, however, are cases where both sides are reasonably well informed. The typical case is a commercial contract between two businessmen or two corporations, either under circumstances in which the two parties regularly make use of arbitrators or where the contract is large enough so that it is worth their trouble to become well informed for that particular contract. In many cases, of course, both of these conditions apply.

Under these circumstances, the parties will know fairly accurately the capacities of the arbitrators, and we can therefore reasonably pause to inquire what type of arbitrator they will choose. Note that at the time the contract is undertaken, the two parties have no significant conflict of interest with respect to the desirable qualities of an arbitrator, although later, when and if a violation is alleged, their differences may be very great. At the time the contract is negotiated, the two parties want the joint profit of the contract to be maximized, albeit they have differences of opinion as to how this profit should be divided. Therefore, selecting an arbitrator who, in terms of both cost and accuracy, maximizes the value of the contract is in their mutual interest.

It is not at all obvious that either of the parties would, in fact, want an arbitrator who is biased in his direction if the other party knew that the bias existed. The other party could insist on the other terms of the contract being changed in such a way as to compensate him for the bias of the arbitrator. Thus, only if hiring an arbitrator with a particular kind of bias were efficiency-promoting would the person who is to benefit from the bias be willing to pay the other party the cost of that bias.

There are special cases where this condition is met. If, for example, one of the two parties is more risk averse than the other, he might be willing to pay for an arbitrator who is biased in his direction by giving the other party to the contract advantages in other areas of the contract. In a way, this is like the policy mentioned above by which most retail merchants give the customer the benefit of the doubt in complaints. The merchant can combine a whole number of such complaints into an actuarially predictable cost, and hence he runs no significant risk. He provides for his customers, then, a reduction in their risk, because they do not have this possibility of actuarial combination.

In most cases, however, it seems likely that the two parties would prefer an unbiased arbitrator who would invest the "optimal" resources in determining the outcome and who would use the most efficient methods. The use of the most efficient methods would probably mean that the personal characteristics of the arbitrator—especially intelligence—would be taken into account.

Once an issue arises between the two parties, it is no longer necessarily desirable for both of the parties that the arbitrator be intelligent and impartial. Since we are currently talking only about issues of fact and not of issues of the law or interpretation of the contract, it is highly likely that the party in the wrong knows that he is in the wrong but sees a good chance to profit from pushing this particular case.[5]

At this point, both of the parties would like to win, and both will be disappointed if they do not. Under the circumstances, the arbitrator, of necessity, is going to annoy one of them. It is not at all obvious that this will reduce his future business. Remember that, ex ante, both parties to a contract want much the same thing from the arbitrator.[6] Thus, even the party who is very disappointed by the decision of an arbitrator in a given case may regard the decision of the arbitrator in that case as good grounds for hiring him in the future.

The arbitrator, then, under the circumstances we have described, has a good reason to do an efficient job, in the sense that the cost-accuracy ratio of his decision is optimized for the two parties. In the real world, it is not always true that arbitrators are well known by all parties to the arbitral contract. In many cases, there is some differential knowledge. The same is also true, however, of professional judges; and indeed judge-shopping is one of the activities of a good lawyer. Further, most contracts can be drawn in such a way that the actual court to decide is determined in the contract. When this is so, the same problem of differential knowledge of prejudice of judges would apply. Although this is a real problem, it does not seem to be a major one either with regular courts or with arbitrators.

The major problem with respect to the use of arbitrators as a general technique, however, is simply that by no means all litigation concerns contracts. In a very large number of cases, the litigation occurs between two parties who have not made any preliminary agreement, and whose first contact is the act which causes the legal dispute. There is an automobile accident, and A wishes to sue B. At this point in time, there is no motive for either A or B to favor an impartial arbitrator. Each would want one prejudiced in his favor, if that were possible.[7] A second example is the average crime. The district attorney and the man he is prosecuting might have difficulty agreeing on a suitable arbitrator. There are many other cases. Parties to a dispute over property very commonly have no previous contract. Parties to a dispute over a will may not have, although in this case presumably the testator could specify an arbitrator.

In all of these cases, there is no point in time in which both parties would have motives leading them to select an efficient and impartial arbitrator. We have thus turned to a social contrivance in which the parties, in essence, agree to a system under which arbitrators—hopefully efficient and unbiased—are automatically provided. We call this system the courts and the agreement was made very long ago.

Note, however, that although we do have this system to provide some means to adjudicate disputes between parties who have not made a specific contract, there is no strong reason to believe that it is optimal, or that it must take the form it does take. Under present circumstances, the dispute is settled either by a permanent government official or by a group of conscripted private citizens. There is no reason why other techniques might not be tried.

To take an extreme example, in Roman law if the case turned out to involve a difficult point of law (not of fact), it would be referred to a private citizen, called a *jurisconsultus*. He was prohibited by law from receiving any direct payment by either party but could anticipate that the party for whom he decided would eventually make a suitable provision in his will. Since this technique of turning over part of the law cases to a private citizen was the foundation of the great Roman law, it is hard to argue that it is impossible. It was, after all, these *jurisconsulti* whose decisions and general writings shaped the Roman law, not any formally appointed official.

Thus, there is no intrinsic reason why we could not use some method under which the government, instead of maintaining a set of judges and juries, simply maintained a procedure for appointing an arbitrator for each case. But if there is no reason why this could not be done, it is not at all obvious that it would be a desirable system either. The arbitrator would presumably be primarily interested in his fee, not for the instant case but for future cases, and therefore he would tend to behave in a way which would make it likely that whoever appointed him (in this case, a government official) would reappoint him. Presumably, the appointing official would have no reason for wanting the arbitrator not to be efficient in the strict sense, but he might prefer some sort of bias. Since the same type of officials appoint our present judges, there is no reason to regard this as necessarily a fatal objection.

Assume, then, that we have a system under which, when a case arises, the parties may agree on an arbitrator, or a board of arbitrators or, for that matter, a board of twelve citizens with no special training. In cases in which they reach agreement, we simply respect that agreement unless there is reason to believe one or the other party has been defrauded. In cases in which they would not reach agreement—the district attorney, for example, and the murderer having great differences of opinion as to who would be a suitable person to decide whether or not the murderer shall be hung—we must turn to another procedure.

The second procedure involves two steps, the first of which is determining the compensation for the arbitrator(s) and the second is actually selecting the individual(s). The first one is fairly simple. We could permit the two parties to decide individually how much they will contribute. Presumably the one who is in the right would be interested in contributing more, because he is interested in hiring a more accurate judge, and therefore he wants more resources invested in the trial. There is no reason why the two parties must put up the same amount. Indeed, in the case of the district attorney and the murderer, presumably the murderer will be unwilling to put up anything, unless he were given a guarantee that the judge would be biased in his favor. The arbitrator would know how much his fee was, but would not know which of the two parties had contributed the largest amount to it.

The total fee of the arbitrator now being determined by simply summing the amount that the two parties are willing to invest, each party recommends one person or group as arbitrator. The arbitrators are then interrogated as to whether they are willing to work for the fee suggested, and assuming that all agree,[8] the choice between the two arbitrators is referred to some government official, perhaps whoever selects our current judges.

Let us look at the incentives which this system provides for the parties. First, the judge who makes the ultimate decision between the two nominated arbitrators has no more incentive to do a good job or work hard or be unbiased than our present judges, but he also has no less. Those who have confidence in our present judges should have confidence in his judgment; and those of us who do not, should not. For the second group, however, it should be pointed out that the choice is both a relatively easy one and, as we shall see, not all that important. It is fairly easy to keep abreast of the general reputation of a limited group of men engaged in this kind of activity.

Where it is not easy to do it directly, there presumably would be reference books, as there are today for labor arbitrators in the United States. These catalogues as they now exist for labor arbitrators, and as they would exist for general arbitrators under the proposed procedure, simply attempt to transmit information, because that is what the person who might buy such a catalogue wants. Under the circumstances, they are likely to present a fairly good picture of the capacity of the arbitrator, although not a perfect one. However, they are generally better information than is available when a man is appointed as a judge under our present system, simply because they are based, not on a guess from character as to how well he will do, but from observation of his performance in a number of actual cases. Someone trying to break into the arbitration profession, instead of trying to get a politician to back him as he does today if he wants to be a judge, would simply have to start with small cases, which he offered to handle at low prices. As his reputation improved, he would rise to better and more important cases.

I said above that the job of choosing between the arbitrators would be neither very difficult nor very important. The reason it would not be very important has to do with the motives of the parties themselves. Each will present a potential arbitrator, and the final decision procedure is simply to choose between these two. Each party is motivated to choose as his nominee someone who is at least reasonably likely to be acceptable to the judge. If my cousin is my candidate, it is likely that the person chosen by my opponent will be selected. This technique was originally suggested for labor cases, in which it was proposed that both parties to the labor dispute simply present their demands and that a government board then make a selection between the two—the board being prohibited from either trying to compromise or from working out its own decision. It was pointed out that this would put pressure on both parties to be moderate in their demands, because it is likely that the more moderate of the proposals will be adopted.

Similarly, the technique I have just suggested would lead each party to suggest someone who was just a trifle on his side—perhaps simply because he had selected him as his nominee—in hopes that he would be the one selected, rather than the one nominated by the other party. We would anticipate, then, that the two people suggested to the judge would be reasonably competent people with no very obvious defects. The decision between them would not be a very important one, since either would do.

This brings us to the question of the motivation of the arbitrators themselves. They are going to make the ultimate decision and are, therefore, the important people in the system. They would think, when making their decision, of its effect on employment in two stages: their nomination by one of the parties to a dispute; and the selection between the two by the government official who makes the ultimate selections. It is clear that diligence and accuracy would pay off in both of these decision processes; bias, on the other hand, would not.

We thus have a system in which the people making the decisions are, to at least some extent, offered positive rewards for accurate decisions, albeit not in an ideally efficient way. Whether it is better or worse than the existing systems is a question I will leave for future consideration.

As a general rule, then, most legal systems have depended not on positively motivating judges and juries to reach the right conclusion, but on attempting to avoid perverse motivation. The substitution of positive incentives clearly would be highly desirable; the only problem is whether we can design an institutional structure which does offer such positive incentives at a reasonable cost.

Chapter 9

Criminal Procedure

Although this book is devoted to court activity, in the particular case of the supression of crime, it is best to consider the activity of all of the government bodies which deal with this issue. Thus, we will consider the situation from the time a crime is reported to the police until the parole board makes a final determination as to the amount of time the criminal must serve in prison. Further, as a general rule, I will confine my discussion to the American criminal investigation procedure, because that will be more familiar to most readers.

Let us suppose, then, that a crime has been committed and reported to the police.[1] The beginning of the process is a police investigation. Unless the police come to the conclusion that some person is both guilty and provably guilty, nothing further happens; and, indeed, for most American crimes this is the outcome. Thus, for either an innocent person who might conceivably be charged with the crime, or for the person who actually committed it, the police investigation is of considerable importance. One basic difference between European procedure and Anglo-Saxon procedure is the result of a recognition of this fact, and hence the formalization of the investigation process on the continent.

Let us look at the matter from the standpoint of an outsider. For this purpose, let us write down an equation indicating probability of arrest (P_A).

$$P_A = f(R_D, E, I) \tag{9.1}$$

The equation shows that the probability of arrest for any given individual (P_A), called the defendant here, is some function of the resources he invests in the investigative processes (R_D), the physical evidence that exists (E), and the resources invested by the police (I). In practice, the defendant, or potential defendant, will invest very few resources at this stage.[2] There are two reasons for this, one of which is that he simply has not much opportunity. If the police ask questions of a number of potential witnesses, they will not permit the defendant's attorney to go along with them. Only under special circumstances can he have access to this part of the investigative process.

The second reason for the defendant investing few resources at this stage is that any significant investment on his part is apt to attract police attention. If a crime has occurred, and the police begin going around asking potential witnesses about it; and one person at this point hires lawyers to make efforts to check up on the police—the police would almost instantly (and quite properly) come to the conclusion that he was their prime suspect. Indeed, it is usually undesirable for an individual who is involved in a crime to invest any of his own resources at all *until* such time as it is clear that the police have already selected him as their primary suspect. Even at that point, it is probably unwise to do anything very much in the way of commitment of resources to the investigative process, because this is apt to convince the police that their initial suspicions are correct.

There are methods of investing resources which may not have this effect. For example, an offer of a reward for evidence in the case, with the decision as to whether the reward will be given or not in the hands of someone other than the potential defendant, would probably not raise any great suspicion on the part of the police except insofar as *any* unusual behavior may raise suspicion. Indeed, this particular technique is sometimes used by wealthy people who are interested in getting a good public image with respect to some crime for which they believe they are suspected.

In any event, the process covered by equation (9.1) proceeds until the police either decide to charge someone or drop the case. It should be emphasized that the overwhelming number of people who might possibly be suspected of a crime are eliminated at this stage. For one thing, the police normally arrest only one individual or group for each crime, although very commonly at the time they start their investigation, there will be a number of alternative suspects. Second, in a very large number of cases, they come to the conclusion either that they do not know who did it or that although they know who did it, the evidence is not sufficient to obtain a conviction; and, hence, they drop the matter.

Suppose, however, that the police do decide who did it and that the evidence is adequate. They will normally then make their arrest and turn the matter over to a government attorney, whom I shall refer to below as the district attorney, although his actual title varies.[3] In the United States, this is, in a way, the most important single stage in the investigation. The district attorney decides not to proceed (technically called "no-papering") in about five-sixths of all the cases the police bring to his attention. In all of these cases, of course, the defendant is cleared.[4] Of the remaining one-sixth of the cases in which the district attorney proceeds, approximately 95 percent end in convictions, albeit not necessarily in prison sentences. In equation (9.2), we show the probability of trial (P_T) as the variable which is of interest to the defendant.

$$P_T = f(R_D, E, I, R_G) \qquad (9.2)$$

Once again, it is some function of the resources used by the defendant (R_D), the physical evidence (E), the investigation which was conducted by the police (I)[5] and the resources invested by the government (R_G), in the form of the district attorney's time. Note that there is again no formal procedure. The defendant is able to employ some of his own resources if he has them, because the prosecuting attorney is usually willing to talk, at least for a short period of time, with the defense attorney. Normally, this discussion takes the form of bargaining about the possibility of a guilty plea, but it is possible for the defense attorney to argue that the district attorney should not proceed with the trial. So far as I know, however, this particular use of resources is characteristically very small.

In most cases, however, the district attorney looks over the file and decides whether or not to proceed, without any significant input from the defendant. In Europe the procedure is rather more formalized, but it is true there, also, that it is an essentially inquisitorial procedure, in which a government official makes the decision in terms of the evidence, and in which the defendant has relatively little opportunity to invest resources in affecting the outcome. Note that in this case, the defendant would normally be prevented by the district attorney from making any major investment. Suppose, for example, the defendant hired a very expensive lawyer, who wished to make a careful, two-day presentation to the district attorney for the purpose of convincing him that he should not proceed with the case. It is doubtful that any district attorney would permit this. They presumably would be willing to permit the attorney to give them a long written report on the subject, but I doubt that it would be read with any great care. In other words, the resource investment by everyone—including, to a large extent, the defendant—is controlled by the government at this stage.

The stages described in equations (9.1) and (9.2) winnow out most potential defendants, and the trial process in the United States has relatively little direct effect on the outcome. As I said above, 95 percent of the people who get through the screening process of equations (9.1) and (9.2) are convicted of the crimes with which they are charged. However, the potential trial process does have a major effect on the decisions made, first, by the police; and, then, by the district attorney. The courts *can* refuse to convict; hence, there is not much point in bringing a case to trial if this is likely. Thus, although the actual winnowing-out process—the decision as to who will be convicted—is largely a matter of police and prosecutorial discretion—this discretion operates subject to a framework of court power. The police and the prosecutor attempt to predict what the court will do, and it turns out that they are quite accurate.

The prosecuting attorney wins about three out of four of those cases that go to trial. Apparently, that is a policy variable selected by the prosecuting attorney. It would appear that prosecuting attorneys, most of whom are elected in the United States, feel that they require a success ratio of about that level in order to be reelected. Therefore, they refuse to take cases without a 0.75 chance of conviction.

It should be pointed out that by the time an individual has proceeded through equation (9.1) and equation (9.2), he has received a very severe punishment from the state. He may be held in prison in lieu of bail (although this is not as common as it was previously); he faces (if he has enough money to hire an attorney) a very heavy legal expense, and he also faces at this stage of 0.95 chance of conviction (0.80 by way of plea-bargaining and 0.15 by trial), which, even if it is not by any means certain to be followed by actual incarceration, is certainly nerve-racking. In reality, it may be that a very significant part of the deterrent effect of American law is achieved here, rather than in the actual court process.

Once through these procedures, the defendant goes to court. If he provides his own attorney, then his probability of conviction is shown in equation (9.3).

$$P_C = f(R_D, R_G, J, E) \qquad\qquad (9.3)$$

It is some function of the resources invested by the defendant (R_D) and the resources invested by the government (R_G) in prosecution, the resources invested by the government in the quality of the decision-making process (J) (we can call this latter either the judge or the jury), and of the evidence (E). If the defendant is innocent, then as resources for J are increased and as the evidence gets better, the probability of acquittal is higher. The same is true as resources are increased by the defendant, but the increase in resources by the prosecutor makes it more likely that the trial will go wrong—in this case, a conviction.

So far, I have assumed that the defendant will provide his own defense from his own funds. If he has the funds, this is no doubt the best way to handle it; but, in recent years, the practice of providing "free" defense attorneys at government expense has steadily grown. It is obvious that resources are not unlimited, and hence the defendant cannot have as many attorneys, or as good attorneys, or as many appeals as he wished, provided by the government. There is no real pretense that the public-defender system gives the defendant a free hand in the government till to hire legal advice.

There must be some rationing device. In one way or another, the public defender must decide how much of his energy will be devoted to each of his cases. If the public defender's office is large, some senior official will decide which defendant gets which attorney, a decision which may have a very great effect on the outcome. Once assigned, the attorneys must decide whether they are going to accept the prosecution's plea-bargaining offer or go to trial, which is a major resource decision.

I have been unable to find any serious discussion of the way these decisions are made.[6] The literature more or less implies that the public defender behaves like a private attorney, but this is absurd. The private attorney's decision as to the size of the resource commitment is not his own; it is made by his employer. He merely makes the decision as to how a given bundle of resources will be allocated during the trial. Presumably, he is willing to ask for as many appeals, rehearings, etc., as his employer will pay for. If legal services are free, as they are to a person with a public defender, obviously the beneficiary of those services would want an infinite quantity; and, equally obviously, it cannot be provided. In this case, then, there must be a decision as to how much resources will be

given to an individual defendant. Equation (9.4) shows the decision
process undertaken by the man making this decision.

$$R_D = f(E, R_G) \qquad (9.4)$$

He should take into account the evidence (E) and his estimate of the
resources which will be invested by the prosecution (R_G). He will
probably have good information on the latter variable. The public
defender and the prosecutors are very commonly housed in the same
building, and they have fairly continuous contact. It should be noted that
the decision as to the resources which will be assigned to the defense of a
given person will no doubt affect the resources assigned by the prosecuting attorney and vice versa. If, for example, the public defender decides
to assign his best man to a given case, the prosecuting attorney may well
do the same. Further, if the case is subject to a fairly large resource commitment in the form of careful preparation by one of the two sides, the
other is apt to increase resources also.

In the case of the public defender, there are some special issues that do
not arise with the private attorney. First, suppose the public defender
feels that the prosecution's offer of a plea bargain is in the interest of his
client, but his client rejects it.[7] Let us further assume (which might well be
true) that he is convinced that the reason his client rejects it is simple stu-
pidity. Suppose, for example, that the public defender feels that he has
about a one-in-four chance of winning the case if it goes to trial, and that
the sentence normally administered in such cases is five years. The
prosecutor, however, has expressed willingness to accept a guilty plea
under circumstances in which the defendant would get only six months.
Actually defending the case in court will not only consume government
resources but make the defendant worse off.

Under current law, the defendant's government-paid attorney cannot
literally force his cleint not to go to trial.[8] Suppose, however, that the
prosecutor comes to him with a proposal: if the public defender will agree
not to push his case very hard, with the result that the prosecution's success is certain, the prosecutor will see to it that the sentence is not more
than nine months. It clearly would be in the best interests of the client for
the government-appointed defense attorney to accept this deal, but it is
not obvious to me that this is what our present rules say should happen.[9]

In practice, I imagine the matter is not of much significance, because I presume that when the government-appointed defense attorney goes to his client with a bargain he thinks is advantageous,[10] the client really has no choice. For example, the public defender may subtly make it clear to the client that he is going to get a very poor defense if he chooses to go to trial. I have no evidence that this is so; it simply seems to me a reasonable outcome. In any event, I have been unable to find any clear discussion of the way in which public defenders are supposed to allocate their resources.

The second special problem with respect to the public defender concerns the guilty defendant. The lawyer is supposed to defend a client even if he thinks he is guilty. This is indeed the reason why defense lawyers are prohibited from making statements in court as to their own personal beliefs regarding their client's innocence.[11] But should a public defender vigorously defend a man whom he knows to be guilty?

Suppose, for example, that A robbed a bank and is now on trial for the robbery. He has a public defender. There is an eyewitness prepared to identify A as a participant in the robbery; but A, after all, was also there, had a better vantage point of the robbery than the eyewitness, and since he was engaged in his normal profession was not as excited as the eyewitness. In consequence, he knows that the eyewitness has made several mistakes on some details of his testimony. It is obvious that if his attorney concentrates on these mistakes in his cross-examination, he may be able to reduce gravely the credibility of the witness.

But can the bank robber tell his attorney that he was in fact guilty and, therefore, has this special information which will be of use in his trial? In the case of a privately hired attorney, there is no problem. The defendant informs the attorney and the attorney makes use of the information.[12] In the case of a public defender, however, it would seem that this government official should have an interest in a correct outcome. The prosecuting attorney, after all, is supposed to refrain from bringing cases if he believes the defendant is innocent, no matter what the evidence is; and, on parallel grounds, it would seem that the public defender should be unwilling to defend if he believes the defendant is guilty.

This is clearly *not* the law, but there is still the issue of the situation which arises when the defense attorney is certain the defendant is guilty because the defendant has told him so in the course of assisting in the preparation of his defense. Even more significant in this case, private attorneys sometimes will devote a good deal of time to the preparation of their client for his own testimony. Can a public defender assist his client, whom he knows to be guilty, in preparing perjured testimony? The only suggestion I have heard about this particular problem is an oral one: an attorney told me that a public defender should not participate in perjury, and therefore he would not put the defendant on the stand if he knew the defendant was going to perjure himself. Since the defendant can get on the stand by himself if he wishes, this is not very helpful.

Note that the problem here is the mystique of adversary proceedings, not anything of greater importance. Presumably, we wish to have guilty people convicted. A legal rule which makes it necessary for guilty people to conceal their crimes—not only from the court but also from their own attorneys—would surely increase the likelihood of guilty people being convicted without injuring innocent people. However, this is *not* the Anglo-Saxon rule. Unfortunately, I am unable to find out what the Anglo-Saxon rule is. I find that if I discuss this subject with lawyers, most of them begin by giving me a very definite statement on one side or the other. After some discussion, they give me an equally definite statement on the other side. Some of them, the more clever ones, change the subject quickly.

Leaving this mystery aside, the decision that the government will provide a defense attorney for some defendants seems to be based on the assumption that the provision of a prosecuting attorney is somehow a fact of nature. In fact it is not, and there is no reason why a court has to have either a prosecutor or a defense attorney present. Even if we do not want to completely abolish the attorneys on both sides, it would still be possible to reduce their influence.

Suppose that we have a court system in which the government is in the habit of providing prosecuting attorneys. Some of the defendants appearing before this court cannot afford defense attorneys. It is now suggested that the government provide defense attorneys for these defendants. There is another possibility, which is to do away with the prosecuting attorney or, in any event, to reduce sharply his allotment. Indeed, for example, one could take whatever resources were previously used for the prosecuting attorney in the case and divide them evenly between a prosecuting attorney and a defense attorney.

So far as I know, this has never been seriously suggested. I believe the reason is simply that almost all of the advice we ever receive on such issues comes from lawyers, and they have much to gain by the increasing demand for their own services.[13] Since judges, members of the bar, and most commentators on legal matters are all lawyers, as are many legislators, their strong material motives for expansion of the demand for legal services is obvious. Unfortunately, it has not been obvious to most people making policy decisions in this area, insofar as these people are not themselves lawyers.

Even the general counsel of General Motors would be in favor of government provision of free attorneys for anyone who wishes to sue General Motors. It is in his interest to have such counsel provided, although it might not be in his interest to say so openly within the hearing of his employers. If there are more suits brought against General Motors, the legal division will be expanded, and its head will probably find himself with a higher salary, larger office, etc. As a general rule, in making decisions as to the governmental allocation of resources for hiring attorneys, the one group that is most influential is the attorneys themselves. It is not surprising that we find an increasing share of our resources being spent in litigation.

So far as I know, the only argument against the kind of reduction of legal resources I have recommended above is one of accuracy. It is alleged that as resources are increased on both sides of a case, the probable accuracy of the outcome increases. I believe that this is true, although no doubt the increase is very slow. A doubling of the fees to the attorneys on both sides surely does not double accuracy.

Granted, however, that accuracy can be increased by increasing the resources on both sides, this is only certain if the resources are increased proportionately. If the resources on one side are increased more than those on the other, then the increase might contribute to inaccuracy. Suppose, for example, that there is some trial procedure to which the prosecution would contribute resources equivalent to, let us say, $1,000 if there is no public defender. If a public defender is appointed, the public defender would normally contribute resources worth $1,500, and the prosecution, raising its bid because of the existence of a public defender, goes to $2,000. Assume that this is the allocation of resources which—granted the fact that we do not purchase infinite accuracy because accuracy costs resources—is optimal for this society. Lowering the resources to $1,000 for the prosecution and $750 for the public defender could leave the same conditional probability but decrease accuracy.

Leaving the conditional probability unchanged while decreasing accuracy seems paradoxical, but this is (I think) the best way to describe a rather odd situation. In order to explain it, I have made up a set of probability matrices. Note that the specific numbers on these matrices were selected for the purpose of making a mathematical point with the minimum complication. A more realistic matrix would not have the neat straight-line characteristics of the ones shown here, but it would still be possible to make the same point. Figure 9.1 shows the situation in which we have some person accused of a crime. As outsiders, we think there is a 50-50 chance that he is guilty or innocent, and we happen to know that this court is a very simple court in which all decisions are made by flipping a coin. There are four possibilities: the court can convict a guilty man, acquit a guilty man, convict an innocent man, or acquit an innocent man. Granted there is a 50-50 chance of the defendant being innocent or guilty, and the court flips coins, there is a one in four chance for each of

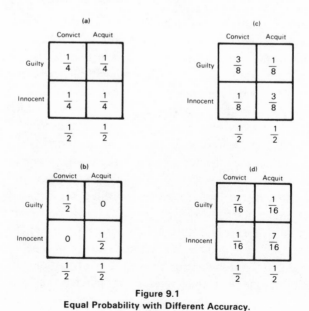

Figure 9.1
Equal Probability with Different Accuracy.

these possibilities, as shown in figure 9.1a. Note, however, the 50-50 break between convictions and acquittals.

In figure 9.1b, we show the situation in a court which has divine guidance and therefore never makes mistakes. All of the decisions are either to convict the guilty (one-half of the decisions with a 50-50 probability of guilty), or to acquit the innocent (the other half). Note that the probability of conviction or acquittal, however, remains one-half on either side. From the standpoint of the person on trial, however, these situations are radically different. He is, of course, the only person in the courtroom who knows for certain whether he is guilty or innocent, and hence from his standpoint the probability of conviction in figure 9.1b is either 1 or 0. For the outsider, however, it is one-half/one-half. Figure 9.1c and figure 9.1d show more realistic situations, in which the court is either accurate three times out of four, as in 9.1c, or seven times out of eight, as in 9.1d. Both of them provide conditional probabilities of one-half from the standpoint of the outsider. But the conditional probabilities are three-fourths/one-fourth and seven-eighths/one-eighth for the defendant, who starts with knowledge of his innocence or guilt. The more resources we invest in a court, the more accurate it will become; and hence with increased resources, we move from 9.1a through 9.1c and 9.1d, and perhaps to some approximation of 9.1b.

Since accuracy is not infinitely desirable, as we have demonstrated in earlier chapters, we will not make any serious effort to proceed to 9.1b. Indeed, in the type of adversary procedure we are now talking about, we will reach an equilibrium between the two parties far short of that which would prevail if the parties were investing their own funds. If we wish to consider a social decision on one or both parties' resources, however, the matter is much more difficult. Indeed, there seems to be no reason to believe that the amount that private parties would put up is the optimal amount from the standpoint of society as a whole. This was discussed in chapter 6.

The problem is that optimality requires that the decision on resources for both the prosecution and the defense be made simultaneously, instead of by two separate institutions. Currently, we have the prosecuting attorney deciding whether to go to trial and how many resources he will commit to the trial. There is, then, another decision on the same facts by the public defender's office, in which they decide not whether they will take the case, but whether they will try to impose a negotiated settlement upon the defendant, and if they do go to trial, how large the resource investment will be. There is, then, a third investigation—i.e., the formal trial process itself—so we have three different government officials involved, each one investigating the case. The first two make the basic decisions as to the amount of resources which will be committed to the case, which surely has an effect on the outcome of the decision in the third process.[14]

Granted that we have two different officials making the decisions, one on each side, then the prospect of error is great. Suppose, for example, that the prosecution has decided to invest $2,000, but the public defender's office decides that $1,250 would be adequate for the defense. This not only lowers the accuracy, but it also moves the center of distribution—it makes the likelihood of conviction of the defendant greater than it would have been under the $1,000–$750 allocation of resources.

So far as I know, my suggestion that we lower the resources given to the prosecuting attorney instead of providing a public defender has never been canvassed before. There does not seem to have been very much careful thought given to the problem of providing public defenders, etc. I incline to the view that the reason for this is simply that it is contrary to the best interests of the attorneys, as a class, to consider such matters. They also normally, as a result of their education, are not trained to consider it, and the decisions are, in our society, heavily influenced by them. Thus, they are in a position where they can use public funds for the purpose *both* of increasing their incomes and increasing the respect accorded them in the community, because these cartellike activities are thought to be highly moral.

But if we should be skeptical about lawyers advising us to hire lawyers, it does not follow that we know what the optimum solution is. In chapter 6, I argued that Anglo-Saxon procedure has little or no tendency to operate at the most efficient level when the two parties hire their own lawyers. In this chapter, I have discussed the situation when the same party—the government—is hiring lawyers on both sides. Here, optimality would clearly be possible for the same reason that optimality is possible in Europe—the basic decisions are made by a third party, rather than by the two parties to the controversy. There is no reason to believe that our actual system is optimal or that it even aims at optimality. It seems to be based instead on the idea of "fairness," with "fairness" always obtained by an increase in resource allocation rather than by a reduction.

The only argument for this kind of increase in resources would appear to be increasing accuracy: we should have enough resources present to provide the optimal balance between cost and error. In order to have this trade-off, it is necessary not only that the total resources be optimal but that their division between the two parties (indeed, between the two parties and the decision maker) be optimal. It seems hard to believe that our present institutions even make any effort to attain this optimality.

However, there are no doubt people who argue that our present criminal justice system does seek, and does achieve, optimality. If it is optimal, and I gravely doubt it, then it most certainly would be true that those suits in which the parties themselves provide the resources for both sides would not be optimal. Thus, arguments for either subsidizing or taxing the provision of legal services in private litigation would also appear to be sound. Basically, however, the problem is that there has been little scientific investigation. Vague ideas of "fairness," together with the self-interest of lawyers in expanding the resources involved in litigation, seem to have been the main drives. It should be possible to do better.

Chapter 10

Trial Technology: Miscellaneous Matters

This chapter will deal with several important matters that do not seem to fit in anywhere else. The first two are rules of evidence and the somewhat related problem of expertise, or what to do if a case involves a dispute about something the judge does not understand, such as molecular biology. One of them—appeal—might have gone into the chapter on the motivation of decision makers, but I thought it best to defer its consideration. Lastly, there is the question of what should be done if the case will affect third parties who, either through ignorance of the existence of the case or through public-goods problems, are unlikely to take an active role in litigation.

Rules of Evidence

Anglo-Saxon rules of evidence are massively more complicated than they are anywhere else in the world. Indeed, it is an oversimplification, but not a dangerous one, to say that rules of evidence exist only in the Anglo-Saxon world. There are, in fact, some minor rules in most other places. Primarily, these minor rules concern the issue of expertise, or insuring relevancy.

In the Anglo-Saxon world, these rules of evidence fall roughly into one of three categories. Category 1: these are rules which prohibit the use of things which are thought to be poor evidence. The explanation for these rules in general is that the jury might be misled by this kind of evidence. Two examples, one very old and one quite new, are the rules against hearsay, and the rules against the use of the lie detector. Category 2 contains those rules intended simply to reduce the cost of the proceedings by preventing the parties from wasting the time of their opponent, and of the court, on matters which have an evidentiary value less than their cost. Most of the rules relating to relevancy are of this sort. Category 3: these are the rules which are developed essentially for reasons extraneous to the proceeding itself. For example, our rules against the use of evidence obtained by torture come basically from the fact that we do not want people tortured. Similarly, we do not want to press women to testify against their husbands (and vice versa), nor do we want people opening letters and eavesdropping on our telephone conversations.[1]

In this last area, we are not really attempting to affect the court proceeding but to enforce rules which exist for normal life. The court attempts to prevent certain police activities by refusing to admit certain evidence into the court proceedings. This is not intended to improve the efficiency of the court but to put sanctions on certain police activities.

Note that I have said above that torture is something we want to avoid for its own sake. There is not very much discussion of the matter in the literature, but what discussion there is frequently implies that evidence obtained under torture is unreliable. Thus, the prevention of torture would fall into our category 1 instead of category 3. My reason for putting it in category 3 is that the unreliability of evidence obtained under torture is no greater than that of evidence obtained under two other conditions, which are, in general, perfectly legal.

First, the prosecution may offer a reduction in prison sentence in return for testimony. It depends on the length of the present sentence and what particular method of torture is being discussed, but it is clear that this reduction offers exactly the same likelihood of generating inaccurate evidence as does the use of torture. In both cases, we can expect people to lie in order to avoid suffering.

Similar to the above is the direct payment of money for testimony.[2] This is common in England and not particularly common in the United States, although in the United States there is nothing to prevent private parties from making such payments; it is only if the government makes them that the evidence is likely to be banned. Nevertheless, this kind of information clearly has defects because of the motive for making it up.

In all three of these cases—information offered to avoid torture, information offered in order to reduce sentence, and information offered in return for payment—we should be suspicious of the evidence, but it is not obvious that we should throw it out entirely. In all three of these cases, we should test the evidence carefully and, in particular, look for extrinsic confirmation or contradiction of it. The accuracy of the evidence obtained by torture, however, would not appear to be very much different from that obtained by, let us say, letting the individual off scot-free, instead of giving him fifteen years, if he turns state's evidence against his confederates. The revulsion generated by the use of torture, then, is based simply on a revulsion from the use of torture, not on a feeling that evidence obtained by torture is particularly inaccurate.

The whole issue of whether we should use judicial proceedings as a way to enforce other parts of the law is an open one. Smith commits a murder. When tracking him down, the police tap a telephone, and the telephone tapping is criminal.[3] Hence, we now have two crimes, the murder and the violation of the law prohibiting telephone taps. It is not obvious that releasing the murderer is the appropriate technique for dealing with this problem and, in fact, the rule is a relatively recent invention of the American courts. It is only in the most recent years that any other courts have adopted it. Most of the world's courts do not use it. Clearly, if we had great confidence in our law enforcement apparatus—if we thought that it would enforce the law against both of these crimes—we would never even consider this particular technique. Both the murderer and the policemen who tapped his phone would suffer the appropriate penalty in jail.

It is only lack of confidence in our legal system, particularly the feeling that the district attorney would probably not prosecute the policeman who tapped the phone and/or that a jury would probably think that he had done nothing very wrong, and therefore would not convict, that leads to our present rules. In a way, the judges trust themselves and do not trust other people; hence, they are attempting to enforce this particular set of rules directly, rather than letting a jury and an elected official (district attorney) participate in the decision process.

Returning to our category 1, keeping out "misleading" evidence must depend on a feeling that we know more about the probitive value of evidence than the people who are actually making decisions. Originally, it was discussed in terms of the jurors being not quite bright. They were "simple people," and might be easily misled. It would seem that if the jury is poor enough in evaluating evidence so that they can be misled by hearsay, they probably evaluate other evidence badly, too. In other words, they are bad decision makers. In any event, most courts in the world make use of hearsay but give it much less weight than direct evidence. This is the way we behave in everyday life, and it would seem to be the sensible rule.

In general, these rules in category 1 involve a sort of intellectual mistake. We give decision-making power to a body which is not thought capable of properly evaluating evidence, and then we remove from its consideration evidence which has some value, but which may mislead this not-very-bright decision-making body. It would seem more sensible simply to assign people to make the decisions who are not easily misled. This is indeed the procedure used throughout most of the world and, to a very large extent, the procedure used in arbitration proceedings in the United States.

The second category of rules of evidence, those which simply attempt to reduce the cost of proceedings, arise because the cost to a particular party is not the same as the cost to society. Suppose that I am the defendant in a criminal case and pay for my own attorney. In the United States, I do not pay for the opposing attorney, the use of the court and judge and jury and, in general, I do not pay for the time of witnesses.[4] The last is particularly important, since, in our court system, the witness cannot be told in advance the exact time he will be called. Under the circumstances, he may spend a great deal of time simply sitting around and waiting. Since he is either not compensated at all for this or compensated at a much lower rate than his actual time is worth, this is a considerable burden on him.

The individuals in the court proceeding, then, pay only a small part of the total cost. They would, if unconstrained, surely use resources to the point where their private cost was equivalent to their private benefit, rather than making the social cost equal to the benefit. Assume, for example, that a defendant in a criminal case who provides his own legal service will pay 25 percent of the total operating cost of the court. Clearly, he would be sensible to use court resources to the point where the private gain to him was equal to 25 percent of the total cost of the court. This would lead to an overinvestment of resources. There is also the point made in chapter 6 that his activities are not only wasteful but, from the standpoint of the opposing party, they are directly counterproductive. Each time one party invests $1 to improve his likelihood of winning, he also *reduces* the likelihood that his opponent will win by exactly the same amount. This may also lead to great overinvestment of resources.

Under the circumstance, some method of restricting this wasteful investment of resources is desirable. Most of the courts in the world depend primarily on a procedure in which the parties themselves do not have basic control over the proceedings. This means that the courts can get by without very much in the way of procedural rules and, in fact, they have relatively few of them. Think of the proceeding as consisting of an investigating commission in which a board of three judges is attempting to find the truth. There may be various defects in the process; but the possibility that the parties will be able to force overinvestment of resources is not likely to be serious.

Thus, we find that in cases which use the Roman law or its "descendents," or in Oriental countries which simply have their own legal system which works out procedurally much the same way, there are not many procedural rules. Further, the procedural rules that exist tend to concentrate mainly on the problem of the composition of the investigating body, rather than on what happens in the courtroom. Even in the civil proceedings on the continent of Europe, however, the parties have at least some influence on what happens. Thus, some restrictions on the type of evidence they can present are still called for in terms of economizing.

Once an elaborate procedural-rule system develops, then it becomes possible for the attorneys in an adversary system to make use of this for strategic purposes. It is my impression that the principal real function of the procedural objection, so common in American courts, is to interrupt the judge's and jury's train of thought so that the testimony of the witness loses effectiveness. This is particularly important for the judge, who must actually role on the procedural objection, and therefore must devote at least some thought to it. The jury, of course, can simply "tune out" during the period in which the procedural squabbling goes on.

If this is so, then the procedural rules, while limiting the use of time by the parties, paradoxically also provide them with a way to waste time. The attorney for the defendant, who makes it hard to follow the testimony of a principal prosecution witness by raising twenty-seven procedural objections during the course of the testimony, is engaged in an almost perfect example of the use of the court resources to the benefit of one party with a net social waste. Attorneys attempting this strategy, of course, must be careful. Too many objections can annoy the jury enough to counterbalance their other advantages.

Still, one objective of rules of evidence is cost reduction. The judges, needless to say, are not very adept at explaining this rule, but it is a sensible one. A particularly interesting case of this sort occurs when a party wishes to call a witness who is only temporarily unavailable, and who would become available if the trial itself were delayed. The Watergate case, for example, involved a request by the defense to call ex-President Nixon. At the time, Nixon was ill, but it was clear that he would recover shortly. The judge refused to delay the trial until he was available. The Harris trial involved somewhat similar circumstances, because the witness (Patricia Hearst) the defense wished to call was at the time undergoing psychiatric diagnosis at the request of the federal government. Either interrupting the diagnostic procedure to make her available, or delaying the trial until the procedure was complete, would seem to have been quite possible.

Note that in both of these cases, however, the resource saving is a clear consideration. It is dubious that the defense attorneys in either case thought that the witness they were attempting to call would contribute very much to their case. In fact, they were probably trying to delay proceedings or to provide themselves with a possible reversible error for appeal. Thus, the court decisions were probably fairly clear-cut examples of the efforts of the sort we are now discussing. In both cases, delay of the case would have been to the defendant's advantage, and there would have been no cost to the defendants in presenting the particular witnesses, who might even have been helpful to them.

The situation is shown diagrammatically in figure 10.1. On the left axis, we show the cost and value of any given piece of information, and all information has been arranged in terms of its probitive value for the truth, with the best cost/value ratio at the left and the worst at the right. Since some information is positively misleading, it has a negative value, although still a cost. This information falls below the zero line on the figure. Thus, the information to the left supports the stand of the party who is in the right, and the information on the right supports the stand of the party in the wrong.

In a sense, we could say that all information supporting the party in the wrong is undesirable, but the court will not know in advance which party is right or wrong; therefore, the court will presumably consider at

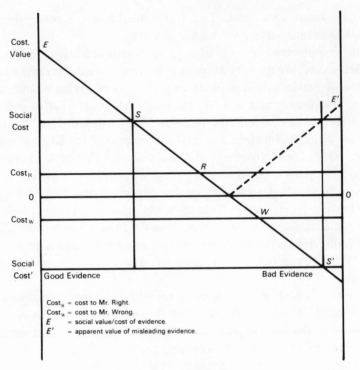

Figure 10.1
Social Cost of Evidence.

least some information which, if taken by itself, would point to a decision for Mr. Wrong. The social cost of information is shown by two lines, the standard social cost line above zero and the social cost prime line which is an equal distance below zero. All information to the left of the vertical line at S has a positive cost/benefit outcome, and hence it should be presented. The same is true of the information to the right of S', even though this information is misleading. This is because, at the time the litigation is underway, the people who are ultimately going to decide do not know the identity of Mr. Right and Mr. Wrong.

The parties, however, do not have to take into account the entire cost. The cost to Mr. Right is shown by the line $Cost_R$ and the cost to Mr. Wrong is shown by the line $Cost_W$. Mr. Right would want to introduce all information to the left of point R, and Mr. Wrong would want to introduce all the information to the right of point W. The information between S and R and between S' and W contributes less than its social cost.

If the reader finds the extension of the evidence line below 0 unintelligible, he can think in terms of the dotted line E', which goes up to the right from the 0 line. All of the intersections of this line are vertically above those of the original line. Indeed, the court, not being able to determine which party is right until it has heard the evidence, but having some idea as to the probitive value of the evidence, would probably have something like the dotted line in its mind.

Thus, if we leave aside the theory that the people who are making the decision are stupid or easily misled, then the basic argument for most rules of evidence would be that they tend to exclude information which lies between S and S'. The information between R and W would be excluded by the parties voluntarily, since their private costs in that area are greater than their benefits, but the private costs/benefit ratio is favorable and the social/benefit ratio unfavorable in the rest of the area between S and S'; the parties therefore will probably put the information before the court.

Consider figure 10.2, which is another presentation of the same point. In this case, we have put the evidentiary value on the vertical axis, and the cost of any given piece of information on the horizontal axis. Those bits of information where the value is greater than the cost—those which lie above the S (45°) line—are the ones we like to have in the court. However, there is a private-cost line shown as P, and the parties will be motivated to introduce all information above the P line. The area between P and S, then, contains socially undesirable information which in an adversary system will tend to be brought forward. Information in the area below line P will be brought forward by no one because it is too expensive, both from the private and the social standpoint.

The laws of evidence, insofar as they have any sense at all (it will not have escaped the reader that the author does not think they have very much), can be explained on the grounds that they have a tendency to ban information between S and P, while not banning information in the area above S. Clearly, they could only have a tendency in this direction, since they do not directly address the problem. It may be, however, that as rough rules of thumb, they have some value. This argument can also be applied to some of the rules in our first category. Suppose, for example, that we collected and somehow or other evaluated the cost and evi-

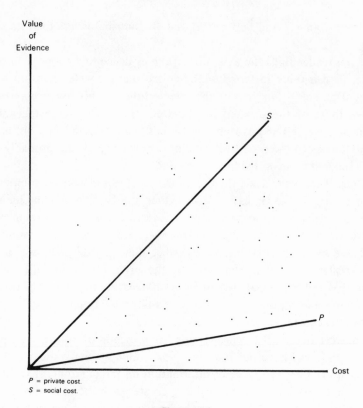

Figure 10.2
Rules of Evidence.

dentiary value of a collection of bits of hearsay information, and we found that they fell in the positions shown by the dots on figure 10.2. It will be clear that banning hearsay under these circumstances would ban more information which is socially undesirable than that which meets the cost/benefit criterion. Thus, in a rough-and-ready way, and over many cases, the net effect of the hearsay rule would be to improve efficiency.

Is there a better way? There is a conceptually simple (although practically difficult) solution. Suppose that the parties were charged the full social cost of the court facilities. Under these circumstances, their own interests would lead them to select only information that lies above line *S*.

How could we do this? It does not seem likely that we could do it exactly in the real world, but suppose that each party were required to pay a fee of so much per minute for the entire time that he is presenting a case, whether this presentation takes the form of testimony by witnesses or oral argument. He could also be charged a page price (intended to approximate the study time needed) for written material such as briefs.

It would not be necessary to have the individual pay his opponent's lawyers. He would have to be charged the cost which he is inflicting on his opponent by compelling him to have his lawyers work longer; but it is not necessary that this money go to the opponent—it could go to the state in the form of tax. Further, there is another very important cost which clearly could not be charged. If I introduce witnesses who tend to prove my case, the largest cost this imposes on my opponent is the increase in the likelihood that he will lose. This is something for which I would obviously not have to compensate him. At most, the compensation would take the form of paying for the increase in legal expenses imposed upon him by these witnesses.

A minute-by-minute charge of this sort would be fairly easy to compute under modern circumstances, and it should seem very natural for most public finance specialists. It is, after all, the usual business of dealing with an externality by imposing a tax. However, there would be certain rather startling consequences. First, it would be necessary to make some decisions as to what would be done about indigent persons; but, leaving aside the restrictions of funds, the two parties could still receive quite different levels of "justice." Suppose, for example, that Exxon sues General Motors about a matter which is small enough so that it is clear that neither one of these companies is even remotely close to its budget constraint. In addition, Exxon may be in the right, but the evidence they have to present is complex and detailed; while General Motors, which is in the wrong, has some very simple but misleading evidence they propose to put forward. Under the circumstances, Exxon, which is in the right, would pay a great deal more in courts costs than General Motors. Though this seems bizarre, it could still be more efficient than our present system.

The last category consists of those situations where we feel that obtaining the evidence involves something we do not want done. As I said above, those cases—such as tapping telephones or the use of torture outside of court—where the unwanted act occurs before the legal proceeding begins would be better dealt with, I think, by straightforward criminal prosecution against the torturer or telephone tapper. If, however, it is thought that our judicial and police systems are not efficient enough to enforce this kind of law directly, then banning evidence which is "fruit of a poison tree" does have something to be said for it. To make this argument, however, one has to have a fairly low opinion of the efficiency of the legal process as a whole, and therefore one might be dubious that any legal proceeding is likely to reach its correct conclusion. There is a very substantial cost involved in the suppression of the information derived from these illegal procedures. Nevertheless, one can imagine specific inefficiencies in our system of criminal justice which would make this system better than its alternative.

The other set of cases in which we object to certain types of evidence because we just do not think they should be used are matters that actually take place in court. Certain witnesses cannot be asked questions on some matters. Under the Fifth Amendment, as it is currently intepreted, an individual's refusal to answer a question which he claims will incriminate him may not be used against him. In practice, of course, juries will normally take such a claim into account even if it is made by the defendant's simply not taking the stand. Nevertheless, they are always warned not to. This is an example where the person being questioned has to claim the privilege. The restriction on a wife testifying against her husband (and vice versa), on the other hand, applies even if the wife does not object to so testifying. Both of these privileges, which have a most interesting legal history,[5] are generally unknown outside the Anglo-Saxon world, and indeed they are not characteristic of Canada, within the Anglo-Saxon world.

Jeremy Bentham was a strong opponent to what we now call the Fifth Amendment, and there is no point in repeating his arguments against it. Clearly, the effect is to reduce the accuracy of criminal proceedings—and, indeed, of other proceedings—when individual witnesses claim this privilege. It is notable that almost all other legal systems in the world include direct questioning of the defendant as part of the normal procedure. In the less-civilized countries, the defendant may be severely punished for not answering or, indeed, tortured until he does answer. In civilized European countries, of course, nothing like this happens. If the defendant chooses to refuse to answer questions, the judge simply regards this as evidence that he has something to conceal. There are various rules as to how strongly the judge should weigh this evidence, but probably the judge takes the same attitude toward it as you or I would in ordinary life.

In these proceedings, the defendant is not sworn, and hence does not commit perjury if he denies he committed a crime which he, in fact, did commit. Europeans always criticize our system because if the defendant wishes to take the stand in his own defense, he is compelled to commit perjury if he is guilty. Under their system, of course, there is no perjury. In fact, however, under our system the judges and juries do not seem to regard perjurious testimony on the stand by the defendant as calling for any additional punishment.

Historically, the privilege of refraining from self-incrimination has had a bad reception in the courts. The general picture of the history of its development from the time of the U.S. Constitution to the late 1930s was a steady restriction on the privilege. It had a boom in the late 1940s and 1950s, but we have begun, once again, to reduce its importance. I would guess that fifty to seventy-five years from now, it will no longer be of much significance; but, perhaps I am simply being optimistic.

Expertise

A second issue is the problem of expertise. Suppose, as quite commonly occurs, something or other comes up in the course of a lawsuit (whether criminal or civil) which is unlikely to be understood by the decision makers. My favorite example involves the case in which Cutter Laboratories was sued by a number of people who had caught polio after taking some Cutter-prepared Salk vaccine for polio prevention. The plaintiffs introduced into the record a very long affadavit from Jonas Salk, in which he explained that his methods of preparation were perfect, and therefore the polio must have come from carelessness on the part of Cutter Labs. Cutter Labs introduced in evidence another long affadavit from a Nobel Prize-winner, Paul H. Mueller, which stated that the methods designed by Salk for preparing the vaccine were defective. Therefore, there was no reason to believe that Cutter had been careless. It is very doubtful that any of the judges (including appellate judges) or jurymen in this case ever understood what the argument between the two great biologists was about. Certainly none of them was capable of saying who was right. Clearly, we do not want to have this kind of situation arise in court, and the question is how can we avoid it.

Since the capacity of the human mind is finite, we obviously cannot train judges and jurymen in everything nor can we expect them to really become expert on a new subject during the course of the trial. The impossibility of training them during the course of the trial is particularly clear, because the attorneys on both sides are unlikely to want to prejudice the judge and/or the jury against them by telling them that they are wrong about something. For example, if an expert witness is testifying about something or other, and the judge asks a question or makes a statement which indicates that he has misunderstood the testimony, the attorneys are torn between annoying the judge by correcting him and letting him remain ill-informed. Further, normally one of the attorneys is delighted to have him remain ill-informed. Under the circumstances, the judge may not be corrected.[6] But, in any event, trials are simply not long enough to educate properly the judge and jury. In the Cutter Lab case, it is very doubtful that the judge and jury had the intellectual capacity to fully understand the Nobel Prize-winner and Salk, no matter how much time they devoted to studying the issue.

What can we do about this problem? In arbitration, it usually creates no great difficulty, because an arbitrator is selected from whatever field of knowledge is required. For example, in many cases, the question is whether an export or import shipment is up to the required quality. The arbitrator is simply someone who knows the quality, and who goes to look at the shipment, perhaps performing some tests on it, and then from his own expertise says whether or not it is up to snuff. This system, however, can only be used if we are willing to have a very large board of people who can be called upon to make decisions. This is the method we use in arbitration, but not the method normally used in regular courts. Further, in some cases, the problem is only partially one of specialized expertise. Only occasionally, for example, will a murder case turn on evidence which requires a high level of technical competence in order to judge its validity.

In Anglo-Saxon countries, when cases do involve a matter of technical difficulty, the usual procedure is for the parties to call specialized witnesses who testify. The judge and/or jury are then supposed to evaluate this testimony. If there are experts on both sides who disagree, it is very doubtful that the judge's and jury's evaluation of their testimony is worth much. They are not experts and the experts are in disagreement. For an example—from another but related field—if a lawyer observed two leading specialists disagree on a point of contract law, he would not think of entrusting the decision to a group of laymen. He would feel that if two leading experts disagreed, the matter was beyond the laymen's competence.

Note that in this case, the lawyers probably would let an expert, the judge, decide. Although judges are supposed to be experts on the law, no one regards them as experts on nuclear biology, recovery of faint blood stains, dating of documents by chemical analysis of the ink, etc. Thus, they are laymen in these areas.

A technique which Anglo-Saxon courts sometimes use is having the court appoint a single expert who will examine the matter and give his opinion. Although he is referred to as an expert witness,[7] this amounts to taking part of the judicial power and transferring it to someone who is not a regular judge. The judge and jury will simply accept the judgment of this particular expert in his particular field; then, on the basis of his judgment, they will make their decision. It would make no great difference if he were formally part of the judicial staff rather than a witness.

This technique is more highly developed in Europe, where it is normal to rely on the court-appointed expert witness. In the United States, the technique is exceptional and requires the consent of the attorneys. The court-appointed expert may not, in fact, be very much of an expert, so the system does not work perfectly. On the other hand, the judge and jury may not be up to their roles either. There is no particular reason to believe that, on the average, the forensic surgeon appointed to determine the cause of death is apt to be of a lower level of competence in his field than the judge is in his.

The problem, it will be seen, is not really terribly difficult if we are willing to accept realistic standards for decision making, both in the expert's field and in the other fields with which the court deals. Errors are likely in both areas, but there is no reason to belive that they are more likely in one than the other. It would appear, however, that the technique of having two experts testify on opposite sides about a matter which is unlikely to be understood by the judge and jury is inferior to appointing a sort of expert special judge, who deals with this problem.

Note, however, that if this line of reasoning is correct, it carries with it the conclusion that, in general, the specialized expert (who is either a special witness or part of the judicial staff) will make the final decision in the area. Witnesses who criticize his technique, or the outcome reached, would be wasting the court's time, not because they are necessarily wrong or because the evidence is irrelevant, but because the court would not be able to comprehend it. To return to the Cutter Lab case, suppose that Mueller had been appointed special master to look into the technical side of the problem. He has reached his decision, which would be essentially in the defendant's favor (although it did not foreclose all of the issues in the case), and the plaintiff wishes to call Salk to contradict Mueller's evidence. Perhaps Mueller is wrong to criticize Salk's position, and certainly Salk is well qualified.[8] Nevertheless, Salk's testimony will simply waste time, because the judge and jury are not competent to make a decision between the two experts.

These cases are on a par with the general rule that a party may not call an expert witness to argue that the judge is wrong about the law, and that, therefore, that the jury should decide against him. Our reason for preventing this is that we think the jury would not be able to properly assess the arguments. The judge is given (subject to appeal) the position of an authoritative expert in the law in our courts, and there is no reason why other people should not be given the position of authoritative experts in other areas.

Appeal

Let us now turn to the problem of appeal. The issues I wish to raise are whether appeal is desirable and, if it is, whether it is universally desirable. The layman is rather apt to think that these are simple questions. He feels that universal appeal is obviously desirable. Thus, he will think that the answer should be Yes on both questions. The lawyer, on the other hand, is apt to feel equally surprised at having the question raised, but he will feel that the answers should be Yes on the first and No on the second, because he is aware, as the layman usually is not, that this is our present law. We only permit appeals on a certain—and rather narrow—category of issues.

As a matter of history, for a very large part of the history of Anglo-Saxon law, decisions made by the jury were not appealable at all. Since the jury made the basic and fundamental decision of guilt or innocence, and determined all matters of fact in common law, this meant that appeals could be undertaken only in a very narrow range of issues. With the development of the law, however, the courts have worked out various techniques for permitting appeal from jury decisions. It is still true, however, that it is much harder to appeal decisions of the jury than it is to appeal decisions made by judges. Since there is no reason to believe that the judge makes more errors than the jury (indeed, most people would think he makes less), those people who think that the right of appeal should be general would regard this particular distinction as positively perverse.

An interesting case in which appeal is not permitted in federal courts is the actual sentencing decision by the judge. This restriction—which was discussed on the Watergate tapes under circumstances which indicated that Nixon, although a professional lawyer, did not know it existed—is particularly surprising, because the sentencing decision is the only part of the ordinary court proceeding in which the judge receives secret information which is not available to the defendant. He then uses that information as the basis for his decision. On the other hand, it could be argued that the decision is not a very important one anyway; the parole board is much more important than the judge in deciding the actual length of time served by the defendant. The parole-board decision is also not subject to judicial appeal, although in the federal system there is a hierarchy of parole boards.

Let us temporarily leave the problem of what restrictions should be placed on appeal if we decide to have appeal for at least some cases and turn to the question of whether appeals should be permitted at all. Most people regard this as a surprising question but, on the other hand, most people who do not have legal training are under the impression that one can appeal anything, instead of only a few issues. As far as I know, there is little or no public complaint that the quality of justice on those issues which cannot be appealed is worse than on those which can. This is not obvious proof, but it does at least indicate that the average citizen, and indeed the average lawyer, sees no great difference between the functioning efficiency of those parts of our system which are subject to appeal and those parts which are not.

To get a concrete example, let us consider a court system in which there are fifteen courts, each presided over by a judge at $30,000 a year, and an appellate court of three judges, each of whom receives $32,000 a year.[9] Decisions of the judges are appealable to the higher court.[10] The argument for this system would be that the lower courts are more likely to make errors than is the appellate court—and the appellate court can correct these errors. Note that in providing only one appellate court for every fifteen judges, we make it certain that only a very small portion of the cases can be appealed. Thus, we are basically relying on the court of first instance. I am not recommending this course of action; it is, roughly speaking, what we do now.

For this argument, we have to believe either that the people who select the judges, whether they are the electors or some other portion of the government, are capable of telling better judges from poorer judges and place better judges in the higher court; or that a board of three judges is more likely to be accurate than a single judge. Belief in the second is general in Europe, where single-judge courts are quite rare, and boards of judges are normally used. But let us restrict ourselves to the American system, in which there is only one judge plus a jury in the court of first instance. Under these circumstances, the proponents of this kind of system would assume that the judges in the court of first instance make a certain number of errors. A portion of these erroneous cases are then appealed to the higher court, which, having a lower error term than the lower court, corrects more errors than it causes. Suppose, for example, that the lower court will normally go wrong one time in eight and the upper court only one time in ten. The cases that are appealed will, in general, be the more difficult ones and hence—although the appellate courts' error term, if put over the entire collection of cases, would only be 10 percent—it may have a much higher error term for the particular cases that reach it. In a way, it is like the extremely skilled surgeon who has a bad death rate because he handles only the most difficult operations. Still, there seems every reason to believe that the appellate court, when it reverses a lower court, is more apt to be correcting an error than making an error of its own.

Let us now consider briefly a possible reform. We disband the court system as a whole, take the $546,000 which is the total annual salary of the existing judges, and use these funds to hire fifteen new judges for a set of courts of first instance without any appellate court. Judges in this new court will have salaries of $36,000 a year and, once again assuming that people who make the decisions as to who shall be judges are capable of judging quality, it should be possible to insure that these judges are better than any of the judges who sat on the previous court. They will, for example, be paid more than the appellate court judges under the previous system.[11] Thus, we now have superior personnel, and we have paid for this superior personnel not by increasing tax costs but simply by reducing the total number of judges. There would be a further cost saving from the reduction in total litigation time, etc., if we look at the matter for society as a whole. If we added these legal expenses of appeal onto the salary of the new judges, we probably could pay them something like $100,000 a year, therefore obtaining really superb quality personnel.

In the above line of reasoning, I have implicitly assumed that the superiority of the higher courts results from superior personnel. It may be that the superiority, if it exists, comes from the fact that they are boards rather than individuals. Substituting boards of judges for the judge, or judge and jury for the court of first instance; and at the same time abolishing appeal, is not quite as simple mathematically as our previous exercise. The saving of the cost of the jury would also have to be counted. On the other hand, the number of judges would be multiplied by three. It might well be more expensive than our present system, but at least for that collection of cases that are not appealed—which are the overwhelming majority—it would provide what advantages there are in a board of judges. If we consider the matter socially—including the legal costs of running through an appeal—it seems very likely that even here we could provide higher wages for the judicial personnel from the savings obtained through abolition of appeal. Thus, either argument for the superior accuracy of the higher courts—that they have better personnel or that a board is better than an individual—would seem to fail. There is no point in going through the numbers, but apparently a combination of the two—the higher court is better because its personnel are better *and* it has a board rather than an individual—would also fail.

It could be argued that appellate courts improve justice, not because they themselves are particularly accurate but because their mere existence puts pressure on the court of first instance to be careful.[12] Since the courts of first instance are not in any way penalized for reaching a decision the higher court thinks is wrong, it is not obvious that much pressure is exerted. I suppose an advocate of this argument would say that the judges are made unhappy and their reputations damaged when their decisions are overthrown. To avoid this, they make decisions which they think the higher court will accept. We cannot prove that this is not true, but I would think it would be a fairly weak motive. Further, it immediately raises the question of motivation of the higher court.

The normal lawyer, on reading the above discussion of appeal, will perhaps be disturbed because we have not discussed at all two of the functions which appellate courts are normally thought to serve—making changes in the law and enforcing uniformity on their subordinate courts. Note, however, that at the moment we are still confining ourselves to errors of fact by the courts, i.e., we are talking about courts as engaging in a factual investigation and not as being involved with legal problems. The legal problems will be discussed in a later chapter.

The above argument against appellate procedures is not very conclusive. What I have attempted to do is to demonstrate that there is no a priori argument that appellate courts are a necessary part of the legal system. They may be, or then again they may not. The problem is essentially an empirical one, and it is one upon which, so far as I know, no research whatsoever has been done. The Islamic Muslim system is certainly quicker than the Anglo-Saxon; but whether this speed is more than compensated for by additional errors is a matter upon which no one, so far as I know, has any real information. We need further research. Until the research is done, people should not go about making very firm statements about whether appellate courts are desirable or undesirable.

If we are going to have an appellate procedure, however, and we do think that it improves the quality of "justice," then there does not seem to be very much argument for not allowing appeals on every aspect of the case. This is directly contrary to existing practice in the United States and England, where only certain aspects of the cases can be appealed. But, if the lower court can go wrong in one area, it can go wrong in another; if the higher court can correct these errors in one area, it surely can correct them in another.

It is true that the present method of appeal, in which the higher court operates entirely on the written record of the original proceedings, would make it somewhat difficult for the court to review certain parts of the initial case. There is, however, nothing divinely ordained in this system. Further, the court does not currently review everything which is in the written record. Almost the only thing which is available to the court of first instance, and not to the appellate court, is the demeanor of the witnesses. With some additional cost, the witnesses could be called to give

their evidence for the appellate court, which could make its own judgment as to whether they are lying or not.

It is not worry about these minor costs but mere custom that has
prevented this so far. Further, the custom does not seem to be particularly well thought out. In general, the areas where the higher courts do
not take appeals—for example, length of sentence or a decision by the
jury as to which of two witnesses is lying—are probably areas in which
the basic lower courts are particularly likely to go wrong. There has been
a good deal of publicity recently about the radically different sentencing
standards apparently used by different judges. The difficulty of detecting
lying, and the probability that the jury does a bad job of it, have been less
emphasized, but I take it that these points are fairly obvious once one
gives the matter any thought.

So much for the appellate procedure. I have not provided, and I did
not intend to provide, a definite answer; but I think that I have raised a
number of questions which should be investigated.

Affect on Third Parties

The final topic in this chapter, which fortunately can be dealt with
briefly, concerns cases in which the matter at issue will affect third
parties. The current procedure in this area is to permit a third party who
knows that he will be affected to file an *amicus curiae* brief. He is not,
however, permitted to call witnesses or introduce evidence. Since the two
parties do not perfectly represent the third party, it is possible that this
can lead to severe errors. For example, the Detroit busing case involved
litigation between a pro-busing group and the school board. The school
board was also pro-busing but less so than the pro-busing party.[13] The
two parties were both agreed on certain views with respect to educational
technique which are, to put it mildly, controversial. As a result of this,
the judge never realized that there was any doubt about the matter at all,
and he made a decision which would severely affect a very large number
of parents on the basis of what he thought were clear facts but which, in
fact, were extremely muddy facts. He might, if he had been presented
with all of the information on the point, have reached the decision but
then, again, he might not.

Fortunately, cases of this sort are fairly rare; but they do occur, and it would seem sensible to permit third parties not only to file briefs but to present evidence and to take an active role in the proceedings when their interests are at stake. The only argument I can see against this would be that it would be quite hard to identify valid third parties; but, since they will be putting up their own money for the case, it is unlikely that very many people will volunteer to enter into legal proceedings if they do not have a real interest.

A more difficult problem occurs when, as in the Detroit case, the third parties at interest are a dispersed group, no single member of which would be motivated to do anything very much about the case. The usual public-good arguments would indicate that the parents of the children who were in danger of being bused, and who objected, would not be able to get together to hire expensive counsel for the purpose of making a presentation before the court. In fact, of course, they did not.

It is very hard to think of a way around the problem, and I have no solution to suggest. One could not leave it to government, because the government body with appropriate jurisdiction was one of the two sides in the case described above. It was, therefore, one of the parties who was concealing the actual lack of clarity of the educational evidence. It is unlikely that if it had been given the responsibility of representing those of its citizens who objected to busing, it would have provided vigorous advocacy.

This chapter concludes my discussion of the theoretical problems raised by trial of the fact. In general, I have not been able to prove anything very much, but I have been able to push the investigation forward considerably, I think. In many cases, I pointed out that the conventional arguments for a given practice are unconvincing, and that in some areas, the a priori arguments would seem to call for a change. Nowhere, however, have I done more than start the debate. A great deal of further research—and, in particular, a great deal of further empirical research—is necessary before we can deal with these problems in a conclusive way. It is one of the depressing characteristics of modern law that serious research has only very recently begun. Under the circumstances, we probably have a very long way to go before we can feel any high degree of confidence that we have an efficient court system.

Chapter 11

Interpretation

So far, we have dealt mainly with the court as a method of determining fact. Most lawyers will be rather surprised by this. Law libraries consist of immense collections of books having to do with the interpretation of the law, but there is very little material in existence on the actual determination of facts. Further, what literature there is tends to be discussions of the rules of evidence, in which the lawyer is told what kinds of evidence he may use, rather than instructed in the fine points of fingerprint identification.

If we look at the actual proceedings of courts, however, it is fairly obvious that the determination of matters of fact takes more of their time than legal interpretation. The courts are, in essence, engaged in historical research, trying to find out what happened in the past, in order to apply the law to it. In most cases, there is relatively little doubt as to what the law is. This is fortunate, because if the law were questionable in most places where it applies, people would have no guide to action.

When I first began working in this area, a number of lawyers told me that I should not use examples with Mr. Right and Mr. Wrong in a lawsuit because there was no Mr. Right or Mr. Wrong until the lawsuit was over. They assured me that the parties did not know who was right or wrong until after the law had been determined by the court. I can think of no more serious condemnation of a legal system than that a man does not know whether braining his wife with an ax is illegal until after a court has so decided. Surely, in most cases, the parties are well aware of their legal responsibilities. The common problem is not that the parties do not know the law, but that the court does not know exactly what it is that the parties did.

This statement is contrary to the existing conventional wisdom, which emphasizes legal interpretation. If one thinks about the conventional wisdom, however, one quickly realizes that it is derived (more or less) from the existence of an appellate court system which pays relatively little attention to determining whether the facts have been decided correctly in lower level courts, and a great deal of attention to determining whether the *law* has been correctly interpreted.[1] This means that most higher-court decisions, which are of great importance in Anglo-Saxon law, are concerned with legal interpretation; and lawyers studying these decisions necessarily devote most of their attention to that issue.

There also seems to be a general feeling that trying matters of fact is not something that requires any special intellectual effort. We frequently entrust the ultimate decision on the facts to a group of average men and women with absolutely no training.[2] The opposing attorneys themselves normally have had no technical training in such matters as ballistics, forensic medicine, identification of forged documents, etc. By the time a particular case comes to trial, they may have taught themselves enough about the factual area of that particular case so that they are quite expert. In most criminal cases, however, this is not so. Only important cases involve extensive pretrial preparation. Even in those cases, the extensive pretrial preparation probably does not make the lawyers true experts in the area with which they are dealing.

As an illustration of this point, in recent years many economists have been earning significant amounts of money by appearing as expert witnesses in damage cases. What they do is make computations as to the present discounted value of injuries suffered by plaintiffs, and then they offer this as evidence for the damage award. It is notable that the defense attorneys in these cases, primarily specialists hired by insurance companies, were quite slow in acquiring the technical ability to understand such a calculation, or to cross-examine expertly. Indeed, many of the early calculations were gravely defective, but it seems that the defense attorneys did not realize that fact. With the passage of time, the defense attorneys are learning, partly by calling in their own experts; and economists are being compelled to provide more sophisticated estimates, and to be prepared for effective cross-examination.

But this is a digression. This chapter is devoted to the problem of interpretation of the law and, what is intellectually much the same thing, the interpretation of contracts. The first thing to be said about problems of interpretation is that if a real issue of interpretation arises, the law or the contract has already failed. The parties who are supposed to be bound could not have discovered what their responsibilities were and, therefore, they could not have carried them out except by accident.

Suppose that I consult highly paid attorneys to find out whether or not I can legally undertake some action. They could inform me that it is legal, in which event I go ahead, or that it is illegal, in which event I refrain. But suppose they reply that the law is unclear. "We think that there is about a 50-50 chance that if you do it, you will be found in violation of the law and fined $10,000; and there is about a 50-50 chance that you will not be found to have violated the law, in which event you will lose nothing."[3] They have given me guidance only in the sense that they have pointed out that the act in question is risky.

Suppose, for example, that the profit I would expect from carrying out that act is about $7,000, so that the prospect of a 50-50 chance of paying $10,000 gives me a positive discounted value.[4] Presumably, under these circumstances I would undertake the act and get my $7,000. The court would then determine whether I was to pay $10,000 to the government. Ex post, my legal position would be clear, but not ex ante. It is clear that under these circumstances, the law provides much less guidance than when we know what it is. It is not true that it provides no guidance at all, because the fact that subjective probabilities can be formulated would have at least some effect on my behavior. If I had been informed by my attorneys that the chances were about four out of five that I would be found, ex post, to have violated the law, and only about one out of five that I would not—that the law did seem to cover vaguely the action I proposed—I would have refrained.

What controls my action is not the court decision but my anticipations as to what the court will do. These anticipations may be based upon the opinion of very expensive counsel or may be personal. In any event, however, they are the only things I have to act on. The court may, or may not, be called upon to make a decision in the future, but I do not know what that decision will be at the time that I make my decision. Thus, my decision must be based not on the court's action but on my advance guess as to what that action will be. The eventual interpretation of the law by the court does not control my action at the time I take it; it merely indicates whether I have made a successful, or unsuccessful, gamble. This is true, by the way, even if I do not consciously realize I am gambling. Perhaps I think the law is certain, and I eventually learn, by way of the court decision, that I was wrong. This will make me unhappy, but the eventual decision, once again, has no effect on my initial action.

Let us continue with the assumption that the law is completely vague, i.e., that there is a 50-50 chance that the court will go either way. This is a situation in which the lawyers' skills are most important. Since the actual law does not tell us which side should win, the outcome is partially purely stochastic but it is, to a very large extent, dependent on the skills of the two advocates. This is the kind of case which is likely to lead to a very large investment in legal expenses. This is sensible from the standpoint of each of the parties considered individually, since when he hires a better lawyer, he does indeed benefit himself, even though he injures his opponent. It is not sensible, however, from the standpoint of either society as a whole, or of that very small subsociety—the two parties to the litigation, considered as a group of two. As is characteristically the case in conflict,[5] an individually rational action is socially irrational, because we are in a prisoner's dilemma.

The situation is even more complicated in real life. I have been assuming that either decision is equally probable. Normally, when the law is uncertain, one decision is at least somewhat more probable than the other. Indeed, there are cases in which the only uncertainty is as to whether the law is certain or not. Thus, for example, the law might appear to the average reader to indicate that A is guilty of some crime. A's attorney, however, argues that the law is not all that clear. The first issue to be determined, then, is whether the law is clear or unclear. If it is unclear, it might be only mildly unclear. It might be, for example, that if we presented the case in the law to ten well-qualified jurists, nine would decide one way and one the other. This would be a law which is certainly reasonably clear, but nevertheless it would be a law in which a skilled attorney would certainly be well advised to raise the possibility of doubt. We then have a continuity up to the point where the law is totally unclear, and hence there is a 50-50 chance that either result will eventuate. The latter case would be a situation in which our ten jurists would split five to five.

But before discussing this issue in more detail, I should like to make a very brief digression into the subject matter of the next chapter—the situation in which the decision of the court actually determines law for future cases, as well as settling the outcome of this case. If the court does have this power, then the case will change the law so that the particular uncertainty under decision is reduced or eliminated.[6]

I should like to leave major discussion of this situation until the next chapter. Not because I think that it is unimportant or uninteresting but simply as an organizational decision. Thus, my discussion here is very brief and is intended merely to persuade conventional lawyers to give me their attention for the rest of the chapter, rather than closing the book in disgust.

The view that the courts can make decisions without affecting the law in the future may shock some lawyers. Their shock is misplaced, because the overwhelming bulk of all legal decisions made by the courts are never even entered into the legal reporting system. In a recent case, a lawyer in Chicago attempted to cite as a precedent another case in the Chicago area, and the court of first instance in Chicago refused him permission. He appealed, and the appellate court upheld the trial court. A further appeal to the Supreme Court also upheld the trial court's decision. Notably, and in complete accord with the principle of the case, neither the appellate court nor the Supreme Court wrote an opinion. The apparent explanation was simply that the law was getting so complicated that it was necessary to restrict the number of precedents.[7] Another, more amusing recent case concerned an effort by a grand jury to withdraw an indictment of the Reverend Moon's Unification Church.[8] The grand jury thought that it could withdraw the indictment because it had been told by the judge that it could. The district attorney, in opposing the withdrawal, said, "It's customary for judges to say that to the grand jury, but it's never really been tested before."

Although I do not really know, I doubt that the district attorney made any serious effort to press forward with the case, because if he cannot convince the grand jury that there is a case for prosecution, the prospect of obtaining a conviction is very small indeed. But note that, for years, the Maryland judges have been giving an instruction to grand juries which is not regarded as good law, because it has not gone to the appellate courts.

If we look at the actual court proceedings, we find that the average court of first instance makes many legal rulings and many rulings on the interpretation of contracts. Further, in practice, juries also make both legal rulings and rulings on interpretation of contract, although this is disguised, since they do not have to explain why they reached the decision they did reach.

There is one case in which jury decisions are regarded as good precedents. If the prosecutors find a particular branch of the law—for example, much of the law of conspiracy—such that jurors do not bring in convictions, they will begin acting as if the law has been repealed. As a rough rule of thumb, if three successive juries refuse to convict people accused of some violation of a particular law, the prosecutors will stop bringing cases. Civil attorneys follow somewhat similar principles.

An akin phenomenon occurs if a particular judge has made a particular ruling on a given case, and that fact is known to the attorneys. They are apt to think that he will probably repeat the ruling if the occasion arises, even though it is not in the reporter series. Of course, most lawyers will not know about the ruling at all, and different judges may make different rulings on the same point. Thus, with respect to issue Z, we may find that 25 percent of the judges in the country have, at some time in the past, decided in favor of the illegality; 25 percent have decided against; and the remainder have made no decision at all. Some of the lawyers know at least one judge who has made a ruling against. The lawyers will not only take this into account in advising their clients, but also in judge shopping if litigation arises. Still, it is hard to argue that decisions of this sort have "made law."

Particularly clear-cut cases of this kind of thing come in the interpretation of contracts. The courts have developed a set of rules under which particular forms of language are taken as having particular interpretations. We will discuss this at greater length below. There are many forms of language and many clauses in contracts, however, for which there is no previous judicial interpretation. If these clauses turn out to be ambiguous with respect to some situation that arises in the real world, the court must approach the problem *de novo*. Further, in many of these cases the interpretation is made by the trial court. Perhaps without announcing the interpretation, it makes a decision on the case as a whole. If it was appealed and the interpretation was laid down by a higher court, it may or may not have relevance for future cases, since there is no law that requires people involved in drafting new contracts to follow the same form of words. Anyone who does not like the interpretation can simply insert a different wording in the next contract.

Most non-Anglo-Saxon legal systems do not, in fact, pay as much attention to judicial precedents, even of appellate courts, as we do. Thus, in the world in general, individual court decisions rarely have very much effect on the state of the law in the future. They are simply an effort to interpret the existing law; and if the law is ambiguous with respect to whatever has come up in the particular case, they interpret it but do not do anything which will change the law in the future.

Thus, it is logically possible for courts to interpret an ambiguous part of the law without making any change in the law for the future; and, as a matter of practical fact, *most* decisions dealing with ambiguity do not make any change for the future. In the Anglo-Saxon tradition, however, a small collection of decisions with respect to such ambiguities do become part of the law. Although this is a small portion of the total number of such decisions, its absolute magnitude is large, as anyone who has ever looked at even the outside of a law library can testify. Whether this Anglo-Saxon custom is better or worse than its contrary—the practice in most of the world—is an issue which will be discussed in chapter 12. For the time being, however, and essentially for reasons of logical and structural coherence, let us confine ourselves to interpreting an ambiguous bit of the law as a problem in and of itself, and not inquire whether it is desirable for the court also to *change* the law by its interpretation. Thus, suppose that two parties have drawn up a contract but something has happened which is not clearly covered by the contract. The matter is now taken to court, and the court must make a decision.

The first thing to be said is that if the contract is in fact ambiguous, there is no truly correct interpretation. Similarly, if the law is unclear, it is unclear. The court, in making its interpretation, is either writing a new piece of the contract for the parties or creating a new law. In the latter case—since we are currently assuming that the court decision will not become binding on future cases—it is a very special law, applicable only to these two parties. At the time the matter comes to the attention of the court, the two parties are very much interested in the outcome. Nevertheless, it should be kept clearly in mind that it is unimportant socially. The gain of one party will exactly cancel the loss of the other, and society will be no better off.[9]

Consider the matter from the standpoint of two parties to a contract at the time the contract is drawn. They are aware of the fact that they cannot draft the contract to cover every conceivable contingency. They negotiate a contract which is optimal, ex ante. This contract should provide clear coverage for matters which are sure to come up, but it should omit various unlikely contingencies, because it is not worth the time of the parties to continue negotiation until a clearer provision is made. These will be either totally uncovered or covered in ambiguous language.

One of the unexpected contingencies now occurs, and the parties enter into the expensive process of litigation to resolve it. After the contingency has occurred, the outcome of the case is of great importance to the two parties taken individually, even if not to the two parties taken as a group of two. At the time they drafted the contract, the probability of this particular contingency arising was low enough so that they did not bother to provide for it. Their behavior—both at the time they drafted the contract and later when they invest great resources in the suit—is rational under our present institutions.

Can we not do better? First, as I have said above, one of the problems with special legal provisions for ambiguous contracts is that the question of whether a given contract is ambiguous or not may in itself be an ambiguous question. If great resources were invested in the resolution of this problem, and then there were a subsequent saving once the contract had been declared formally ambiguous, it is not obvious that we would make much of an improvement in the present situation.

Still, there is one thing that can be done. Whoever is making the decision on the contract can simply prevent the parties from investing many resources into argument on points of this sort. The points where the contract is unclear are points where a judicial arbitrariness is desirable. Further, I think we can say for certain that if there were some technique in our law which permitted the parties to contract in advance for such judicial arbitrariness, they would do so. At the time the contract is drafted, the present discounted value to each party of somewhat arbitrary decisions on the exact meaning of the contract involves two components. First, there is the probability that the court will decide against you, which is not changed by the arbitrariness in interpreting an unclear law, because there is no way to tell which way the arbitrariness will go. Secondly, the legal costs if the court devotes much time and attention to the issue are certain, but they can be avoided if the court behaves arbitrarily. The present discounted value, then, of "quick and dirty" decisions on these matters is higher than that of careful thought.

All of this is likely to be considered by most lawyers a most extraordinary recommendation. Certainly, it is directly contrary to our present procedure, where the court characteristically devotes great time and attention to matters of this sort and, indeed, may ask the parties on both sides to submit special briefs. Indeed, these matters, which I have argued should be dealt with hastily and arbitrarily, are given a good deal more careful attention than are matters of fact. As readers of this book will have already realized, I regard this as perverse.

It is fairly obvious, however, why this particular concentration of effort in Anglo-Saxon courts has occurred. Appeal, in general, can only be made on such matters of law and interpretation. Although courts have succeeded in working out a number of ways to deal with factual matters on appeal, they frequently say they will not; and they are certainly not nearly as willing to overthrow a case on the grounds that the original court was wrong on a matter of fact as they are on a matter of law.

Under these circumstances, the judge—not being subject to much prospect of correction with respect to matters of fact and facing a real possibility of appeal on interpretation—is apt to give far more careful attention to the interpretation. Indeed, the whole existing structure of the law implies that these interpretive matters are more important than decisions of fact, although, in my opinion, this is a perverse emphasis. Where the law is clear, it should be followed, and that means we must know what the facts are in order to apply the law to them. Where the law is unclear, on the other hand, it is not possible to follow it, because there is nothing to follow. Under the circumstances, although a decision must be made in a given case, there is no reason to invest great resources in it.

A problem arises not only in contracts but with the law itself. In drafting our laws, we do not make any effort to anticipate every conceivable contingency. Indeed, lawyers will normally say that it is impossible to draft a law code so that all conceivable contingencies will be covered in a clear and unambiguous manner. This being so, a social decision on the length and detail of the law should be made, and the basic principles should be the same as those used in deciding how long a contract will be.[10] The matter will be discussed in the next chapter, when we deal with the problems of courts writing new law, rather than simply interpreting existing law. But it should be pointed out here that it is not obvious that the law should be very long. To repeat, anyone who has ever worked with a complex computer program knows that when an ambiguity in one area is cleared up by a change in the language of one sort or another, or perhaps the insertion of an additional command, it can very easily lead to difficulties elsewhere.

The law is somewhat similar. When we clarify one part of it, the interactions between that part and others may mean that the total law is clearer or less clear than it was before. In our previous example, clarifying point A is almost certain to raise at least some difficulties for points M and Z, and it may well be that these difficulties will be greater than the advantage from the clarification itself. Even if it were possible, we would not want to have an infinitely detailed law, because an infinitely detailed law would have an infinite number of conflicts within it. Lengthening the law by adding detail will improve the clarity of the law up to a point.[11] But, after some point is reached, further details are likely to cause more difficulty by creating conflicts within the law. The point at which this phenomenon occurs—the optimal detail of the law—to a considerable extent is a matter of skill on the part of the draftsman. But, even with the most skilled draftsman, the law can get so complex that an additional rule will cause more difficulties than it cures.

It could be argued that, in principle, the situation in which the law is not clear is no different from that discussed in earlier chapters, in which the law is clear and the evidence is not. Suppose the contract had been drawn up in a completely unambiguous manner, but the two parties were disagreeing about some factual matter which would lead to $10,000 changing hands if the decision was made in favor of Jones. We can assume that the evidence is evenly divided, so that the court has only a 50-50 chance of deciding for either party. It would appear, superficially, that this is a very similar case to the case where the contract is ambiguous.

The resemblance, however, is merely superficial. In the case where there is a problem of fact, there is a right answer. The court resources are being invested in an effort to do what the court should do—i.e., provide the outcome specified by the parties. Where the contract is ambiguous, there is no outcome specified by the parties; hence, this objective is no longer possible. Resource investment in the first case may be sensible, whereas in the second case it is sheer waste.

It may be possible to put into the contract a general clause giving the court instructions as to what to do if none of the specific clauses cover the case. For example, it could be provided that in the event some contingency arises which was not covered by the contract, the court should order that action which maximizes the joint profits or minimizes the joint losses, and then divide said profit or loss evenly between the parties. In order to carry out such a contract, we would need judges, or perhaps special masters, whose training was commercial or industrial rather than legal; but that does not seem to be a serious objection. Presumably, however, there would still be difficult issues in which one party maintains that the contingency which arose is in fact covered by the contract, and the other maintains that it is not. Thus, ambiguity would still exist. Once again, the resource investment in solving such a problem should be low.

A somewhat similar suggestion is frequently made in respect to the law. It is suggested that the court should, if the law does not clearly cover the matter in question, follow its own conscience or "the spirit of the law" or "analogy with the rest of the law." Indeed, in many systems of jurisprudence, there has been no specific law and the judge is supposed simply to apply morals or custom. It seems likely that the English common law developed from this kind of situation.

Today it also seems likely that in ambiguous situations, judges are apt to do something like this, whatever they say. It also seems very clear that juries tend to follow their own ethical codes whenever the law is not clear, and they frequently follow their own ethical codes even when the law *is* clear.

In part, the tendency of juries to ignore the law and follow their own ethical code depends on the fact that they do not know what the law is. The lengthy instructions characteristically given to them by the judge are normally much too long for them to remember and are couched in difficult technical language, which is intended to resist overthrow on appeal, rather than to inform the jury. Indeed, in many cases, standardized instructions are given to the jury in language which is now obsolete, and therefore is misleading to the layman who has not carefully read all of the previous cases.

But if the jury sometimes follows its own conscience because it does not know what the law is, it may also follow its own conscience, albeit directly contrary to the law. In the Coppolino case mentioned above,[12] the jury found the defendant guilty of unpremeditated murder, although it is quite impossible to imagine how the careful selection of a poison thought to be undetectable, and its subsequent injection, could be unpremeditated. The apparent reason was simply that the jury felt that the penalty for premeditated murder was excessive. The jury may, of course, have been very dubious about its own decision, because it realized it did not understand the evidence.

Although there are cases where the court does apply sort of general ideas of justice to cases where the law is not clear, it might be possible to do something better in the way of specific instructions. Some technical problems having to do with pollution, for example, have perfectly good technical solutions even if the law is not clear. It might be sensible in these cases to tell the court that when the law is unclear, they should select the technically best solution. In many cases, this would be a relatively easy thing to do, because the lack of clarity in the law comes from the fact that it was drafted some years in the past, and science has progressed, so that we now know more than the drafters of the law. In other cases, it would be very difficult. Note that this is only a suggestion for a very specific detailed area. I have no general suggestions for what judges should do when presented with a problem in which the law is not clear, except that, in most cases, they should not only invest few resources of their own in the decision, but they should also make every effort to prevent the parties from wasting socially valuable resources by investment in it.

In the case of the law, as in the case of contracts, there is an optimal length and detail. After awhile, the law gets long enough and detailed enough, so that the resources invested in extending it by one more clause are greater than the benefit. This is particularly true in the case of the law, because it is binding on many people, instead of just the parties to a contract. Thus, if one adds one paragraph to the length of the law, one makes it harder for a very large number of people to find out what the law is. Even if the law is unambiguous and covers the matter at hand, it may not be easy to find this out. Indeed, the existence of highly trained lawyers who spend much of their time giving advice on matters in which the law is not in any great doubt is evidence of that.

Of course, there are dubious places in the law, too, and lawyers deal with them. But the very large part of a lawyer's duty consists of communicating to laymen what the law is, because the layman does not know and would have great difficulty finding out on his own. The longer and more complicated the law, the more lawyers are needed for this duty and the more time they must take in answering questions. Thus, the cost of adding a paragraph is much more than the mere matter of drafting and printing. It is also the additional search costs which that paragraph imposes on citizens trying to find out what their legal rights are. Offsetting these costs is the benefit that the law can be found out. This offsetting would lead to an optimal length of the law, just as a similar process leads to the optimal length and detail of the contract.

An important problem remains: what do we do if the law is clear to some people but not to others? I have already mentioned the situation in which the lawyers and the judge regard the law as perfectly clear, but the jury is totally unable to understand it. This is not the only example. The average citizen probably is not capable of keeping in mind the details of a complex legal system, even if it has been explained to him. Lawyers have devoted a great deal of time and energy to studying the problem and are normally of above-average intelligence, so they can keep a much larger volume of law in mind. Another group is intellectuals in general. For example, most readers of this book, even if they are not lawyers, would find it no great task to look into the English translation of *Justinian's Digest* and find the Roman law with respect to transfer of real property. It would be a very great trial indeed for the average citizen. Thus, if the law is as complicated—or even much more complicated—than Justinian, this very fact gives intellectuals an advantage over the rest of the population. Presumably, it is an advantage which they will be willing to defend.

Note, however, that if one has a jury, it is not at all obvious that these legal complexities make much difference. Indeed, this may be one of the reasons why modern court systems are moving to deemphasize the jury and switch many decisions to a judge. The jury will not understand complicated provisions of the law, will forget them (even if the judge tells them what they are just before they retire), and are in fact likely to ignore them quite deliberately *if* they think that they are "unjust." It seems likely that juries characteristically enforce a rather simple view of the law, which is more or less the average man's view. They are unlikely to find someone guilty of a crime if what he did does not seem bad to them, regardless of what the law says. They are also likely to find someone guilty of a crime if they decide he is a bad person, even if there does not seem to be anything on the statute books which exactly fits. They are, after all, judges of the facts and can decide that one did something that he did not do if they think he should go to prison.

Most intellectuals will prefer a judge here. Nevertheless, there is something to be said for a jury which effectively enforces a simple legal system. An extremely complex legal system, which no one actually knows, imposes costs, benefits, and punishments upon people at random. Suppose there is a clause in the laws of Virginia providing certain conditions of work for the casual day laborer. In total ignorance of these clauses, I hire a man to cut some wood for my fireplace. He also is in ignorance, but Mr. Busybody, a legally well-informed person, passes by and observes the law being violated. He complains, and the law is enforced.[13] From my standpoint, and from that of the man hired as a day laborer, the situation is very similar to that which would have occurred if a completely arbitrary Oriental despot had chosen to decree a new law on the spot. The law cannot control my action unless I know what it is and, if the legal code is extremely complicated, it is impossible for me to know everything in it.

When I was in law school, we still believed in holding every man responsible for knowing the law. In recent years, the law has become so extremely long, and so extremely complicated, that the courts have begun to develop, slowly, a legal system which deals with what we might call nonculpable ignorance of the law. So far, this branch of the law is not very well developed, and the possibility of being caught for a crime of which you were unaware is still real.[14] Further, it seems likely that it will continue. If we excused people from knowing what the law was if they could demonstrate that most people in their situation did not know the law, by that single act we would be repealing something like 90 percent of our existing legal structure. It seems doubtful that we will do this, although it might be a good thing.

It is not necessary that everyone knows the whole law. There are large parts of the law which deal only with certain classes of people. For example, a sanitary code for butcher shops need interest only butchers. Thus, the law can be a good deal more lengthy than any person would be able to carry in his mind and still not be beyond practical use. All butchers would know that part of the law which applied to all citizens plus that part which applied to butchers only. Bankers would know nothing about the butchers' code but would know the banking sections. Provided only that there is some fairly good method of informing people as to which subsections of the code they should know, this would permit a law which is much longer than that which any citizen can be expected to carry in his head, because the citizen only has to carry selected portions of it. Nevertheless, it is likely that our present law is massively too voluminous even by this scheme.

Granted that the law is—as I think it is—very long, and that the average citizen taking action does not know all of the laws covering any action, and granting, further, that portions of the law are also confused enough, so that even with good legal advice he cannot be sure what his legal position is, then even the activity of finding the law may be of relatively low value and something upon which we should waste few resources. Suppose again the situation given above, in which Mr. Busybody has accused me, and a laborer working for me, of having violated an obscure clause in the law. Clearly the law had no effect on our behavior until he brought it to our attention. Is it even worthwhile to have the judge find out whether Busybody's allegations as to law are true or false? The law has already failed to provide guidance and control for the citizens, because the citizens did not know what it was.

The above question would have been absurd in earlier times when the law was fairly simple and, for the bulk of those clauses which might affect the average citizen, very close to the existing moral code. Under such circumstances, acting as if the citizen knew the law was sensible.

Today, however, the law is very long, and situations frequently occur in which some party, or group, takes some action in total ignorance of the fact that there is a law dealing with it. In some cases, we can legitimately say that they should have regarded themselves on notice to find out what the law is, but that is by no means the general case. It is presumptuous of a judge who has never read his insurance policy, or the full text of the conveyance transferring to him the house in which he lives, or the full text of the federal code, to argue that the parties before him should know the law.

Under present circumstances, judges (and more particularly juries) do indeed take ignorance of the law into account. If there turns out to be some aspect of the law which applies to the case at instance, and it is fairly clear not only that the parties did not know that law, but that they cannot be blamed for not knowing it, there seems to be no very strong reason why the law should be applied.

It could be argued that under these circumstances, applying the law is harmless. The parties were in ignorance of the law, and therefore they had no particular idea of what would happen. From their standpoint, anything that does happen is roughly random. This would be true if the parties literally were in total ignorance of the law. If, however, there is some general rule which the parties did know, and what they did not know was an exception which turned out to cover their activities, then that argument would be false. They would be under an excusable misapprehension as to the law and would have acted upon that misapprehension.

All of the above deals with the law code which is unnecessarily long. Such a code inflicts considerable cost on society, because it leads to competitive investment of resources in efforts to find out what the law actually is under circumstances where the matter is of little social consequence. Reducing the resources invested in this activity would be socially desirable. We should try to minimize an investment of resources which has no social product, and, where it does have some social product, we should inquire whether the resources invested in obtaining that social product are greater than the size of the product itself. In other words, does the benefit exceed the cost or is it smaller than the cost? This is a complicated empirical question and one which, so far as I know, has not been dealt with.

In general, however, my conclusion is that where a contract or the law is ambiguous and it is necessary to make a decision, the decision, in general, should be made by some low-cost method. This is because the law or the contract has already failed: it has not been able to offer guidance or control to parties, because they did not know what it was. From their standpoint, at the time they took the action which later leads to a lawsuit, any outcome of the court will be essentially a random variable. There is, therefore, no reason why we should pay great attention to seeing to it that the variable is nonrandom from the standpoint of someone else, let us say a Supreme Court justice; we should consider the parties that the law is intended to control, not an outsider.

Where the law is clear, but the legal code is so lengthy and involved that there is no reason to believe that the parties know the law, somewhat the same argument should be applied. In this case, the resource cost of determining the actual law in court is not apt to be very great, since the attorneys on both sides will appreciate the clarity and therefore not invest many resources into arguments on it. Even here, however, resources may be invested in competitive legal search before the contract is drafted. For example, if one of the parties to a contract can insert in it a clause which has previously been interpreted by a high-ranking court to mean something rather different from what it appears to mean on the surface, and the attorney on the other side does not notice, the party who hired the first attorney may have a very decided advantage. Thus, the two parties are motivated to hire attorneys to engage in a privately profitable game—attempting to outwit each other in the contract-drafting stage. In all probability, with skilled attorneys on both sides, the outwitting rarely occurs; but the resources invested in this high-quality legal attention are socially wasted, even if they are of value to the two parties. Thus, there are considerable wastes involved in an overcomplicated law, even if it is clear.

We can never draw up any law which clearly covers all possible contingencies, but the theme of the above discussion is that we should not try. We should have the detail of our law expanded to the point where the costs—and they are very real—of extending it further match the benefits. This would mean a very sharp curtailment of the length of our present law.

Granted that both in the laws we observe around us, and in a theoretically optimal law, there would be many cases that were not covered in any clear way by the law; it is certain that the courts will have to deal with them. The theme of this chapter is that how they deal with them is relatively unimportant, and that we should attempt to expend only very modest resources on it. This is directly contrary to our current practice. It is also, the reader will remember, a conclusion drawn only under circumstances in which the court's interpretation of a given case simply determines the outcome of that case and does not write law for future cases. The question of whether the court may write law, and how it should be done, will be the subject of the next chapter.

Chapter 12

Courts as Lawmakers

Apart from serving as interpreters of the law there are the other duties that courts (at least in the United States) assume: the making of law and the enforcement of the Constitution against the other branches of government. In recent years, the courts have rather loosely interpreted the latter duty; they seem to feel that they have the right not only to enforce the Constitution but to change it from time to time. This chapter is devoted to the lawmaking activities of the courts and not to their constitutional role—a subject with which we will deal in the next chapter. It should be noted in passing, however, that, on occasion, the constitutional role calls upon the courts to make law; for example, they interpret an existing law in a way which, on its face, is ridiculous, because that is the only way to interpret it and be in accord with the Constitution. Further, their lawmaking is sometimes controlled by whatever they happen to think the Constitution means at the moment they make a particular law.

Some time ago I wrote an attack on the lawmaking power of the courts.[1] I do not wish to withdraw anything I said in that paper; indeed, most of it will be recapitulated here. On further thought, however, it has occurred to me that although the courts are not very good legislatures, the legislatures also are not very good; and executive rule-making, which is the third alternative under our Constitution, also has fairly severe drawbacks. However, this is a book about the courts, and therefore I propose to concentrate on the courts as lawmaking bodies. It is true that logical coherence will require that I discuss briefly the legislatures and the executive rule makers, but I propose to make that discussion short.[2]

Turning, then, to the courts as lawmakers, there are a number of arguments in favor of this role of the courts in the literature. I shall go through them more or less in chronological order, starting with a very traditional argument, which I met first in law school. This argument is simply that the outcome of the law—i.e., the common law—seems to be pretty good. Since much law is, as a matter of fact, legislative rather than judge made, and since other laws are administrative, the fact that the law is "pretty good" is hardly an argument for one particular technique of making the law.   .

Further, in connection with this argument, it should be kept in mind that we do not really have any way of saying whether our law is "pretty good" or "pretty bad." We would need a careful comparison of our judge-made law with some set of other laws generated by other methods, in order to find out whether ours was above or below the mean. This would involve major empirical study and no one has done it.

There is a variant of this particular argument contained in Posner's *Economic Analysis of the Law.*[3] Posner has gone through a very large number of legal rules, arguing that in very many cases—of course not in all—the existing law is economically efficient. In general, his efficient examples tend to be cases of judge-made laws, and his inefficient examples tend to be cases of legislative laws, although of course this rule is not unvarying.

There are several problems with his demonstration, although the intellectual achievement of the book must be admitted. First, obviously the cases discussed are not a random sample, so it is not clear that even if we accept all of his arguments, superiority of judge-made law would be demonstrated. The second problem is the character of his arguments. In general, he justifies various rules by arguments dealing with transactions cost. I find most of these arguments quite plausible, but to say that they are quite plausible is quite different from saying that we can be sure that they are true. In most cases, I think I could invent another—at least reasonably plausible—argument indicating that the rule should be different from the one approved by Posner. Nevertheless, my offhand guess is that when and if the immense body of detailed empirical study necessary to test Posner's views about transactions cost is carried out, most—but not by any means all—of his conclusion will stand up. I think, however, that legislative law and executive regulations would do about as well—but, of course, that is merely a personal opinion.

It is possible to justify on grounds of pure efficiency much of the general outlines of our existing law. Indeed, I have done so.[4] However, this general structure is common to most, albeit not all, legal systems and, hence, cannot be used to prove the superiority of one particular technique of lawmaking. When we turn to the more detailed legal provisions, which do differ from one law system to another, in general very elaborate empirical studies would be necessary to determine which was better. In a way the argument that our law system is "pretty good" is merely a statement that we are accustomed to it and have adjusted to it so that changes might be inconvenient.

In my opinion the strongest of the arguments for the superiority of courts as lawmakers is contained in Bruno Leone's *Law and Liberty*.[5] Leone, an Italian lawyer trained in the Roman tradition, realized that the bulk of the Roman law had been created by *juris consults*, who if they were not actually judges, nevertheless had developed a common law from the consideration of real cases. He offered three strong arguments for the efficiency of this process.

Unfortunately, two of these arguments are not applicable to the United States today. One of these was that a case did not become a true precedent until it had been considered several times by several different judges, all of whom had reached the same conclusion. In Roman law, there was no truly binding supreme court decision, although it was possible to appeal individual cases to the emperor or the senate. Only a few cases were, in fact, appealed to this level; and those that were, were not regarded as necessarily binding precedents.

The same was true, as Leone pointed out, of the common law up to about 1800. The British government before the Benthamite reform is best described as an organization, which, like Topsy, "just growed," without conscious design. There were, although it seems incredible to a modern lawyer, actually competing courts. Once again, appeal to the House of Lords was at least theoretically possible, but it was rarely undertaken; in addition, the decisions of the House of Lords in any given case were not necessarily regarded as law for other cases. Thus, judges felt little reluctance in overthrowing decisions by other judges—perhaps in a competing court system—of which they disapproved. The common law was composed not of all of the decisions but of those decisions where the same matter (more or less) had come up several times. There was sometimes an exception to this, where a judge in the first hearing had made a particularly compelling argument for his point of view.

It would appear that the end of this system was an American invention, albeit an accidental one. From the standpoint of the lawyers, having several different decisions on the books but knowing that the precedent was not yet actually binding, was inconvenient. The lawyers who played such a large role in drawing up the Constitution of the United States wanted a court of last resort which could make binding rulings, and hence make their lives easier. The Supreme Court was the result, and it regards all of its decisions as binding. Of course, it can change its decisions; but until it has changed its decision, the previous decision is law.

It is not my purpose here to argue that this is wrong but simply to point out that it eliminates one of Leone's arguments for a type of common-law system, i.e., that there is careful consideration of a given point in several cases before it becomes a general law. Of course, under the older system, the decision of the judges in the individual cases is binding on the particular parties, but it is not binding on future parties until the matter has been repeatedly considered.

Leone's second argument for the common-law system is one which, for the present-day lawyer, must sound strange. He pointed out that, in general, it is thought desirable that the same law apply in one place as in another. It seems to me that the arguments for this are not as strong as Leone indicated, but, still, it is true that it is easier to know the law if it does not vary from place to place geographically. Leone argued that the same thing should apply to changes over time. In other words, he argued that it was desirable that the law, insofar as possible, be uniform over time as well as over space.

Naturally, Leone, who was a very intelligent man, did not want law to remain permanent and unchanging. He did, however, feel that it was highly desirable that the law change only slowly. This would make it much easier for people to know the law, because most of what they had learned ten years ago would be true today.

Using this basic argument, Leone pointed out, quite correctly for his time, that courts tend to change the law less rapidly than legislatures. Hence, he argued that there was an advantage in judge-made law. In this case, although Leone's arguments were certainly correct at the time he made them—there were signs that they might become incorrect in the future—it is not obvious that they are correct today. Judges certainly change the law a great deal; and legislatures, being largely tied up in other things, very commonly leave laws unchanged for fairly long periods of time. Under the circumstances, it is an empirically unresolved problem whether the legislature or the courts are more likely to change the law quickly. Certainly, neither of them change it at the very slow—indeed glacial—speed that Leone thought was optimal.

But if Leone's two arguments are no longer valid, his third argument can still be pressed. This argument is the claim that the circumstances of a lawsuit are particularly good for making decisions about the law. There are two parties who have real matters at stake, and who are willing to invest considerable resources in presenting the best arguments possible. There is a judge in the court of first instance, and boards of judges in the appellate courts, whose decisions are really necessary to make the law a law. They have (we hope) no personal interest in the matter and, therefore, are open to the strong arguments presented by the two sides. The fact that the judges know that their decisions will make law for the future is a motive for care, although it is not clear that it is an adequate motive. Indeed, this is one of the situations we discussed in chapter 4, in which the parties are highly motivated; but it is not obvious that the ultimate decision maker (in this case, usually a board of judges in an appellate court of one sort or another) has suitably strong incentives to make such a decision properly.[6] Further, the interests of the two parties may not represent all interests. Nevertheless, it has to be conceded that this is indeed a strong argument for judicial lawmaking.

However, before comparing this argument for judicial lawmaking with the countervailing arguments for legislative lawmaking or executive regulation writing, let me briefly pause to throw out one particular argument for judicial lawmaking which was pressed very hard when I was a student at law school. It is alleged that the legislature cannot produce a detailed-enough law, and therefore, of necessity, the courts are required to produce detailed glosses on the legislative decisions.

The first comment about this is that under present circumstances, in which the courts very commonly throw out legislative acts as a unit and impose new basic policies, it seems a little odd that we should talk about their making detailed decisions. *Brown vs. Board of Education* was certainly not a mere minor detail.

Second, if the judicial decision-making process is particularly suited for drafting laws, then it would appear to be one that we should use generally, not confining it to very minor parts of the law. Advocates of the common law favor this, of course. Third (and I take it the reader has anticipated this), it is not necessary for the courts to make new law if they find themselves confronted with an area where the legislative law is not clear. They can decide the given case and not impose the judgment as a rule on future cases. This is what they usually do; it is only in exceptional cases that the issue gets to the appellate court and a new rule is made.

Fourth, the legislatures are frequently extremely detailed in drafting rules. Indeed, if one reads the acts of Congress, one is continuously surprised at the variance in the degree of detail. In one place, very fine administrative rules will be presented; and in another place, some very general statement of policy will be enacted into law. Although this may be thought surprising in the first instance, it should also be said that the courts do the same thing. Very commonly, for example, the higher courts will instruct the lower courts to do various things; but will say that, of course, judicial discretion is necessary in each individual case. The same mixture of broad policy decisions and fine detail is found in court decisions as in legislative ones.

A particularly good example of the court's use of broad, general concepts is the "all deliberate speed" in *Brown vs. Board of Education*. This is a case in which the legislature eventually provided the details for a general policy decision by the courts, just exactly the opposite sequence from that which was used to justify judicial decision-making in the law school classes that I attended.

In general, there are various sources of laws. The first (and this is a very general broad category) is *extragovernmental*. The clearest cases are theologically determined laws. I have mentioned Muslim law above; and there was the situation in New England in which, for a number of years, the "Law Moses" (the Bible) was enforced.

On a broader level, there is *customary law*. International law is a particularly good example of customary law, in which the custom is not generated basically by the government but by the international society as a whole. Obviously, in our system, in which juries do play a major role, this type of law is important. Lawyers, who know this, spend a good deal of time when arguing before juries claiming that their side is ethically in the right. This type of law, however, is very hard to control; in a way, it just develops on its own. If we want to control it, we would normally turn to propaganda or the educational system in order to change general views.

The remaining sources of law are all *governmental;* they are the three branches of the government as defined by Montesquieu: the executive, the legislative, and the judicial. We are trained by our own history (and, in particular, the way the historians have presented it) to regard the legislature as the basic source of law. It draws up general laws or detailed laws as it wishes, and it is free to change them, subject only to constitutional restrictions in the United States, and to nothing in England.[7] It is interesting to note that at the present time, the American legislatures are showing signs of surrendering their right to make laws to the executive branch and retaining for themselves only a somewhat qualified veto power of the executive's acts. For example, they will provide that the executive may draw up regulations with respect to some subject or other and then require that these regulations be submitted to Congress before they become law. In most cases, they become law not as a result of a positive act of Congress, but as a result of inaction by Congress. Notably, sometimes the inaction that is required is inaction by both Houses and, in other cases, it is inaction by only one.

In a way, providing that the matter must be resubmitted to Congress is merely driving home the obvious. It would always be true in such cases that Congress could change the rulings by positive legislation, and giving Congress a negative veto power makes relatively little difference in the matter.

Executive regulations are another law source. Historically, kings could simply make laws. In the Anglo-Saxon tradition, this particular power was, for many generations, thought to be undesirable, and the king was, to a large extent, deprived of all direct lawmaking power. Only the king in Parliament could make laws, and, in the United States, the king's assent was not even (strictly speaking) necessary.

The gradual, but now very large, swing of lawmaking power back to the executive branch in the twentieth century is a most interesting phenomenon. Today in the United States, although the fundamental structure of the laws is not only legislative but enacted by state rather than national legislatures, the total volume of executive regulations is many times as great as the total volume of the regular law. Indeed, when President Carter first became president, he ordered all members of his Cabinet to actually read the regulations which each of their departments promulgated.[8]

It was quickly made evident that it was impossible for the Cabinet members to do this. The real time involved in reading the regulations they promulgated would have made it impossible for them to carry out their other duties. Indeed, in some cases, it would have been physically impossible for one person to read all of the regulations regularly promulgated by a department. Carter, therefore, backed down, and announced that he did not really mean his initial order—it was just a way to dramatize his concern over the length of the regulations. He may be concerned with the matter, but the regulations certainly have not become briefer since he became president. Today, the number of regulations is truly gigantic. It is doubtful that there is anyone who knows all of them, and, indeed, it seems likely that it would be a very difficult research project to find them all.[9]

The making of administrative regulations is characteristically rather tightly circumscribed on the continent of Europe, where special collegial bodies are responsible. They meet in public conclave, listen to arguments if there are any, and produce detailed glosses, which are the administrative regulations. The most famous one perhaps was the supreme administrative court of France's formal decision as to how large a G-string a striptease dancer must wear. This was, of course, in a former period in which French striptease dancers wore G-strings.

In the United States, provision for the drafting of the regulations are much less formal, but it is generally true that fairly senior officials at least read them with some care. There does not seem to be any regular arrangement by which interested parties can present their points of view to the officials; but when the interests are such that a formal lobby can be maintained in Washington, I presume that informal methods are available. The problem is that such informal procedures are open only to organized interests, and, for reasons pointed out by Mancur Olson,[10] this is only a portion of all real interests. But, on the other hand, the same restrictions would make it unlikely that these unorganized interests would appear at an open hearing. Indeed, where we do have open hearings—for example, utility regulations—it is clear that the kind of people who are well represented in the state and national capitals are the only people (in most cases) who turn up to argue before the commissions.

The last source—and the one with which this book is mainly concerned—is judicial rule-making. It is of some interest that apparently courts originally did not realize that they were making rules. They thought they were simply stating clearly a customary law. It is not clear when they began to realize that far from stating a customary law, they were making a new law of their own.

I should not like to argue that my list of sources of laws is exhaustive.

Indeed, since it seems to me that all four of these sources are defective in various ways, I would be very anxious for the discovery of other methods which would work better. Nevertheless, for the purpose of this book, I propose to stick to these four or, to be more precise, to the judicial, legislative, and executive, since these three are the only ones from among which we can choose. As long as we retain the jury system, the first one will still be important in our system; but it is not really a policy variable. I am, as readers of *Logic of the Law* know,[11] not an admirer of the jury, but it seems to me that the arguments against the jury are basically to be found in other fields than those which we are now addressing.

What, then, are the advantages of these three sources of law? First, I should like to point out that by tradition in the United States, judges—once on the bench—are rather insulated from elections. The exact form of this insulation varies from place to place, and it can be quite weak. There is a judge in a juvenile court who, at the moment of this writing, is facing a recall election, not because of any of his decisions but because of something he said in a proceeding—which, by law, was secret—that was leaked to the press, probably by way of the prosecuting attorney. Still, in general, we do tend to insulate our judges from popular pressure.

So far as I know, this insulation is never argued for on the grounds that it leads to superior production of new laws. The normal argument is that we do not want the judge biased in his decision of a given case by conflicting interests or the need to seek election. In other words, the arguments for insulating judges from political pressure largely turn on the kind of considerations with which we have been dealing in the earlier chapters, rather than on their ability to make law. Most students feel that laws should be highly responsive to popular opinion, because they think that is democratic.

My point in bringing up this matter, however, is not to take sides on the basic issues but to point out that it is really irrelevant to the question of whether judges or legislatures should make law. There is no intrinsic reason we cannot have elected judges who are not insulated from popular pressure, nor is there any reason why we cannot have a legislature which is as insulated as present-day federal judges. For example, if the legislature members were elected for life, they would be—like federal judges—politicians who are taken out of the sphere of politics and given a lifetime tenure in order to insulate them from political pressures in the future.

The arguments I have given above for the superiority of the courts as a way to make law have to do with the incentives of the parties arguing before them and the fact that the judges are confronted with a real conflict, which tends to concentrate their minds. The fact that they may well be free of any particular bias in the case does not mean that their views on the case are different from those of the voter but that they are not biased by special aspects of the case, such as whether their cousin is the defendant. This could easily be worked out with elected judges if we simply had a conflict of interest law.

Note that it is not strictly necessary that we have elected judges for all cases in order to have elected judges for those cases in which the law is to be written. A rule under which parties took their cases to a board of elected judges only in those cases in which, for some reason, it was thought desirable to change the interpretation of the law, or make it more detailed, or in some other way change it, and otherwise took them to courts which did not change the law would be quite possible. Presumably it would operate on much the same set of rules as the current Supreme Court system. In any given case, of course, it might be quite difficult to tell whether we are dealing with a simple interpretation or a change in the law.

The above merely indicates that it is possible to have judges write the law. I have been assuming that the question is whether they should write the law—including making changes in it—rather than whether they should simply clarify it when it is not clear, because if the judicial process is in fact the superior way to write laws, then it should not be confined to the clarification function. If, on the other hand, it is an inferior procedure for making law, then, although the judges would have reached decisions in individual cases, these decisions should not become law, and whatever superior procedure exists should be used to provide the additional details. All of this is contrary to received Anglo-Saxon traditions, but I do not believe that what is, is necessarily right.

It might be true that the courts are a particularly good way to write detailed provisions into law but not to settle general policy. People who feel that this is the appropriate rule should be annoyed about *Brown vs. Board of Education* but favor the vast library of decisions with respect to minor rules. Granted the discussion of the degree of detail we want in the law (in the last chapter), we would not want every judicial decision to make law or to clarify law, simply because we do not want the law to be all that finely defined. The cost of search through a highly detailed law is much greater than the benefits which can be obtained from the details. Today, of course, computer technology makes the search for detailed provisions cheaper than it would have been in 1890, and hence we could have a more detailed law. We would like to have the details in the law written in by some agency which takes into account the total size of the law, rather than by a court which reaches decisions on each case and adds a little bit to the law as a by-product.

What about the courts as basic lawmakers, not simply adding a gloss on the superior wisdom of the legislators? To repeat what I have said before, I am not convinced that the legislatures are perfect, nor that the administrative bodies which produce detailed regulations—and which would be the obvious competitor of the courts if the courts confined themselves to minor detail—are perfect either. Nevertheless, in this chapter I am going to talk mainly about the courts themselves as sources of law, rather than these two major competitors. This is not because I think nothing can be said about the other methods, but because this book is, after all, about judicial procedure.

Let us pause here to distinguish between two general lines of reasoning which may be used to urge the efficiency of judicial procedure. The traditional argument turned on the fact that the judge was interested to some extent—obviously not solely but to some extent—in the efficiency of the law. The two parties, having strong motives for offering strong arguments for their respective positions, would include efficiency arguments among those arguments which they presented to him. Since this was one argument in his utility function, they would, over time, have an effect on the development of the law in a desirable direction. I have no quarrel with this argument, per se, although I suspect it is of relatively low practical importance in making judicial decisions. It should be pointed out that the same argument would indicate that the legislatures and administrative officials would tend toward efficiency for the same reasons. They, too, are recipients of arguments from interested parties and are, to some extent in any event, interested in efficiency.

The new arguments reverse field.[12] Instead of arguing that the judge will take efficiency into account, and that hence, over time, judicial decisions will have at least some tendency towards efficiency, they argue that a tendency toward efficiency comes out of the actions of the parties. Simplifying the matter a great deal, the argument is that the party who has efficiency on his side is apt to put in more resources in litigation than the party on the other side. The judges are then seen as largely passive mechanisms, responding to the resource investment of the two sides.

Instead of going through in detail the various models produced by Rubin, Priest, Landes and Posner,[13] I should like to introduce a model of my own, which is easier to understand and basically the same as theirs. Assume two parties, A and B, and assume that A is suing B for some sum of money. Regardless of who wins, the decision will have some effect on precedents and hence on future law cases. This effect on other law cases would normally be only a trivial consideration in the minds of the parties, since they do not know whether they will be involved in any of the future lawsuits or on which side they will be. In some cases, however, one or perhaps both of the parties might regard precedent setting as a matter of some importance. For example, a company which is regularly the defendant in suits of this sort might regard the establishment of precedent as of interest to it. Under these circumstances, the resource commitment of the party to the suit might to some extent be effected by its evaluation of the impact on it of the rule change. In most cases, this will be a trivial effect. In almost all cases, the resource commitments which would be called for in order to deal with this effect will be considerably less than the resource commitments for winning the given case.

So far, we have said nothing about efficiency. If there is a change in the future rule, however, it should either increase or reduce social efficiency, albeit perhaps in a trivial way. The bulk of any such efficiency effect will, of course, fall on people other than the parties to this particular decision. Indeed, they may feel no important part of that effect. Nevertheless, insofar as they do feel this effect, both parties would be benefited by an improvement of social efficiency. This, again, would be taken into account in their investment of resources in pressing their side of the case. Here, however, the results are rather different from the previous effects of the case. Both parties will gain from an increase in social efficiency, albeit not necessarily to the same extent. Therefore, if the decision for the defendant will increase social efficiency, that fact should lead the defendant to put up a little more in the way of resources to win—because he gets this additional gain from winning—and the plaintiff should put up a little less in social resources—because the increased efficiency if he loses will, to a very small extent, compensate him for his loss. Thus, so argue Landes and Posner, resources on the side of efficiency would be greater than the resources on the side of inefficiency, and, over time, there will be a tendency for judges to be pushed in the direction of efficiency.

The above argument seems to me to be perfectly correct but also probably trivial. Surely, in most cases, the resource commitments by the two sides are primarily an effort to win or lose the instant case. In those cases where they are thinking of future precedents, they are far more interested in the transfer effect—i.e., the change in wealth which results from that to one side or the other—than in the effect on social efficiency. Thus, although I do not quarrel with the logical rigor of the model, I do not think it has much real-world relevance.

It should, however, be kept in mind that insofar as this model does indicate that judicial proceedings would tend toward efficiency, it indicates that both legislative and executive rule making would have a much stronger tendency. The reason is that, in these cases, the second and third motives for investment of resources by parties at interest—i.e., changes in future laws which might raise or lower one person's wealth, and which might change efficiency—are the only reasons for investing resources in attempting to influence the outcome. There is no instant case which tends to dominate the resource-investment equation. The lobbyists who approach congressmen or government regulators are only interested in the future, and general, impact of whatever change they are urging; and, hence, the efficiency considerations should play a much larger part in decision making at this level than in judicial decision making. But although I do not see any strong reason to believe that the judicial method of law making is better than the legislative or executive, still I will talk here mainly about the judicial process. Since I will have a number of things to say which appear to be critical, I should like to reemphasize that I am not arguing that it is inferior to the other methods of making law. It does have disadvantages, so do the others; but this is a book about court procedure.

Let us begin with the problem of resource investment. The reader will recall that I argued above that if the court is confronted with an area where the law is unclear but it must nevertheless make a decision, and it is not attempting to make law, then a very low resource commitment is optimal. Clearly, if it is attempting to make law—it is laying out rules for the future—there is a positive externality and a higher resource commitment would be called for to obtain a correct decision. Presumably, the size of this resource commitment would vary with the importance of the issue. Note that when I say the "importance of the issue," I do not mean the importance of the issue for the two parties to the current litigation but the importance of the issue to other people in society, who will find themselves bound by this new law or interpretation.

We have pointed out above, however, that, in general, private parties to a litigation which involves an unclear point of law will be motivated to invest large resources if they are not prevented from doing so. Where the outcome is simply settling a case between the two parties and not setting law elsewhere, the investment will be greatly in excess of that which is socially optimal. If, however, the outcome of the case is going to set a legal precedent, then greater resources are desirable; hence, this additional investment by the two parties is not so readily criticized.

Note, however, that there is no reason why the parties should be investing the socially correct amount of resources in the litigation. Presumably there are cases in which the value of victory to each of the two parties is very great and the social value of the rule is very small. On the other hand, there are, no doubt, cases in which the value to the parties of winning is very small and the social value of setting a good rule is very great. Although I am not basically discussing the regulation setting or the legislative way to make law, there is also no argument there that the optimal amount of resources from the social standpoint would be invested.

There is another peculiarity about the resource investment when the courts are used to make law, and that is that it comes from a rather odd source. In essence, two private parties are being called upon to bear a considerable part of the burden of investigating and making decisions as to optimal law. The problem is put in its most dramatic form if we assume that we have two kinds of lawsuits. First, there are those in which, although the law is unclear and the judge must interpret it, the interpretation will not make future law. This should be distinguished from the other cases, in which the judge will be called upon to make a law binding on the future. The second case could be where he is simply changing the law. In the first case, as we pointed out above, it is optimal to have very little in the way of resources invested in making the decision. In the second case, on the other hand, much more resources should be invested.

Let us assume that we can distinguish between the two cases, and where case one—the case where little resource investment is desirable—occurs, we prevent resource investment on a large scale; but, in case two, we say to the parties that they are now to be subject to a special tax: we will throw them into a game situation, in which each of them will be motivated to provide quite large resources for this case, not because they benefit from the decision (indeed, they would be better off with a smaller resource commitment), but because society will benefit from their commitment of resources.

This would be a most peculiar way of using private resources for the public interest. But to say that it is peculiar is not to say that it is not optimal. The parties would be motivated to invest large quantities of resources, and these would surely lead to better decisions on the law than could be made without such resource investment. As we have said above, there is no obvious reason to believe that the resources would be optimal in quantity, but we are not likely to get the exactly right quantity of resources anyway.

Note, however, that any approach to optimality requires that we can distinguish between those cases in which we are going to make new law and those where we are simply deciding a case. It seems fairly certain that it is highly inefficient to invest very large resources into all cases merely because, in a small subsegment of them, we need fairly large resources in order to get careful discussion of the matter.

Further, if we are interested in large resources in these cases, the traditional common law and Roman law view was that the point should be tried several times—i.e., it must come up several times in somewhat the same context before there is a valid precedent. Perhaps this is a better method than our present single case in the Supreme Court rule.

We must also note here that the traditional argument for the judicial method of making these decisions (that the argument is presented by people who are strongly motivated) has rather slurred over the prospect that the motivations may not be socially optimal. Suppose, as I imagine is the case in most real situations, that there are some fifteen or twenty possible ways in which the law on a given point could be written. One is optimal from the standpoint of the plaintiff and another from the standpoint of the defendant. But if we are talking about future law for society as a whole, still a third is better—indeed, there may be several which are better than either of the two that are most useful for the two parties. Neither of the two parties, then, will be arguing for what is actually the best law from the standpoint of society.

To a very small extent, this problem can be dealt with by permitting third parties to enter as friends of the court; but note that friends of the court would either be arguing for a particular interpretation which from their standpoint was optimal (which, once again, might not be socially optimal) or, if they are arguing for the socially optimal position on grounds of pure goodwill, they would not be motivated strongly because there would not be too much riding on it for them. Once again the regulation and law-writing process of the legislature suffers from the same defect. In all of these cases, it is, in practice, possible for almost anyone who feels like it to get his arguments heard.[14]

We turn now to what is, in my opinion, the most serious of the arguments against court proceedings as a way to make law for the future. The law will not only bind future parties; it will also bind the two parties who are now before the court, and whose arguments are framing the law. This is a necessary requirement if we are going to have those two parties strongly motivated to frame good arguments and to make strong efforts to win, which is part of the argument for judicial lawmaking. But the position of the parties in the future, after the law has been made, is different from the position of the parties before the court. The parties before the court face either a vague law or a law which the court is being asked to change. Suppose, to take an extreme case, that the defendant in the instant case carried out the law to the letter, but the plaintiff is arguing that the law was unwise and should be changed. Let us suppose that the arguments do indeed convince the judges that a new law (or new interpretation) is better than the old one. Changing this law for all future cases may well be wise, but it seems hard on the defendant in this case.

Once again, note that if we make the new law only for future cases and make a different decision in the present case, then we cannot argue that judicial lawmaking is desirable because it places strong incentives on the parties to press their cases. Suppose that the current law provides for A and a better law will provide for $\bar{A}$; if the rule is that the parties to this particular litigation will be bound by the previous law but the court will also issue a new law, the parties would presumably concentrate their arguments on the present law and ignore the advantage which other people in the future would gain from $\bar{A}$.

This problem is not significant in the case of laws made by legislatures and regulations made by executive branches, because they characteristically have only prospective effect. In recent years, however, regulations have begun to have retrospective effect in some cases. Indeed, a number of laws changing the nature of titles with respect to natural resource or amenity considerations are, in effect, very strongly retroactive. In these cases, an individual who has bought a piece of land under a clear, straightforward idea of its value may find that a change in the law greatly reduces that value. Of course, he may also gain a great deal from a similar change in the law. Still, retroactivity of court cases is more clear-cut than the retroactivity of legislative acts. In particular, if we are going to argue that the court is a particularly good place to change laws (or to improve their interpretation), because the parties are strongly motivated to produce all the evidence for a good law or a good interpretation, then it is necessary that these parties be retroactively bound. In the case of legislation or regulation, no similar argument applies.

The proponents of the court system could reply that this may be hard on the two parties, but it does make certain that strong arguments will be offered by the two sides, whereas there is no similar assurance in the case of legislation or administrative acts. Once again, a tax of a rather peculiar nature is being imposed upon the parties, but it is not obvious that this tax is not an optimal institution, in spite of its rather peculiar nature.

Occasionally, imposing upon parties the need to take a great risk and invest large resources for the benefit of the future well-being of the society would be hard on them, but it is very similar to a random tax. Most economists would argue that random taxes, provided that they are not very heavy, carry only very slight excess burden. For example, suppose we had a rule that one hundred names would be drawn from a hat every year, and that each of the people whose names were drawn would be taxed half of his personal fortune. It is hard to think of an argument for this particular tax, but it is also fairly certain that the cost to society would be light. The prospect of this occurring to any person would be small enough so that people in general would not engage in any particular activity to lower their tax liability. There might be a slight reduction in total savings because of the slightly greater risk, but this would be small. The institution that we are describing, in which individuals are occasionally called upon to engage in lawsuits to change the law at great risk and expense to themselves, would have somewhat the same characteristics.

There is a special problem here, however, which is that the institution may put special strains on the court itself. The court finds itself deciding a case between A and B not in terms of the relations between A and B but in terms of the rule for future cases dealing with other people. For example, choosing an optimal law for future cases will severely injure B, who merely carried out to the letter an existing law which A argues was a poor law; or A is now arguing that a vague law should be interpreted differently. If the court accepts A's arguments, it will impose a very great cost on B, who is physically present in the courtroom, even if it will benefit a number of other people in the future. Surely, most courts would give considerable weight to the well-being of poor B, and therefore they might choose a less efficient law for the future, simply because they feel that the parties directly before them, who took their action under the old state of law, should not be punished for it.[15] Here again, the legislature or the regulatory authority, with no need to impose any cost on people for past action, is in a somewhat superior position.

The rationalization for this rather peculiar tax, however, might be good enough so that we will be willing to impose it. We can say to each individual, "Interpret the law not in terms of what it says but in terms of what it should say. Only thus will you be safe, because only thus will you be able to argue in court that the law should not be changed at your expense."

There is finally, however, another problem when it comes to the writing of new law by the courts, whether this new law is interpretation of the old law where it is vague, or literally changes it. This is that judges in general are not very well trained for this activity. Legal training consists very largely of learning what the law now is. There is almost nothing in the way of training in desirable techniques for determining what is a good law. At best, there is a good deal of ethics chopping—i.e., the students are called upon to argue that one or another position is ethically right. In my own case, this tended to strengthen what was already a fairly strong tendency toward ethical relativism. The fact that ethical arguments could be made for almost anything (and, indeed, *were* made for almost anything by one or another of my classmates) tended to undermine the authority of ethical systems.[16]

But for those who are satisfied with ethical arguments as a foundation for at least some law, the fact remains that a good deal of the law deals with areas where there just is no ethical position. Most rules in the law of contract, for example, simply set the language which is to be used by parties in future contracts. It is hard to argue that this is an ethically important issue.

The immense bulk of current law and regulations is largely concerned with technical matters, where ethics is of little or no assistance in determining the optimal rule. Thus, it would appear that if we are going to have judges make these decisions, we would want them trained rather differently. They should have a good background in statistics, economics, ideas of administrative efficiency, etc.

Once again, although this would be ideal for judges making law, it has to be said that the legislators who make legislative law, and executive employees who currently write administrative rules, are equally lacking in these skills. Indeed, it is possible to argue that the executive employees have negative information in these areas. Characteristically, their approach is extremely one-sided, with the result that we have such aberrations as the Federal Communications Commission's effort to make the development of cable television hard or impossible; the Civil Aeronautics Board's long history of strong efforts to maintain high air fares for American citizens; and the Federal Drug Administration's indulgence in mass delay of approval for new drugs which would sharply reduce the death rate. To put it mildly, it is not obvious that the courts would do worse. Still, if we are planning to have the courts write our laws, there should be a change in the training of judges.

Basically, this chapter has dealt with the courts as legislatures and has argued that they are not by any means ideally adapted for the making of new laws or for the clarification of existing laws. On the other hand, as we have pointed out, the alternative methods of making new laws or clarifying existing laws seem to have defects too. There does not seem to be any very strong argument for any one of the three standard methods or, for that matter, even argument that one of the three is the least of the evils. One of my main themes throughout this book has been the need for further research, mainly empirical research. Here the problem does indeed involve some empirical work, but I also feel that further theoretical developments are necessary before we can solve the problem. Meanwhile, no doubt the courts will continue writing new laws and clarifying old ones. The process of writing new laws and clarifying old will, no doubt, add further elements of confusion to the total law in unexpected areas.

I do have one reform, however, which I think could be argued for very strongly. The current method by which courts write new law is to write a sort of essay on a case. They begin by describing the case, characteristically (I think) cheating a little bit on the facts so that the ultimate decision they reach will seem more reasonable, and then they reach a decision on those facts, with some discussion of why they reached it. The total length of this essay may run fifty or sixty pages, although usually it is shorter. Further, as a general rule it is very far from a masterpiece of English exposition. Here there are occasional exceptions; there have been judges who are great masters of English prose. The general level, however, is low. Indeed, I would argue that, on the whole, judges write at least as badly as economists.

This lengthy essay is then bound, classified, and indexed according to an indexing system which essentially was invented by the West Publishing Company—it is also put into loose-leaf services by several other publishers—and is computer indexed; and it becomes part of the law. The classification system is markedly better than the classification system used in any other area of knowledge, but that is unfortunately not great praise. Further, the existence of this very long essay as the basic law means that finding the law is much harder than it would have been had the court been compelled to simply put the intended change in the law (whether that change is an interpretation of an unclear spot in the existing law or a literal change) into a relatively short paragraph. Indeed, in some cases, simply changing one word in the existing statute would be adequate.

There seems to be no reason for this custom of writing essays of great length in order to make what are in most cases very slight changes in the law except that it is custom. There is no reason why the judges may not, if they wish, make speeches about the laws they draft. It is the general rule that the citizen is not compelled to have read all the speeches by proponents of a piece of legislation when he is deciding what are his legal duties.[17] The same should be true with respect to judge-made law. Judges should be compelled to put the change in the law in as brief a form as possible, which normally would be one or two sentences or less. But they have freedom of speech. If they wish to write a lengthy essay, there is no reason why they should not do so; they may even find a publisher. But this should not become part of the law. The shortening of the body of the law from this simple reform would be immense. The only cost that I can see would be compelling a small collection of elderly men (the appellate court judges) to change the habits of a lifetime. Since the change in habits would reduce their work load, I do not imagine this would be very difficult.

Thus, although in general this chapter does not reach any firm conclusions on major matters, on a minor matter—a mere matter of expression—I have offered a reform, and it seems to be one that would be very hard to argue against on any grounds except custom.

Chapter 13

Constitutional Problems

It is one of the peculiar characteristics of American law that our judges—particularly the judges in the higher courts—are much concerned with constitutional problems. They may declare acts of Congress unconstitutional, and, in recent years, they have gotten around to ordering Congress (and, for that matter, the president) to do things on the grounds that, in the view of the court, are their constitutional duty. This latter is a fairly recent doctrine, since, until very recent times, it was normally believed that the courts could not issue orders to these coequal branches. The judges themselves could refuse to carry out orders from the legislature and the president by refusing to enforce laws which they thought unconstitutional, but that was as far as their power was thought to go.

Most Americans do not realize quite how unusual this particular judicial activity seems to the world as a whole. England, from whom our legal system descends, knows nothing of this doctrine, and their judges are bound, simply and straightforwardly, by any act of Parliament.[1] That very democratic country, Switzerland, actually has a specific provision in its constitution prohibiting the courts from overruling the legislature or a referendum.

The history of this provision is amusing. The 1848 revolution in Switzerland was won by a group who were great admirers of the United States Constitution, and who proposed to establish a similar constitution for Switzerland. It turned out that this admiration was not based on much knowledge, and, when they began investigating the United States Constitution in detail, they discovered the constitutional powers of the Supreme Court. This shocked them to the point that they inserted the specific ban in their constitution.

If we turn to the rest of the democratic world, once again we find few courts acting as constitutional enforcers. Today we find more than we would have found fifty years ago, since the custom has spread, partly as a result of military conquest and partly by imitation. Since the last fifty years has also been a period in which democracy itself has become rarer on the surface of the globe, it is not obvious that this institution has become very firmly entrenched. There are many dictatorships which are decked out with formal constitutions, including the power of a court to declare the acts of the dictator unconstitutional—if they dare. It will perhaps be recalled by history buffs that shortly after Lenin took power in Russia, the Russian Supreme Court formally found his government unconstitutional.

Of course, the fact that courts with the power to declare acts of government unconstitutional are rare does not mean that it is a bad idea. There are a number of difficulties with the use of courts for the protection of the constitution; but the fact that these difficulties exist does not necessarily mean that we have other procedures which will work better. Once again, as was suggested in the last chapter, the difficulties faced when the courts take up this duty are matched—and perhaps more than matched—if we attempt to give it to other agencies.

The problem here is one which has become known in the new discipline of public choice as the problem of the self-enforcing constitution. A constitution is characteristically composed of two parts. One of these parts is the set of specific rules, which we may simply call "important laws." For example, we have the constitutional guarantee of free speech, the prohibition on export tariffs, or the right of the citizens to bear arms. The Bill of Rights is an example, but the original Constitution also contains a number of very specific provisions of this sort. The second major part of a constitution is a design for government, and a set of rules as to how government decisions shall be made.

The problem faced by constitutional designers is making certain that their second set of rules will be self-enforcing. Suppose, for example, that the constitution provides (as the Chilean constitution did provide) that the president shall be elected by direct vote but that, if no candidate gets a majority, the legislature shall elect the president. The legislature might, as the Chilean legislature did, develop a habit of always electing the candidate for president who had the most votes in the popular election; thus, in essence they eliminated both the majority rule and the legislature's own powers. Incidentally, it is this particular custom on the part of the legislature, together with its application in a case in which Allende led but had only 36 percent of the popular vote, that set in motion the events which eventually led to the end of Chilean democracy.

Clearly, the original designers of the Chilean constitution did not intend that plurality voting be substituted for majority voting, but they did not draft the constitution well enough to prevent it.

A more surprising case comes from the kingdom of Laos, which had a constitution of the parliamentary type—it provided that when the prime minister lost the vote of confidence, he should resign, and then a new prime minister would be appointed by the king. Prince Souvanna Phouma, then prime minister of Laos, lost a vote of confidence but refused to resign. He agreed that it was his constitutional duty to do so, but he argued that the constitution provided no remedy in the event that the prime minister failed to resign, because the king was not permitted to appoint a new prime minister while there was still one in office. This rather bizarre crisis led to Prince Souvanna Phouma's finding it necessary to flee the country while still claiming that he was prime minister; and, once again, it was one of the important events leading to the end of what little chance Laos had of becoming a democracy.

But we need not go to these distant parts of the world to see cases in which the constitution has been changed from its original meaning. The founding fathers undeniably intended that the central government have only very restricted powers and that most governing be done by the states. This is clear from the original document, and it is even more clear in the Tenth Amendment. Today, alas, little remains of this particular constitutional provision.

In none of these cases is it obvious that the rule drafted in the original constitution was necessarily the best or the wisest. I merely point out that it is hard to design a constitution so that it enforces itself. We do not have any way to get divine assistance in enforcing the Constitution; it must be enforced by the people who are in the government itself. How do we prevent these people from doing things which will increase their power—or simply carry out their ethical principles—if these things violate the constitution? It is a difficult problem and the solutions which are quite widely believed to work in the United States are at least partially illusionary. Unfortunately, I shall not be able to suggest a better system, because I know of no system which guarantees a solution to the problem.

This is particularly unfortunate, because one of the results òf the development of the new discipline of public choice is that we now have fairly good ideas as to how to design efficient constitutions.[2] However, how can we make such an efficient constitution work the way that it is designed? Until we have solved this problem, we cannot feel very confident that our superior constitutions will work the way they are intended.

Having said that we do not understand fully the problem of designing a self-enforcing constitution, I should point out that, as a matter of fact, a good many constitutions seem to have worked for fairly long periods of time with only very modest changes in their structure. The longest lasting, as far as I know, was that of Venice, which lasted about one thousand years without any really violent changes in its governmental structure. This does not mean that it was not changed at all, but the changes were gradual and almost imperceptible over any given century.

The United States Constitution was also moderately successful for a very long time. It seems likely that if the founding fathers had returned in 1914, they would have found no great changes from their original design. The failure of the original process for electing the president, which led to constitutional amendment, and the direct popular election of senators—once again, by way of a constitutional amendment—might have surprised them but not have seemed undesirable. The elimination of slavery would have been regarded by most of them as a distinct step forward, which, due to the political situation, they were not able to make at Philadelphia. It is very likely that even the southern representatives to the Constitutional Convention would share this point of view.

But to say that the Constitution in 1914 was much as it had been in 1789 is not necessarily a compliment. Changes in the Constitution might have been highly desirable. Similarly, the rather rapid changes in the form and scope of our government which have occurred since 1914 are not necessarily undesirable simply because they depart sharply from what the founding fathers had in mind.

It is not at all obvious that the founding fathers had all wisdom, although, as a matter of fact, on the whole they did a rather good job. So, for that matter, did the Swiss in 1848, in spite of their prohibition of judicial review for constitutional matters.

Presumably, what we would want if we could have our "druthers," would be a constitution which at any point in time was of optimal efficiency for that point in time, taking into account the cost of changes. This would, I imagine, involve at least some changes if for no other reason than that our knowledge of constitutional design would improve with time.

Note that it is not, in general, necessary to change the constitution when some technical development occurs, because it is usually possible to design the constitution in such a way that adjustment to changing technology or natural situation can be done by simple law. The basic problem with a constitution is how decisions are made, not the specific policy that is carried out. Thus, the United States Constitution provides, first, vast scope for enactment of laws that deal with all sorts of problems and, second, makes it possible, through the amendment process, for this scope to be either expanded or contracted if that seems desirable to a sufficiently large part of the population.

Here we should pause briefly to say that one of the apparent arguments for judicial review in modern times has been simply that a change is desired which probably cannot be obtained through the constitutional-amendment process, because the popular support for it is not great enough. This particular attitude or explanation is rarely stated frankly; but it can be seen not very far beneath the surface when people argue that the Supreme Court adjusts the Constitution to changing needs, or that the abrupt change in the Constitution brought about by *Brown vs. Board of Education* was desirable, although it would have been impossible to get through an amendment for that purpose. The previous decision had left policy on school segregation to the elected representatives of the people, rather than imposing a constitutional duty upon them.[3] It would have been possible to change the policy, either by a simple legislative act, or if it was intended to coerce Congress, by an amendment. It was thought to be politically impossible to do either of these, and therefore another and easier route was used. The arguments for the change are largely that the new decision was the right one, even if it was a change in the Constitution imposed without going through the usual channels.

Brown vs. Board of Education is a particularly strong case, but the Court has, in recent years, done this same kind of thing quite frequently. I find that people's judgment with respect to such judicial action characteristically turns on whether they think the outcome is desirable, rather than on their views about procedure. For example, in the 1930s, most liberals thought that the Supreme Court should be very strongly curbed and its constitutional power reduced. They favored a plan to pack it in order to change the voting majority. Conservatives, on the whole, were on exactly the opposite side in all of these issues. In the 1950s and 1960s, these people had changed sides.[4] Liberals were taking the view that the Court must be obeyed regardless; and conservatives were talking about restrictions on the Court, and threatening to impeach the Chief Justice. With a further change in personnel, the Court has now changed in some of its policies; and, once again, we now sometimes find liberals remarking that the court seems to be ignoring the Constitution, and conservatives are urging changes.

This is not to criticize the people who feel this way; after all, the only thing which can possibly justify the means are the ends achieved,[5] and if one likes the ends, he may favor the means. It does mean, however, that the Court has, at any given time, a number of people who are urging it to make changes in the Constitution, and a number who think that this is improper. The people in each of these camps change from time to time, depending on what the Court is doing. This, in turn, means that we cannot depend upon the Court to "protect the Constitution," because the Court is one of the bodies which may decide to change it.

Thus, if we were to design an optimal constitution, together with some optimal device for making changes in it, we could not depend upon the Court as a protection for that constitution. Once again, this is not necessarily a criticism of judicial review. Other bodies might change it, too.

Insofar as the founding fathers had any ideas on this matter—and it is not obvious that they did—it seems likely that they intended to rely on the tension built into the government for the defense of the Constitution. They did not specifically give any powers to guard the Constitution to any particular branch, but each of the branches was sworn by oath to obey the Constitution. The president was given a more complicated and thorough oath than the other officials, but all were compelled to swear. When Mr. Chief Justice Marshall, in *Marbury vs. Madison*,[6] first formally put the power of refusal to enforce a law into our constitutional doctrine, he based his reasoning on the oath he had taken.

The actual history of the review power is a much contested matter. Alexander Hamilton favored it and said, in the *Federalist Papers*, that it was part of the power of the Court. He also, in an early case before a state court, argued what appears to have been the first case in which judicial right to reverse a legislative decision was urged. At the time, he seems to have thought that this was an original argument.[7] Fragmentary reports in local newspapers indicate that there were at least a few other cases which might be argued to be precedents to *Marbury vs. Madison*; but Marshall certainly did not mention any of them in his opinion and probably was not aware of their existence.

It seems likely, however, that the actual precedent which was at least in the back of the minds of the writers of the Constitution and of Mr. Justice Marshall—although none of them mentioned it—was a colonial custom. Each of the colonies had its own legislature which passed laws. These were sent to London where they were examined by the law officers of the Crown to find out whether they were in accord with the laws passed by Parliament. If they were, they became law in the colony which had passed them; and if they were not, they were thrown out by the law officers. They threw out about 5 percent. It seems likely, although it is not certain, that this power—very reminiscent of the present role of the House of Lords in dealing with the acts of Parliament which serve as constitutions for some members of the Commonwealth—was in fact the real basis for the idea of judicial review.

Marshall did not mention it and hardly could have. The review was not by judges but by members of the executive branch; it referred not to the supreme government but to inferior governments. Indeed, the constitutional theory of the time held that there were no restrictions on the government of England. Last but by no means least, colonial laws were not thrown out for violating the constitution but for violating ordinary acts of Parliament. There was also no trial but simply a quiet investigation in the law officer's study. It would be hard to argue that all of this was a particularly good precedent for judicial review.

The particular circumstances of *Marbury vs. Madison* also rather cast doubt on whether Marshall was really following precedent or simply creating a new law out of whole cloth. Jefferson, together with his Secretary of State, Madison, on the first day of his presidency violated the law in a rather spectacular way by refusing to transmit the commissions of a number of government officials (which had been signed the night before by President Adams) to the officials. One of them brought suit for a writ of mandamus compelling the delivery of the commissions, and it was clear that the Court would have considerable difficulty avoiding a decision against the president.

Marshall, however, did not want to bring in a decision against President Jefferson. The two men were old enemies, and Jefferson had made it very clear that he was going to disregard any decision that Marshall made in the matter. Under the circumstances, Marshall, who did not like being defied, was in severe need of an argument which would make it possible to avoid ordering Jefferson to deliver the commissions, with its resultant defiance and reduction in the power of the Court. Marshall turned to the doctrine of unconstitutionality. Note, as I have said above, that he based his argument on the oath he had taken, and not on anything else. Although the decision was based narrowly on the oath, it seems to me sound, although the drafters of the Constitution may not have realized that the oath provision would have this consequence. The real difficulty that Marshall faced was that the law which gave him the power to issue the writ—and which he was about to call unconstitutional in order to get out of his dilemma—did not, on its face, appear to have anything particularly unconstitutional about it. Thus, his arguments that he should not enforce an unconstitutional law seem to me clear and straightforward. His arguments that this particular law was unconstitutional, on the other hand, are crabbed and twisted in the extreme. Still the situation in which he found himself was a difficult one, and we cannot blame him for not being able to produce an ideal solution.

The power to declare acts unconstitutional started with *Marbury vs. Madison*, and has grown exponentially. It was relatively little used up to about the 1870s and 1880s, when there was a burst of important cases; then it fell into partial disuse—although still much more actively used than it had been in the early part of the nineteenth century—until the 1930s, when a number of basic acts of the New Deal were declared unconstitutional. The people whom Roosevelt appointed to the Court were rather reluctant—although not totally unwilling—to declare acts of Congress unconstitutional, but they developed a very strong tendency not only to declare local and state laws unconstitutional, but to issue positive orders to the local governments.

Although, so far as I know, no Court has ever actually announced that it has the right to change the Constitution, most students of the courts today would say that this is what the Court is doing. Note that I have selected neutral language here, because some of the students disapprove of this and others, of course, are in favor of it. Thus, one group is apt to say that the Court is forming itself into a continuing constitutional convention for the purpose of imposing its own opinions of policy, and the other group is apt to say that the Court is undertaking the task of adjusting the Constitution to the modern world.

In a way, the basic problem of enforcing the Constitution is the impossibility of getting a court to operate in the way that the first group of critics (those who simply want to enforce the Constitution) say that they want it done. Note that I emphasize "say that they want it done," because there is no evidence whatsoever that many of these critics who are opposed to the Court's efforts to change the Constitution would be pleased if the courts suddenly began enforcing the Constitution in accord with its literal meaning, using an eighteenth-century dictionary to find out what that literal meaning was. Few of the current students of the Constitution actually want the original document enforced in its full meaning as it was at the time.

The real difference between these groups is exactly which changes in the Constitution they regard as desirable, and which as undesirable. Indeed, in a way, the whole debate is simply about current policy, with both parties wanting to use the Supreme Court to enforce their ideas of good government. It is, thus, from the standpoint of both parties, an effort to evade the use of the amendment process as a way to change the Constitution. In fact, the Constitution has already been changed quite drastically, so that it is quite different from what it appears to be on the surface.

All of the above is descriptively accurate, I think, and it is not intended as either praise or criticism. It is intended to get rid of a number of mythological views which are current, so that we can turn to a more careful discussion of the entire problem. I must also dispose of two more myths before turning to an analysis of the actual problem. The first of these is simply that the Court is not capable of damaging—or not likely to damage—the Constitution by its own decisions. This sometimes takes the form of simply saying that it is impossible, as a matter of definition, for the Supreme Court to make an unconstitutional decision; because the Supreme Court decides what the Constitution means. I have never found any proponent of this point of view who was willing to go along with it if an extreme case was stated to him.[8]

Judges are like other people and like to increase their power and influence; further, unlike the top officials of the other branches of the government, they are not subject to removal by the electoral process.

Thus, it would be particularly dangerous to entrust all power to them, and the formal definition of the power of the Constitution as "what the Supreme Court says it is"[9] would be giving the supreme power to a board of nonelected and nonremovable persons. So far as I know, no one wants to do it.

The second myth is that the Constitution requires, of necessity, a single group making decisions about constitutionality or unconstitutionality; and that body is the Supreme Court. This point of view is held so strongly that a rather lengthy discussion of it is desirable.[10] We must return therefore to the decision in *Marbury vs. Madison* by Chief Justice John Marshall.

This case concerned a "plain violation" of the rights of five individuals. The Court refused to take action to redress the wrong to these individuals, because it held that the act which gave them the right to sue before its bar was unconstitutional. In other words, it put enforcement of the Constitution above human rights. The reasoning upon which it did so is still the foundation of the doctrine of unconstitutionality.

Marshall's arguments may be summed up by one paragraph from his decision.

Certainly all those who have framed written constitutions contemplate them as forming the fundamental and paramount law of the nation, and consequently, the theory of every such government must be, that an act of the legislature, repugnant to the constitution, is void.[11]

Clearly this paragraph would make as much sense if the words *executive* or *judiciary* were substituted for *legislature*. The view that the executive or the judiciary is not bound by the Constitution would as much subvert the document as the view that the legislature is not so bound. It is true, of course, that we must not expect to find the Court announcing that its own acts are unconstitutional, any more than we should expect to find the legislature passing laws which it explicitly states are unconstitutional. In each case, the constitutional check is imposed from the outside, not by a given branch of the government judging its own acts.

The same principle will be found to fit the remainder of *Marbury vs. Madison*. Marshall was a judicial officer engaged in deciding whether he would obey a law duly passed by the legislature and signed by the president. As such, he confined his language to this particular problem and did not discuss the complementary problems which would arise if the court made an unconstitutional determination. Nevertheless, his language is still convincing if it is applied to the converse problem. As an illustration, let us make the necessary changes for two and one-half paragraphs.

If, then, the [executive] is to regard the constitution, and the constitution is superior to any [judicial decision], the constitution and not such [decision], must govern the case to which they both apply.

Those, then, who controvert the principle that the constitution is to be considered [by the executive], as a paramount law, are reduced to the necessity of maintaining that the [president] must close [his] eyes on the constitution and see only the [decision].

This doctrine would subvert the very foundations of all written constitutions. It would declare that . . . [a decision] which, according to the principles and theory of our government, is entirely void, is yet, in practice, completely obligatory. . . .[12]

The contrary view, that decisions of the Supreme Court are superior to the Constitution because "the Constitution is what the Supreme Court says it is" has never been claimed by the Court, although a man who later became a Chief Justice once said this in a speech.[13] The Court in its decisions always claims that it is bound by the Constitution. It does not purport to have the power to change the Constitution, only to interpret and to apply it. It is, of course, true that the Constitution is a rather short document and almost two hundred years old. Interpretation under these circumstances may frequently involve filling in the gaps in the law. In fact, this is the main function of the Supreme Court. There is, however, a great difference between deciding what the Constitution should mean in an area where it is unclear and deliberately going against the plain words of the document. For example, ruling that the Senate must be elected according to population would clearly and obviously be unconstitutional.

Marshall, however, had one more problem after he had demonstrated that the Constitution was superior to the acts of a branch of the government; he had to show that the Court was charged with a duty of enforcing the Constitution. His method was simple: he pointed out that the Constitution "direct[s] the judges to take an oath to support it": "This oath certainly applies in an especial manner, to their conduct in their official character. How immoral to impose it on them, if they were to be used as the instruments, and the knowing instruments, for violating what they swear to support!"[14]

Continuing this line of reasoning, the final full paragraph of his decision reads: "Thus, the particular phraseology of the constitution of the United States confirms and strengthens the principle, supposed to be essential to all written constitutions, that a law repugnant to the constitution is void; and that *courts*, as well as other departments, are bound by that instrument."[15]

The argument, again, makes as much sense if the name of another department is substituted for that of the judiciary. Marshall explicitly recognizes this in the last full line of the above quotation. The same sentence of the Constitution which requires judges to support the Constitution also requires legislators, and other officials of the government, to swear to support it. Surely the oath is not more binding on one class of officials than on another. Let us experiment by substituting the executive for the judiciary in two more paragraphs of this fundamental decision:

"Why does . . . [the president] swear to discharge his duties agreeably to the constitution of the United States, if that constitution forms no rule for his government? If it is closed upon him, and cannot be inspected by him?

"If such be the real state of things, this is worse than solemn mockery. To prescribe, or to take this oath, becomes equally a crime."[16]

It is hard to see why this is less reasonable as a matter of constitutional law than the original version. If Chief Justice Marshall's reasoning was correct for the judiciary, clearly it is also correct for the executive and the legislature.

My argument that the Congress and the executive also have responsibilities for preserving and protecting the Constitution, although it would have been acceptable to such liberals as Justices Black and Douglas in the late thirties, will be vigorously contested today. The argument which may be offered against it is that there must be a single ultimate authority to decide constitutional problems, and that the Supreme Court is that authority. This can be divided into two parts, an argument that a single authority is logically necessary and that the Constitution established such an authority in the Supreme Court.

The first, or logical, argument, although superficially plausible, is fairly easily answered. It would, of course, be impossible to have two or three bodies each issuing authoritative interpretations of the Constitution if these interpretations were equally binding upon the citizen and likely to conflict. We are not, however, faced with the necessity of choosing between two equally unattractive alternatives: the one involving multiple and possibly conflicting authorities, and the other involving a single arbitrary authority. If the founding fathers had seen the problem in this light, they would surely not have set up an appointed body as the ultimate sovereign. They had just fought a war to free themselves from the control of appointive royal governors. Surely they did not wish to place themselves and their descendants under the complete control of a body of men who were not removable, no matter how bad their decisions.

That the drafters of the Constitution did not think in terms of giving ultimate power to the Court can be readily seen from the provision of the Constitution that "the Supreme Court shall have appellate Jurisdiction, both as to Law and Fact, with such Exceptions, and under such Regulations as the Congress shall make" (Article III, Section 2). The right of Congress to make exceptions in the jurisdiction of the Supreme Court, upheld by that Court in *Ex Parte McCardle*,[17] a case involving civil rights, is clearly inconsistent with the view that the Court is the ultimate authority on constitutional questions.

If we return to *Marbury vs. Madison*, we see that Marshall did not claim any sort of ultimate authority for the Court. He simply said that where he thought the Constitution and a law conflicted, he would carry out his oath of office and refuse to enforce the law. Until very recently, this purely negative concept of the duty of the courts in constitutional questions was the dominant theory. The whole subject was traditionally described under the rubric of "judicial review," and that review amounted to "little more than the negative power to disregard an unconstitutional enactment."[18] This negative view of the problem of protecting the Constitution raises none of the logical problems of conflicting determinations of constitutionality, while at the same time avoiding the grant of ultimate power to one body.

Normally, any act of the government will require the cooperation of two or three of the main branches of government. If the act initiated by one branch is constitutional, the other branches are required to cooperate. If the initial act, on the other hand, is unconstitutional, then the other branches are required, by the oaths that their officers have taken to uphold the Constitution, to refuse to play any part in destroying the constitutional guarantees. This is the famous system of "checks and balances," which the drafters of the Constitution thought more desirable than dependence upon the goodwill and self-restraint of a small body of men.

In practice, of course, the bodies initiating action in our system have normally been the legislature and the executive. The courts, until very recently, seldom took the initiative. This meant that most cases on the point have been resolved through refusal by the courts to carry out unconstitutional acts of the legislature, rather than through refusal by the legislature or executive to enforce unconstitutional decisions of the courts. The only major effort at judicial legislation prior to the last two decades was the Dred Scott case, which was, quite rightly, not enforced by many state governments and reversed "on the slight, bare slopes of Gettysburg."

The recent outburst of judicial activism, which contrasts so strongly with the restraint characterizing most previous Courts even in the exercise of their negative power of judicial review, has raised an essentially new problem. Although the Court still talks the language of simply applying the Constitution, it now acts as though it were a sort of superior legislature, not only imposing new laws but also actually changing the Constitution by its decisions. No longer are constitutional decisions largely limited to refusals to enforce laws: they now frequently take the form of positive orders to other branches of the government and general rules for the control of citizens. Most of the civil-rights cases and the reapportionment decisions are of this nature. Under these circumstances, the right of the other branches to "check" the Supreme Court by refusing to apply its decisions when they violate the Constitution, a right long in abeyance, becomes a matter of first importance.

Even if a supreme authority is not logically necessary in a system where each branch checks the others, it might still be true that the Constitution did establish such an ultimate arbiter in the form of the Supreme Court. This is, however, not the case, for there is nothing in the language of Article III of the Constitution which directly assigns to the Supreme Court the enforcement of the Constitution. If the Constitution conferred such special powers on the Court, it did so implicitly, not explicitly; and it is hard to see where supreme power is implied for the Supreme Court. The judiciary is given "the judicial power of the United States." If they had been written in 1979, these words might be construed as implying arbitrary power of the Court to interpret the Constitution in any way it sees fit. But this mythological view of judicial power was not held in 1789. Nor did Marshall claim such power. He made only the following claim:

> So if a law be in opposition to the constitution; if both the law and the constitution apply to a particular case, so that the court must either decide that case conformably to the law, disregarding the constitution; or conformably to the constitution, disregarding the law, the court must determine which of these conflicting rules governs the case. This is of the very essence of judicial duty.[19]

The statement of the role of the Court is acceptable; but it is also a duty of the executive to decide which of two conflicting laws is to be enforced, especially if one of these laws is the Constitution itself.

The president holds a unique status, in that the Constitution itself specifies the content of the oath he must take on assuming office. This oath concludes with the words "[I] will, to the best of my ability, preserve, protect, and defend the Constitution of the United States." The obligation devolving on the president is clearly more weighty than the mere duty "to support" the Constitution, the requirement specified for oaths to be subscribed to by all other officials, including judges. In carrying out his duty to execute the laws, the president must, of course, make constitutional decisions. If he feels that a given law enacted by Congress is unconstitutional, he may veto it; and this is one of the reasons given by presidents for their vetoes. If an unconstitutional law is passed, he must follow his oath and refuse to enforce it. This, although it may appear novel, is simply a description of what presidents have always done. The attorney general frequently considers the constitutionality of various laws, and his rulings on such points are normally accepted by the executive arm.

The members of Congress are not only sworn to support the Constitution, they also run heavily to lawyers, and hence are apt to be interested in constitutional questions. The question of whether a given measure is constitutional is frequently discussed on the floor of the two Houses, and a consensus seems to prevail to the effect that unconstitutional acts should not be passed. If the president requests legislation which appears to the members of Congress to be unconstitutional, they should refuse to pass it. It is always a little hard to determine exactly why Congress has taken any given action, since there will normally be many different arguments offered by different members; but it is reasonably clear that there have been occasions when legislation has been rejected, or modified, for constitutional reasons. Again this involves no usurpation of judicial prerogatives. Congress is unique in that the Constitution specifically limits its power to making "Laws which shall be necessary and proper for carrying into Execution the foregoing Powers, and all other Powers vested by this Constitution in the Government of the United States. . . ." Surely congressmen asked to appropriate money for a purpose they believe to be unconstitutional may refuse to do so. The view that Congress should refrain from considering constitutional questions is not only absurd, but also directly contrary to the established practice of our government.

Thus, it is not only the Constitution, but long-established practice, which gives to each of the three branches of the government the right to check the others if their acts are unconstitutional. The Supreme Court has seldom experienced such checks, but this simply reflects the fact that it has seldom taken positive action. Surely the restraint of previous judges does not give the present Court positive powers to do anything it wishes.

We pointed out, before, the extreme difficulty involved in a self-enforcing constitution. It would appear that the founding fathers had at the back of their minds an idea which, if far from perfect, was in any event as good as any I can think of. They thought if they established a government so that it was not at all clear who had ultimate power—i.e., a number of different bodies would compete for power—then squabbles would occur, and the actual text of the Constitution would always be an argument which could be adduced in the course of these squabbles. Granted that there would always be someone losing as well as someone winning in the squabbles, this particular argument might have considerable weight. The Constitution, to a considerable extent, might be self-enforcing by this mechanism.[20]

Note, however, that there is no reason to believe that the founding fathers (or anyone else, for that matter) wanted the Constitution to remain totally unchanged. They wanted improvements to be made as they were discovered, and probably also wanted the Constitution to adjust itself to popular opinion, even when the change in popular opinion is simply a shift and in no sense an improvement. They provided a formal amendment process, but it seems doubtful that they were naive enough to believe that the Constitution would change only by that amendment process. Many of them, for example, were lawyers and were aware of the fact that the English common law had changed over time, albeit very slowly.

Further, the amendment process they specified did not put any restrictions on amendment, except to make amendments hard. Any amendment would, of necessity, be the result of a considerable period of discussion; it would only go through if it had a very wide measure of popular approval. The founding fathers probably hoped that the same criterion would apply to the other changes the Constitution would undergo—i.e., its gradual change by interpretation, which they surely anticipated. Thus, they organized government in such a way that different parts of the government could stop changes if they objected to them—Congress by refusing to appropriate money, the president by vetoing or, in some cases, simply refusing to carry out decisions.[21] One of these blocks was the Supreme Court's power to refuse to carry out acts of Congress.

On the whole, this system worked, in the sense that few government changes were made without widespread public support, although it is notable that, in recent years, the Supreme Court has succeeded in imposing a number of changes in the Constitution which have evoked very widespread opposition.[22] Presumably, this simply reflects the fact that the Supreme Court, unlike the other governmental agencies, is free of the prospect of being voted out of office if its actions are sufficiently unpopular.

It should be pointed out that in one area—an area in which this type of tension was not built into the original Constitution—the change has been quite rapid. This is the contest between the states and the federal government for power. The recent very sharp increase in the power of the federal government has largely taken the form of bypassing the potential conflict between the politicians who run the state governments and the politicians who run the federal government. In most cases, the state governments are not actually ordered to do anything by the federal government, they are simply offered money. Since he who pays the piper calls the tune, this does give the federal government control, without facing the type of conflict which made it almost impossible for the various branches of the federal government to win out in their struggles with others.

It may be that the existence of three branches in the federal government—any two of which may be expected to unite against one growing in power—provides a better structure for preventing the switch of power than the situation between the state and federal government, where there are only two sides. With only two power groups, if one grows in power, it is automatically in a better position to grow further than it was before the change.

It seems likely that some such general process is, in fact, all we can do in this area. In any event, it is all I can think of. A structure of government such that the different people at the top will tend to be brought into conflict with each other, hence making it difficult for any basic change to be made, does make certain that basic changes will be thought over carefully.

Students of constitutional history will recall that in the Constitutional Convention, the first act of the Convention was to constitute itself in a committee of the whole to consider the first proposals for the Constitution. This was a well-known, fairly old technique, which insured that the whole Constitution would be examined twice, once by the Constitutional Convention sitting as a committee of the whole, and once by the Constitutional Convention sitting as a Constitutional Convention. Looked at from the standpoint of a modern mathematical social scientist, this seems redundant, since we tend to assume perfect information. If, however, the objective is simply to be very careful and to assure widespread support, then some mechanism which assures that the discussion take a lot of time may be wise.

The organization of the federal government into three competing branches insures a good deal of tension, stress, and disorderliness in the decision-making process. It also makes it very difficult, however, to get changes through which will increase the power of one of the branches at the expense of the other two. Note that I say it is difficult, not impossible. The fact that it is difficult and time-consuming means that the matter will be discussed with considerable vigor and for a considerable period of time; and in this vigorous and lengthy discussion, the parties who have the actual Constitution on their side are given an advantage which is greater than they would have if the discussion were quicker and less subject to multilateral veto.

Not only is the Constitution in itself important, but it seems likely that this structure of struggle between the various branches often precludes a simple majority from winning. Normally, a good deal more than a majority is necessary; although as one of the coauthors of *Calculus of Consent*, I realize that in the logrolling context, the phrase "majority" has a somewhat ambiguous meaning. The particular change that goes through may in fact be supported only by a minority, but they will find it necessary to buy off not just 51 percent of the votes but probably something like 70 or 80 percent if the change is "constitutional."

I have pointed out, above, that the original arrangements seem to have failed to protect the power of the states, although they certainly held for very nearly 150 years. There is another area where the original arrangements seem to have failed, and this is an area where no one apparently gave the matter any consideration at all.

It is customary these days to say that the executive branch is much the most powerful. This is frequently taken to imply that the president is more powerful than Congress. This is quite untrue. The change that has occurred has been a rise in the power of the federal bureaucracy, with the president, the courts, and Congress all losing power. It seems probable that the basic change which made this possible was the civil service act, which protected most government employees from any severe disciplinary action by their nominal superiors. Although the various civil service acts are mere acts of Congress and not only can be changed but, in fact, are changed in various minor ways from time to time, it seems likely that any objective discussion of the present United States "Constitution" would hold that the civil service acts were a very important part of it.

With the civil service acts in existence, the interests of the civil servants themselves—their desire to expand their jurisdiction, increase their power, and raise their wages—have achieved a built-in political position. There are enough civil servants, so that their vote is of great importance, and they are the group for whom government policies are most important. Under the circumstances, it is not surprising that the civil service has grown and that its wages have risen rapidly. It is also not surprising that it has, to a very considerable extent, escaped from the control of the president.

It is interesting that as a result of the rise of the civil service and its steadily growing power, there has been a reversal in the roles of the president and Congress. Most general policy decisions today are initiated by the president, but, on the other hand, he has only modest control over what this vast mass of inchoate and competing bureaus do.

Congressmen, on the other hand, find themselves devoting a very large part of their time to supervising the bureaucracy. It is easier for them than for the president, simply because there are many of them, and because, individually, they receive a continuous input from constituents who are having difficulties of one kind or another with the bureaucracy.

If congressmen spend much time supervising the bureaucracy, there is little evidence that they are able to do very much about the general policies followed by individual bureaucrats or branches of the bureaucracy. Acts of Congress may be simply ignored in the administrative realm. What congressmen can do is see to it that individual constituents are given "a fair deal." Frequently, this "fair deal" involves giving someone who is being injured by one bureaucratic act a special privilege with respect to another, rather than eliminating the original injury. Ironically, the congressman is apt to have more influence over the function of government sitting in his office and telephoning various bureaucrats than he is when voting on the floor. On the other hand, one of the reasons he has this influence is because it is known that he can vote on the floor; and if worse comes to worst, he may cut the appropriation.

However, this is a digression into how the system has changed. Note, however, that I have said nothing at all here about any special role of the courts. There are many people who feel that the courts should have a special role in the interpretation of the Constitution, and, granted the way the president and Congress act, I cannot argue very strongly that this is undesirable. What we must *not* do, however, is give the courts a monopoly. The courts have clearly demonstrated a desire to increase their power. No one who has even the remotest idea of the desirability of democracy would be in favor of this particular change.

To say that we must not let the Supreme Court decide its own powers is quite different from saying that we should not give it greater respect in constitutional matters than the president—acting presumably through the attorney general—or Congress (most of whose members are lawyers). It is only when the Court turns to decisions in matters where its own power is involved that we, of necessity, must be suspicious. Unfortunately, this is a large category of decisions; but, still, it is by no means all decisions. Fortunately, also, the founding fathers, who were rather more aware of these problems than many present-day constitutional students, took care of the matter by providing for a suitable set of checks on the Supreme Court. It is true that since 1950, Congress and the president have frequently been reluctant to make use of these checks, but it seems probable that this is merely a temporary phenomenon, and that, with time, the usual disorderly squabble we depend upon for restraint of power in various branches of government will reassert itself. The Supreme Court, too, will find that it is not a constitutional dictator.

Let us now turn to the activities of the Court in a constitutional question. As in the case of writing law, what I have to say below will indicate that the courts are far from ideal in this area. However, it is also true—and again this is similar to the law—that our alternative methods are far from ideal. The attorney general and the president frequently consider constitutional problems when dealing with proposed legislation or implementation of legislation, and Congress frequently deals with it. There is no reason to believe that these alternative methods of dealing with constitutional problems work better than the Court. The court system—as I trust will become clear after further discussion—is far from perfect; but it may nevertheless be optimal in the sense that we have nothing better.

Let us begin briefly by describing how constitutional cases get to the courts. This description will not, I should tell readers now, be identical to what they learned in high school civics, although it will bear some resemblance. The first thing that happens is that someone finds that his interests are injured by a law (or, in some cases, by an interpretation of the law). The interest has to be a significant one from the standpoint of the person concerned if there is going to be any constitutional issue, because of the fact that it is very, very expensive indeed to take a case up to the point where a binding constitutional decision is made.

Note, here, that there is an important public-good problem. There are many matters in which the total interest of all citizens of the United States is many billions of dollars, whereas no individual person has more than, let us say, $500 to $1,000 riding on it. Such cases are, on the whole, unlikely to get to the Supreme Court, no matter how basically important they are or how extreme the violation of the Constitution is. Of course, it should be said that under special circumstances such cases can get to court.

As an example of this kind of thing, I have been told (I must admit this is hearsay) that the Social Security Administration administers the Social Security Act in a way which probably would lead to very great legal difficulties if it were not that the individual decisions which are made so arbitrarily normally involve too small an amount of money to justify a lawsuit. Since I have just admitted that I have only hearsay evidence for this, the reader will (I trust) not take the specific allegation as proved; but it is clear that this kind of thing could happen. If the Social Security officials were deciding all complaints from their customers behind closed doors by flipping coins, it is very doubtful that the matter would get to the Supreme Court, although one can readily imagine congressmen taking action.[23]

The fact that individual cases will go up for constitutional decisions only if they are of some importance to an individual litigant (perhaps, to a specialized pressure group) means that only a subset of all possible violations of the Constitution will ever get into the constitutional track. It is likely that widespread but minor violations of the Constitution are more apt to attract the attention of the attorney general or of Congress, through a large collection of letters saying much the same thing, than they are to be brought before the court.

There is also another area where what we might call "hobbyists" become important. There are a certain number of private foundations—the ACLU and the Right to Work Foundation are examples—which solicit funds from private citizens who make essentially charitable contributions. They then use these funds to pay for litigation on constitutional questions. It is possible for these agencies to carry constitutional matters to the Supreme Court, even if the exact amount in question is relatively small. To repeat, this is a somewhat hobbyist activity. Some areas are subject to this kind of legal pressure and some are not. The ACLU, for example, decided long ago that it would not take on labor unions. In consequence, the provisions in labor union contracts that an employee will be fired if he criticizes the unions are never objected to by the ACLU. Interunion democracy is also a matter that the ACLU has avoided. This is not criticism of the individual hobbyist agency—after all, hobbies do tend to be rather specialized, and these people are engaging in litigation for ends which they think are desirable.

You will note that so far I have referred to the activity as arising because the Constitution is being violated or requires interpretation. There is a third case, in which the people bringing suit (or perhaps the people being sued) feel that the Constitution is incorrect and should be changed. Distinction among these three conditions is of great importance for our purposes, but the Supreme Court pretends that all cases are in the first category or in the second. It does not admit that it is changing the Constitution, even when it very obviously is doing so.

In those cases in which the Constitution is clear, and whatever is objected to in the case coming to the Supreme Court is clearly a violation of the Constitution, the Court may simply carry out a ministerial duty of enforcing the Constitution, providing that it does not decide that the Constitution should be changed in this case. In fact, cases of this sort rarely get to the Supreme Court, since they are normally dealt with at lower levels.

The important cases, then, are cases of interpretation or elucidation and cases where the Supreme Court is proposing, or being asked, to change the Constitution. In these cases, looked at from the standpoint of the litigants, the Constitution has already failed. If it is unclear, they can hardly have known what their duties were. Further, if it is about to be changed, they surely did not know at the time they did whatever it was that led to the lawsuit that a new Constitution was about to be imposed upon them.

Thus, the outcome of the case will, in a way, be unfair to whoever loses, because they may very well have done their best to carry out the Constitution at the time they did whatever it was that led to the lawsuit. In this respect, the situation is very similar to that of the individual who simply does not know what the law is, or who suffers because the courts change the law.

The arguments given above with respect to the individuals concerned in such cases would seem to apply here. If the law is unclear, or if the Constitution is unclear, then it is no doubt necessary to make a decision in this particular case; but from the standpoint of the parties to the case, this decision should be a low-resource-cost/low-accuracy decision, because, in essence, high accuracy is impossible. What we are doing is imposing upon these parties a system under which they must invest very large resources in litigation, and the only argument for it is that we need a fairly comprehensive investigation of the general issue for social purposes.[24] In other words, it is another peculiar tax.

In the case of constitutional change, the tax is particularly heavy because the costs are high, and yet probably it is not high enough. It seems likely that we would want constitutional changes and, for that matter, cases where there is a serious ambiguity in the Constitution that needs to be cleared up, considered much more carefully than legal problems. Thus, it is likely that even granted the large investments involved in constitutional cases, the resources are too small.

Methods to increase investment in this area would be fairly easy to design and, indeed, one very old-fashioned technique would seem to be fairly easy to apply. As we have mentioned above, originally, in both the

Roman and the common law systems, the individual case which first dealt with a given issue was not regarded as determining the law. The same issue had to be considered by several different courts before it was thought to be firmly established law.

A similar rule—that a court decision in a given constitutional area was not truly binding on future cases until the third time—seems to reach the same goal. Note, however, that if it were literally the same court, we would expect that it would reach the same conclusion the second and third times that it reached the first time.[25] However, there is no reason why we could not have several courts of last resort, just as they had in England during the time when the common law was developing. There has been much complaint recently about the Supreme Court being over-worked, and this could be dealt with by creating five Supreme Courts with regional jurisdiction. Supreme Court justices could be appointed simply to "the Supreme Court" and then moved randomly through the set of five at, let us say, two-year intervals. This would provide a system in which there would be final decisions for given cases, probably at somewhat lower cost to the litigants than under present circumstances, and in which constitutional matters would normally not be regarded as settled until several cases had come up with different courts and with different judges sitting on the bench. It would presumably improve the function of the system at modest cost.

Once again, we have serious difficulties in the effect of the decisions on the individual litigants. Surely the courts are going to take into account the fact that the parties appearing before them can be badly injured by the decision. A socially optimal decision might appear, from the standpoint of the parties appearing before the court, extremely unjust, because those parties did not know in advance what the decision would be. This presumably has some effect on the court decisions. Once again, it would seem that the easy way to deal with this is to permit the courts to reach a decision with respect to the constitutional point, which is then enshrined in the Constitution, and a separate decision on the rights of the parties. Once again, however, if we do this, the parties will not be motivated to argue strongly for their constitutional position. Thus, the present scheme must be retained—even though it is clearly unjust on occasion to the parties in litigation—if we wish to use the argument that the courts are useful in making these decisions, because they consider them in the context of a specific case (or, better yet, a set of specific cases) in which the parties make very strong arguments on both sides. Once again, we have a very peculiar and rather arbitrary tax, which is used, in this case, to improve the Constitution.

Here, also, the reform that we suggested with respect to the way in which the decision is made when the court is clarifying or changing the ordinary law would seem desirable. If the court, instead of writing very long decisions about individual cases, simply decided whether the plaintiff or defendant had won in this particular case and then made a brief, clarifying change in the language of the Constitution, or a change which literally modified it, we would be able to study law with much less difficulty in the United States.[26]

The only objection to this particular reform in the constitutional case is that it would require us to face openly the fact that our courts are changing the law and the constitution, rather than merely enforcing it. So far as I know, everyone has agreed that they do this, but it might be that this is the case where a certain amount of verbal hypocrisy is worth retaining. Still, the cost of our present method of reporting the results of judicial decisions for future cases is extremely high.

Last, but not least, in my discussion of the problems of use of the Supreme Court as an agency for clarifying inconsistencies and making changes in the Constitution, is that the Supreme Court justices seem to be very badly trained for this purpose. They are almost uniformly lawyers and have devoted much time either to litigating cases, or to studying the writings of judges who have written decisions in the past. Clearly this is not the ideal training for someone who is being called upon to make basic social policy. It would be far better if they were trained in other fields, such as economics, political science, etc. It should be said, however, that if the justices thought of their duty simply as conserving the Constitution—they did not think of themselves as having the right to change it—then legal training would be ideal. After all, if one is simply conserving something, a conservative point of view and a conservative education are desirable. There are few things more conservative than reading the writings on the interpretation of a body of law by long-dead judges.

Granted that the Supreme Court does not simply conserve the existing Constitution but makes changes in it, then this is not the kind of training we would like our judges to have. Once again, although one would prefer judges trained differently, the actual existing alternative methods for dealing with the Constitution—Congress and the executive branch—are not markedly better. It is true that presidents and congressmen are not all lawyers (although there is a heavy preponderance), but it is not obvious that the type of training that they have had is any better than that of a lawyer when it comes to deciding on basic social policy. President Jimmy Carter, for example, was a naval officer and then a manager of a peanut business. The training at Annapolis is essentially an engineering training, but it is clear that he has a great ability—as any man who gets to be president will have—to pick up a quick knowledge of almost any subject to which he turns his attention. Still, I do not see any strong argument that this background would be better for constitutional interpretation than training in the law. In both cases, it is not what we would hope for.

In general, this is true of all the other objections I have raised above. The method of determining constitutional issues by Supreme Court decisions has a number of severe defects. It is not obvious, however, that these are worse than those possessed by the alternative ways of making such decisions.

Thus, we end with little in the way of proposals for reform. There is one area where clearly present constitutional doctrine is at fault. We should return to the pre-1950 situation, in which the Supreme Court was merely one of three quarreling branches of the government, rather than being considered an ultimate source of control. This is particularly important for cases which involve the power of the Supreme Court, since the Supreme Court is as likely as the president or Congress to attempt to expand its own power. We need a check on the Court as well as on other agencies.

Having left the one area of the power of the Court, however, the present situation is not very good, but it may well be ideal in the limited sense that we cannot do better. Frank Knight is reported to have said, "When the captain of the ship says, 'We are sinking and all of the lifeboats have been stove in,' he may be describing a social optimum."

Chapter 14

Envoy

My readers are no doubt convinced by now that this book is different from other books on legal procedure. They may be convinced that it is superior, but, then again, they may not. I am proposing a radically different way of looking at procedural problems, and anyone making radical proposals must recognize the possibility that he could be wrong. But, although I concede the possibility that I could be wrong, I do not think that I am.

It is my hope that this book will be merely the first step. By applying a totally new approach, I have (I hope), opened a new method of studying legal procedure which will lead to much progress. If the book is a success, it will be followed by other books by other scholars, elaborating on the methods of research suggested here, finding errors (in detail, I hope), and in general moving the scientific examination of legal procedure forward. It is hard to evaluate one's own work; the reader may be in a better position to judge my success.

In addition to developing new analytical tools and a new approach to legal procedure, I have made quite a large number of specific proposals for improvement. Most of these proposals are tentative and are suggested not with the idea that they will be immediately adopted, but with the conviction that they should be carefully studied. In many ways, however, these suggestions are not the most important applications which the book might have. I argue that a great many of the conventional practices are not well founded on scientific reasoning. Further, I argue that many common rationalizations of traditional practice are simply false. In these cases, I am essentially calling for further research. It may be that we can invent nothing better than the present practice, even if it has severe defects, and it may also be that there are other and better explanations of the practices than those currently in use. I hope, however, that major improvements are possible.

The book, then, if it is a success, will provide more questions and topics for research than answers.

Notes

1. WHY HAVE LAW?

1. For another explanation together with an excellent discussion of legal education, see Jerome Frank, *Courts on Trial* (Princeton, N.J.: Princeton University Press, 1949), pp. 225–46.

2. Actually Goldberg was already preparing at the time the issue arose, so he had certainly gotten started earlier.

3. The prosecuting attorney, interestingly enough, asked Anderson not to release secret information, and Anderson agreed to comply, provided that the prosecuting attorney behaved in a way in which Anderson thought was suitable. All of this was reported in the newspapers, and there was no indication that I could see that anyone thought that it was improper.

2. THE SIMPLEST MODEL

1. Note that since the proceeding is always accurate and costless, if a crime were committed, all of the names in the community could be submitted to God and He would find all but one innocent.

2. With our present zero-cost rate, the total elimination of crime or contract violation would be optimal. With a positive-cost rate, which is what we see in the real world, reducing the crime rate to zero is not desirable. See Gary Becker, "Crime and Punishment: An Economic Approach," *Journal of Political Economy* (March/April 1968), 76(2):169–217, reprinted in *The Economic Approach to Human Behavior* (Chicago, University of Chicago Press, 1978), pp. 39–85.

3. Of course, God might take care of this in His other capacities.

4. Although the English courts normally do assess the costs on the loser, there are occasional exceptions to this rule.

5. For simplicity I am ignoring the fact that a portion of the costs are paid for by the general public, i.e., I am assuming that the full costs are split evenly between the two parties.

6. It could be argued that it has behaved immorally, but I think that this kind of consideration should generally be kept out of discussions of enforcement of the law. If we could depend on everyone to behave morally, the law would shrink to a minor and insignificant set of institutions. Its major role is to compel people to do things which "morally" they have a duty to do, but which they propose not to do if they are not compelled.

7. Note that here I am implicitly assuming that only the victim is involved. There is no intrinsic reason why we could not have an elaborate police force which sought out all violations of the law and then carried out the necessary prosecution at no cost to the victim. This, however, will not be discussed very much in this book simply because, so far as I know, no system in the world uses it. Uniformly, someone has to complain to the police, and has to invest at least some resources in getting them to take action. With civil actions, the police are normally not involved at all.

8. This is, as a matter of fact, true for the plaintiff in most American accidental damage suits. His lawyer is working on a contingency fee, but the defendant's is not.

9. Once again, this is an effort to approximate the present state of the empirical data, which I regard as very poor indeed.

10. Note that although all burglars would now get terms that are twice as long, only half as many would be convicted; hence, the total prison costs would be the same. Similarly, although innocent persons who are convicted get twice as heavy a sentence, their number is halved.

3. MORE ON ERRORS

1. We are assuming that it does so because it wishes to produce a particular legal outcome, but we are also assuming that this legal outcome is certain once the court has decided what the facts are.

2. See Sarah McCabe and Robert Purves, *The Shadow Jury at Work* (Oxford, Baso Blackwell, 1974). The book was summarized quite nicely by Peter Evans in the London *Times*, December 18, 1974, p. 4. " ' Shadow' jurors disagree with one court verdict in four penal research report says."

3. The University of Chicago jury project has run somewhat similar experiments in Chicago. I am unable to gain access to their results.

4. See Harry Kalven, Jr., and Han Zeisel, *The American Jury* (Boston: Little Brown, 1966).

5. Fred L. Strodbeck and Richard D. Mann, "Sex Role Differentiation in Jury Deliberations," *Sociometry* (1956), 19:1-11; F. L. Strodtbeck, R. M. James, C. Hawkins, "Social Status in Jury Deliberations," *American Sociological Review* (1957), 22:713-19; R. M. James, "Status and Competency in Jury Deliberations," *American Journal of Sociology* (1959), 64:563-70.

6. John Baldwin and Michael McConville, *Jury Trials* (Oxford: Clarendon Press, 1979). S. McCabe and R. Purves, *The Shadow Jury at Work*, Oxford University, Criminal Research Unit (London: Blackwells, 1974). "Are Too Many Professional Criminals Avoiding Conviction?" *Modern Law Review* (1974a), 37:28-62. This attracted a comment, "The Acquittal Rate of Professional Criminals: A Critical Note" by J. Baldwin and M. McConville, *Modern Law Review* (1974), 37:439-43, and Sanden replied in "The Acquittal Rate of Professional Criminals: A Reply," *Modern Law Review*, 37:444-49.

7. Janusz A. Ordover, "Costly Litigation in the Model of Single Activity Accidents," *Journal of Legal Studies* (June 1978), 7(2):243–61. For further work in the same vein, see John Prather Brown, "Toward an Economic Theory of Liability," *Journal of Legal Studies* (1973), 2:323; Peter A. Diamond, "Accident Law and Resource Allocation," *Bell Journal of Economics & Management Science* (1974), 5:366; Peter A. Diamond and J. A. Mirrlees, "On the Assignment of Liability: The Uniform Case," *Bell Journal of Economics & Management Science* (1976), 6:553.

8. See note 7.

9. Gordon Tullock, *The Logic of the Law* (New York: Basic Books, 1971), pp. 105–35.

4. MORE ON COSTS

1. This might be one which actually costs the government a great deal of money but where the parties are not charged, because the government not only provides the court but also provides them with free attorneys, free people to assist in making up their cases, free expert witnesses, etc.

2. John von Neumann and Oskar Morgenstern (Princeton, N.J.: Princeton University Press), 1944.

3. Thomas C. Schelling, *The Strategy of Conflict* (Cambridge, Mass.: Harvard University Press, 1960), p. 21.

4. In actual bargaining, "fake" final offers are fairly common. As long as such a "final offer" is not thought of by the parties as really being a genuine commitment to end the bargaining unless the terms are accepted, it will be treated as an ordinary part of the bargaining process, and distinguished from real binding commitments of the sort which Schelling has analyzed. *Ibid.*, pp. 22–24.

5. It may be possible to reach agreement on some procedure which will keep bargaining costs low.

6. Since such estimates would necessarily be very chancy, this must be treated as a stochastic guess, involving probabilities rather than as an expectation of hitting the two quantities squarely on the head.

7. In bargaining, a failure to respond to an offer may be a "communication."

8. In spite of the improvement over his expectations, the seller is likely to feel that he bargained badly. When the other party accepts what is intended as merely a bargaining offer, the man who made it will normally assume that he could have done better, say $91,500, if he had been more skillful.

9. Strictly, the seller is trying to make the estimated cost function a vertical line, but in most cases his bargaining partner would not be absolutely certain that refusing the offer would cut off negotiations. Hence, I have given the line some curvature.

10. Almost entirely rather than entirely, because it is normally necessary to utilize some resources in convincing your opposite number that you really mean

it. This is a problem to which Schelling has devoted much attention.

11. He had filed an *aminus curiae* brief.

5. OPTIMAL PROCEDURE

1. Perversity is particularly likely if the plaintiff who is in the wrong is able to get the court to compel the defendant to commit an illegal act.

2. Specifically, if any animal test has shown development of cancer.

3. Rita James Simon, " 'Beyond a Reasonable Doubt'—An Experimental Attempt at Quantification," *Journal of Applied Behavioral Science* (1970): 6(2):201–9; and Rita James Simon and Linda Mahan, "Quantifying Burdens of Proof: A View from the Bench, the Jury, and the Classroom," *Law and Society Review* (February 1971):319–30.

4. The principal defect is the failure to realize that many of their experimental subjects may not be very familiar with the percentage method of presenting probability. I should say, however, that my statement that this article contains defects is not intended as a criticism of its two authors. The first study in almost any field inevitably contains defects, simply because it is the first study.

5. Gordon Tullock, *The Logic of the Law* (New York: Basic Books, 1971).

6. It is possible to put line E–E in such a location that equalizing the numbers of type 1 and type 2 errors does not minimize the total errors, but, in most cases, the 0.5 rule will work.

7. Actually, it would increase it slightly because the choice between committing the crime and not committing the crime also involves a measure of the likelihood of being unjustly convicted as a cost on the "don't commit crime" side. In most cases, it is trivial.

8. And, of course, in many cases, although the plaintiff nominally is a private citizen, it is in reality an insurance company.

9. Needless to say, I am using the contract case and plaintiff-defendant only as an example. Where the plaintiff is a large corporation, suing an individual in tort, the bias would likely be in the other direction.

10. In those cases where the insurance company is not a defendant, it is doubtful that the jury knows it. In general, it is not possible to say in the court proceedings that the defendant is actually an insurance company. It is likely that juries assume that all such cases involve insurance companies.

6. THE ANGLO-SAXONS VS. THE REST OF THE WORLD

1. The next few pages are drawn largely from Gordon Tullock, "The Efficient Organization of Trials," *Kyklos* (1975) (Fasc. 4), 28:745–62.

2. See Gordon Tullock, *The Logic of the Law* (New York: Basic Books, 1971) for a "commonsense" argument for the European system as opposed to the Anglo-Saxon system.

3. For calculation method and a set of results, see Gordon Tullock, "Efficient Rent Seeking," in James Buchanan, Robert Tollison, and Gordon Tullock, ed., *Towards a Theory of the Rent Seeking Society* (College Station: Texas A & M Press, forthcoming).

4. Needless to say, it might be wiser to hire a board of judges rather than an individual, a technical specialist rather than a legal specialist, etc.

5. Contributions would have to be restricted to positive contribution. Presumably, Mr. Wrong would be delighted with the opportunity to make a negative contribution.

6. It is my personal opinion that the social benefits would be large enough so that a Pareto optimal move is available, i.e., we could fully compensate them for this loss and still make a gain.

7. For a discussion of the general problem of the undermotivation of government officials, see Gordon Tullock, "Public Decisions as Public Goods," *Journal of Political Economy* (July/August, 1971), 79:913–18.

8. Fred S. McChesney, "On the Procedural Superiority of a Civil Law System: A Comment," *Kyklos* (1977), 30 (Fasc. 3):507–10. J. A. Ordover and Phillip Weitzman, "On the Efficient Organization of Trials: A Comment," *Kyklos* (1977), 30 (Fasc. 3):511–16.

9. Gordon Tullock, "Reply to McChesney, and Ordover and Weitzman," *Kyklos* (1977), 30 (Fasc. 3):517–19.

10. McChesney, "Civil Law System: A Comment," 507–10.

11. *Ibid.*

12. According to the *Economist* (August 12, 1979, p. 94), the British Government drastically changed its arbitration act in 1979 because a great many cases were being heard in Switzerland, Paris, and the United States, and they wanted to improve the competitive status of the English arbitration system.

13. William M. Landes and Richard A. Posner, "Adjunction as a Private Good," *Journal of Legal Studies* (March 1979), 8(2):235–84.

14. *Ibid.*, pp. 251–52.

15. Michael Marks Cohen, "A Venue Problem with the Arbitration Clauses Found in Printed Form Charters," *J. Maritime L. & Comm.* (1976), 7:541; Lynden Macassey, "International Commercial Arbitration: Its Origin, Development, and Importance," *Trans. Grotius Soc'y* (1939), 24:179, 199; Donald E. Zubrod, "Arbitration from the Arbitrator's Point of View," *Tul. L. Rev.* (1975). 49:1054, 1055.

16. Tullock, *Logic of the Law.*

17. See Table 1, Landes and Posner, "Adjunction," p. 251.

18. When I was in law school, we were told that courts would not enforce arbitration contracts, and I remember personally feeling horrified at being informed that the English courts would. That was a long time ago.

19. Richard A. Posner and William M. Landes, "Adjudication as a Private Good," *Journal of Legal Studies* (March 1979), 8(2):252.

7. VARIOUS WAYS OF DEALING WITH THE COST
OF LITIGATION

1. But not all lawyers. See, for example, Mirjan Damaska, "Evidentiary Barriers to Conviction, Two Models of Criminal Procedure: A Comparative Study," *University of Pennsylvania Law Review*, 121:506.

2. The judge might suffer in reputation from a bad enough decision. How frequently this happens and how important it is, I have no knowledge.

3. In recent years, some of the attorneys have begun to charge a higher fee than the traditional one-third. It is only the best attorneys who are able to do this. Thus, the tendency discussed above is now less strong than it used to be. A very skilled attorney, for example, might be willing to take a rather poor case in return for a much higher than normal percentage of collections. This would reduce the efficiency of the system as described above.

4. There is a small and, in my opinion, unimportant organizational difference. In the Angela Davis case, her attorneys played a part in raising the money. In the Watergate case, this was not true. Outside political sources raised money; the attorneys confined themselves to spending it. It does not seem to me that this is of much importance.

There is another difference which might conceivably be of more importance, and which had to do with the publicity given to the two operations. Although it certainly was no secret that the Republicans were paying the legal expenses and living costs of the Watergate defendants, there was no deliberate publicity given to the operation. In the Angela Davis case, there was a public fund-raising drive. The outcome, in effect, involves an interesting inversion. We now know all of the people who made the contributions to the Watergate defense case, but we do not know all of the people who made the contributions to the Angela Davis case, because secrecy, for at least some donors, was better preserved there.

5. In the original Watergate case, this turned out not to be true. Hunt and four Cubans, motivated by heaven only knows what, chose to plead guilty on the first day of the trial. Judge Sirica then prohibited the attorneys for the two remaining defendants from presenting the defense that they had prepared, with the result that, for all intents and purposes, there was no defense at all. In this particular case, it cannot be said that the people who paid for the attorneys actually had any control. Clearly, this was a most unusual case; indeed, I can recall no case in which there has been such obvious judicial bias. Since I am in favor of systems which quickly and easily reach the correct conclusion, and since I do think that the defendants were guilty in this case (also in the case of Angela Davis), I am not objecting to this bias. See, Walter Rugaber, "Liddy and McCord Are Guilty of Spying on the Democrats," *New York Times*, January 31, 1973, p. 1.

6. In some cases, politicians or bureaucrats may indeed want the government to take one side for strictly partisan reasons. In general, however, this is undesirable.

7. Note, I am assuming that the government is helping the plaintiff. It might

well be helping the defendant. This makes no difference in the basic principles we are going to discuss.

8. Normally the contest concerns alimony, custody of children, etc., and not whether or not the divorce will be granted.

9. This 95 percent chance of conviction requires a little explanation. Somewhere between 80 and 90 percent of all people who are prosecuted choose to negotiate a plea of guilty. This normally leads to a lower sentence but, of course, a much greater certainty of receiving the sentence. Of those who actually go to trial, about three-quarters are convicted. I compound these two numbers to get my 95 percent conviction ratio.

10. It is now fairly well known that the police frequently have evidence that cannot be presented in court because of the laws of evidence. This presumably has some effect on jury behavior. Juries realize that there is a possibility that there is further evidence of the guilt of the accused, which the prosecution possesses but cannot present. Since the laws of evidence do not seem to prevent the defense from presenting anything it has, no matter how it was obtained, this particular element is one-sided. One would assume, therefore, that juries (to at least some extent) take this into account when making a decision. Thus, it is by no means obvious that barring this evidence benefits the accused. It surely benefits those particular accused for which there is such illegally obtained evidence, but the accused for whom there is no such evidence may be damaged by the rule.

11. In order to keep things symmetrical, assuming that they chose to represent the wife only and not the husband, the odds would be 95 percent for the wife getting custody and only 5 percent for the husband. I omit the prospect of the legal aid office providing a third attorney to look after the interests of the child.

12. This is apparently the view of Arthur Okun:

In some important noneconomic areas, we do regard whatever results emerge as untouchable, because they are generated by an explicitly accepted ideal process. I do not believe that the winner of an election is always the best candidate, but I believe that it would be wrong to overturn the results. Similarly, I do not care whether a jury finds a particular defendant guilty or not; I care only that justice be done. And I am prepared to respect the jury's verdict, unless I learn that the intended process was violated by tampering or the like.

Arthur Okun, "Further Thoughts on Equality and Efficiency," in Colin Campbell, ed., *Income Redistribution* (Washington, D.C.: American Enterprise Institute for Public Policy Research, 1977), p. 25.

13. This assumes, of course, that the free representation provided to impecunious parties by the various government agencies is, in fact, good representation. I am not convinced that this is so.

8. THE MOTIVATION OF JUDGES

1. With elected judges in the United States, this is not entirely true, since it is at least possible to remove them by the election process. However, most judges

are fairly well shielded from any real risk of this kind by a set of local customs or laws. Thus, on one hand, their own future is well insulated from the consequences of any mistakes they may make on the bench, and, on the other hand, particularly brilliant and effective service will not benefit them.

2. It should be noted that this does not involve dishonesty, since almost everyone is biased about almost everything to some extent.

3. Note that a very large number, indeed the vast majority of all arbitration cases, are not decided by a professional arbitrator but by some businessman who is an expert in the particular trade concerned. A colleague of mine, for example, recently decided that the contractor had done an inadequate job in building his house. Arbitration was proposed and it would have consisted of asking another contractor in the vicinity to look over the house and decide whether it had, in fact, been badly built. The arbitrator would not have received a fee in this particular case. Even if he had received a fee, he would hardly have been a professional arbitrator for whom future arbitration assignments would be an important part of income.

4. We could put on a third round, but that would simply move the problem one stage back.

5. With large corporations, this will be true with respect to "the corporation," but not necessarily with respect to its senior officials. It may be that the junior official responsible is falsely reporting to his superiors in order to protect his job, and his superiors believe him, with the result that the people who actually initiate the litigation on both sides each honestly think that they are in the right.

6. Unless one of the parties has special knowledge which indicates that the arbitrator is biased in his direction, and this knowledge is not available to the other party. The publicly announced decision in a case of this sort would not be an example.

7. Of course, it might be a case which is clear enough so that one of the two parties would feel confident that an impartial arbitrator would decide in his favor. In this case, he would favor the impartial arbitrator, although he might wish to buy a little insurance by choosing his brother.

8. If one or both disagree, the party would be permitted to substitute another.

9. CRIMINAL PROCEDURE

1. Of course, many crimes are not reported to the police; but the system of criminal justice does not actually deal with these crimes.

2. If the defendant is, in fact, guilty of the crime, he may have invested considerable resources at the time of the crime to conceal his identity.

3. In England, in most cases, he is a private attorney, who has simply been hired by the police to handle this particular case.

4. Note that new evidence would normally permit the reopening of a case dropped at this stage. This does happen, although it is rare.

5. The police may be asked by the district attorney to continue their investigation; indeed, in many cases the district attorney has his own little police force for that purpose.

6. There is some descriptive material mainly by sociologists. For example, see James Eisenstein and Herbert Jacob, *Felony Justice* (Boston: Little Brown, 1977).

7. Note that plea bargaining, although it is talked about more in connection with American legal procedure than with any other, is in fact a rather uniform characteristic of criminal law. In general, the accused criminal who cooperates with the accusers will be given a lower penalty than the one who does not. For example, in Communist China:

[t]he principle in dealing with the criminal is to integrate a policy of suppression with a policy of leniency—leniency to those who confess and severity to those who resist. The criminal can lessen the gravity of the crime by making a contribution to the settlement of the case. If the criminal makes a big contribution he can be treated leniently, or even be rewarded . . .

Gerd Ruge, "An Interview with Chinese Legal Officials," *China Quarterly* (March 1975), 61:122.

8. The Charles Manson case and a couple of other cases similar to it seem to indicate that a public defender *does* have the right to prevent his client from pleading guilty even if the client wants to.

9. A reader of the manuscript pointed out that the client might be a risk lover, and hence wish to take the chance of the court proceeding even though the odds were against him. This is, of course, conceivable, but I do not see any reason why government funds should be used to finance gambles, merely because the gambler likes to gamble.

10. It could be to the advantage of the client simply because the public defender's office is hard pressed at the moment and will not have time to give him a really good defense.

11. They are extraordinarily good at implying their beliefs without actually stating them.

12. I may be oversimplifying here. I am sure that his is the correct practice, but it is not necessarily the correct ethical theory. See Monroe H. Freedman, "Professional Responsibility of the Criminal Defense Lawyer: The Three Hardest Questions," *Michigan Law Review* (June 1966), 64 (1469):1485–92, and David G. Bress, "Professional Ethics in Criminal Trials: A View of Defense Counsel's Responsibility," *Michigan Law Review* (June 1966), 64 (1469):1493–98 for a discussion which presents rather neatly how badly muddled lawyers can get when they try to talk about these matters in formal context.

13. "The First Law of Expert Advice states: Don't ask the barber whether you need a haircut"—Daniel S. Greenberg, "When Quackery Dons a Starched White Coat," *Washington Post*, August 2, 1977, p. A19.

14. If it does not, obviously we should drop the public defenders because if their resource commitment to defense is not of much significance to the outcome, we can save money without having much effect on the outcome.

10. TRIAL TECHNOLOGY: MISCELLANEOUS MATTERS

1. Actually, the word *we* here is perhaps too inclusive. Many of us do not want these things. It should be noted, however, that the desires are apparently not very strong. It was recently discovered that the Russians have established an elaborate facility for the purpose of eavesdropping on literally millions of American telephone conversations. There would be real, although not gigantic, costs involved in forcing them to stop; for example, there would be some risk that they would compel us to close our embassy in Moscow. It turns out that most people think that retaining privacy of telephone conversations is not worth that rather modest cost.

2. Note this is payment for a particular sort of testimony not intended merely to compensate the witness for his time on the stand. The classical example would be the three shillings offered by England's oldest police force, The Bow Street Runners, for evidence leading to conviction on charge of murder. Evidence disputing the guilt of the accused would not have been similarly compensated.

3. This is a technical matter; at some times and places and under some conditions it is a criminal act, and at other times and places and under other conditions it is not.

4. Most expert witnesses are, in fact, paid by the party who calls them and, indeed, may make a living out of this activity. They are a small part of the sum total of all witnesses.

5. See Sidney Hook, *Common Sense and the Fifth Amendment* (Chicago: H. Regenery, 1963).

6. See William R. Grant, "Community vs. School Integration in Detroit," *Public Interest* (Summer 1971), 24:62–79.

7. Sometimes, he is referred to as a master and has considerably more power than an "expert witness." This, however, is more an illustration of the fact that our law has many ancient nooks and crannies in it than a real distinction.

8. And, of course, had a strong personal interest as well.

9. These numbers are simply selected for convenience. The actual numbers and amounts vary a good deal from state to state and between the state and federal systems. The reader who is familiar with some particular system can simply insert the numbers for that system into my example and work out the conclusion from those numbers.

10. Note that whether there are also decisions by the jury which are or are not appealable is not relevant for our present purposes.

11. This, of course, depends on the exact numbers. We would always get judges paid more than the trial judges, but perhaps less than the appellate jurists.

12. The German system mentioned above in which the promotion of judges in courts of first instance depends on the number of cases in which they are overthrown on appeal would provide a particularly strong incentive.

13. See Grant, "Community vs. School Integration."

11. INTERPRETATION

1. The distinguished trial lawyer, F. Lee Bailey, put the matter in simple language.

Let's start with a hypothetical case; two men, inmates in the same prison, write my office for help. Both have been convicted as participants in the same loan company holdup; the first man says he's innocent. He was tucked in with his girlfriend at the time of the robbery but the jury didn't believe her. The second man doesn't deny taking part in the crime, but complains that he was never told that as an indigent he had a right to free counsel. Jailhouse lawyers have told him that this is sufficient violation of rights offered him by the Miranda decision to win him a new trial.

We write the first man: "There is nothing we can do for you; innocence is not important once you're in the can." But we tell the second man he has a 60–40 chance of winning a new trial. He writes back to say "that's fine," and that a relative will be in with a retainer. "By the way," he adds, referring to the robbery, "the other guy who wrote you wasn't there; I know, because I was."

"The revelation won't change anything"—F. Lee Bailey, *The Defense Never Rests* (New York: Signet, 1972), p. 307.

2. F. Lee Bailey gives another example. Coppolino was twice tried for murder. In both cases, Bailey, the defense attorney, argued that there had been no murder, that the death was natural. In the case in Florida, in which Coppolino was convicted, the allegation of the prosecution was the use of a poison which left little or no trace in the body. The bulk of the testimony consisted of experts in medical research testifying either for the prosecution that very faint traces of the poison had been detected by their tests, or experts for the defense testifying that the tests were invalid and that the defense experts' use of tests, in any event, had shown no signs of a poison. Turning over the decision on such a matter to a group of laymen, who surely did not understand the technical discussion, was roughly equivalent to flipping a coin. It is notable, however, that by accident a retired organic chemist was one of the first jurors called. No lawyer will be surprised to hear that he was rejected, thus assuring that none of the jurymen understood the evidence.

3. Except, of course, my legal fees.

4. The riskiness of the action might mean that I run a risk of legal action even if I am not convicted. Correct calculation would require my putting in the ex ante cost of the legal fees, but let us leave that complication aside.

5. See Gordon Tullock, *The Social Dilemma: The Economics of War and Revolution* (Blacksburg, Va.: Center for Study of Public Choice, 1974).

6. Note that the fact that this particular uncertainty is reduced or eliminated does not mean that the total uncertainty of the law is reduced. As anyone who has tried to draw up a complicated computer program knows, changing a single command in order to clean up a problem in one part of the program may cause great difficulties elsewhere. The law is somewhat similar. Changing the law so that it becomes definite with respect to A may very well create ambiguities with respect to M and Z. Whether the net effect of such a change is to reduce the

amount of confusion in the law or increase it is essentially an empirical problem, and, once again, no work has been done on it.

7. Since there are no opinions, the above case is cited from a newspaper story. John P. McKenzie, "Secret Decisions," *Washington Post*, November 2, 1976, p. A2.

8. Also cited from a newspaper from somewhat similar reasons. Carla Hill, "Jury Asks to Withdraw Indictments," *Washington Post*, July 31, 1977, pp. C1, C4.

9. If the remedy requested by the plaintiff is not payment of damages, but specific performance on the part of the defendant, then it is possible that one or the other party will be injured more by the decision than the other gains. It is not clear whether this factor should or should not be taken into account by the court.

10. For a discussion of optimal contract lengths and the way they should be calculated, see Gordon Tullock, *The Logic of the Law* (New York: Basic Books, 1971), pp. 45–52.

11. Although perhaps not the ability of the average person to obey the law because he may not be able to keep it all in his mind.

12. Bailey, *The Defense Never Rests*.

13. It probably would not have been had a jury been called upon, because they not only would not have known the law existed but would not have blamed anyone else for ignorance.

14. The head of the CIA (Helms) ordered a burglary. The attorney general later ruled that he was not responsible because he mistakenly thought his action was legal. It seems doubtful that a man with less political influence than Helms would have received a favorable ruling even with similar ignorance.

12. COURTS AS LAWMAKERS

1. Gordon Tullock, "Courts as Legislatures," in Robert L. Cunningham, ed., *Liberty and the Rule of Law* (College Station and London: Texas A & M University Press, 1979), pp. 349.

2. Much of my scholarly production has dealt with the legislative and bureaucratic processes. Although I have not specifically discussed their role in making laws of general applicability, my general approach should be clear from such of my works as *The Calculus of Consent: Logical Foundations of Constitutional Democracy*, with J. M. Buchanan (Ann Arbor: University of Michigan Press, 1967); and *The Politics of Bureaucracy* (Washington: Public Affairs Press, 1965).

3. Richard A. Posner, *Economics Analysis of the Law* (Boston: Little Brown, 1972–73). The book has been very successful. There is a second edition in print and I suspect there will be a third edition by the time this book reaches the reader.

4. Gordon Tullock, *The Logic of the Law* (New York: Basic Books, 1971).

5. Bruno Leone, *Law and Liberty* (Princeton, N.J.: Princeton University Press, 1961).

6. Gordon Tullock, "Public Decisions as Public Goods," *Journal of Political Economy* (July/August 1971), 79:912–18.

7. The statement that the acts of Parliament are subject to no control in England is a little oversimple; but the controls are very, very weak and, in important areas, they are nonexistent. Prime Minister Wilson, for example, simply refused to hand in his resignation on one occasion when he lost a vote of confidence. He got away with it.

8. Although the laws vary a good deal, it is normally said that the Secretary shall make the regulations. This has, in practice, been interpreted as "the Secretary shall appoint someone to make them."

9. In a way, the difficulty of finding them is not as much of an indication of size as you might think. At one time, I was in the embassy in Korea. I discovered that no one knew exactly what treaties and agreements we had with the Republic of Korea, even though the history of our relations with them could not have been very ancient, since before 1945 they had been part of Japan and my work took place in the early 1950s. Of course, this was a special case, because many records had been lost due to the fighting; but apparently the sets of records available in Washington were also incomplete.

10. Mancur Olson, *The Logic of Collective Action* (Cambridge, Mass.: Harvard University Press, 1965).

11. Gordon Tullock, *The Logic of the Law* (New York: Basic Books, 1971).

12. They were originated by Paul H. Rubin, "Why is the Common Law Efficient?" *Journal of Legal Studies* (1977), 6:51; and elaborated on by George L. Priest, "The Common Law Process and the Selection of Efficient Rules," *Journal of Legal Studies* (1977), 6:65. The basic work of Rubin is criticized and replaced in William M. Landes and Richard A. Posner, "Adjudications: A Private Good," *Journal of Legal Studies* (March 1979), 8:2. Landes and Posner are basically concerned with replacing the Rubin argument by another and more mathematically rigorous approach. All of the March 1979 issue of the *Journal of Legal Studies* is devoted to this basic paper by Landes and Posner and a large number of comments, with both Rubin and Priest being included as commentators. As a result the general subject is very thoroughly ventilated in that issue.

13. See Rubin, "Common Law"; Priest, "Common Law Process"; Landes and Posner, "Adjudications" and remainder of March 1979 issue of *Journal of Legal Studies*.

14. It is actually more difficult in the case of a lawsuit than in the case of a legislature or regulatory agency, but that is because the operations must be open and aboveboard for court proceedings, whereas there is a good deal of informal contact in the other two. It is not obvious that the court procedure suffers from the comparison, even if it is somewhat harder to get your ideas before a court if you are not a party to a suit than it is to get in touch with your congressman or a Deputy Assistant Secretary.

15. "Hard cases make bad law."

16. To continue with my autobiography, this particular attitude was greatly

strengthened by my later exposure to Chinese civilization, which has a radically different code of ethics than does Anglo-Saxon civilization.

17. Actually, the speeches by the proponents may be made use of by the courts in interpreting the law, but this has always been a somewhat dubious expedient and is surrounded by many precautions.

13. CONSTITUTIONAL PROBLEMS

1. There is also an obscure doctrine of "natural justice" which courts used to sometimes refer to and perhaps are in the course of reviving.

2. James M. Buchanan and Gordon Tullock, *The Calculus of Consent* (Ann Arbor: University of Michigan Press, 1962).

3. See Plessy vs. Ferguson, 1896 (163 U.S. 537).

4. See Robert J. Harris, *The Quest for Equality: The Constitution, Congress, and the Supreme Court* (Baton Rouge: Louisiana State University Press, 1960); and *The Judicial Power of the United States* (Baton Rouge: Louisiana State University Press, 1940).

5. But not necessarily the converse.

6. 5 U.S. (1 Cranch) 137, 177 (1803).

7. Rutgers vs. Waddington. The best account is contained in Julius Goebel, Jr., ed., *The Law Practice of Alexander Hamilton: Documents and Commentary* (New York and London: Columbia University Press, 1964), pp. 282–84.

8. For example, suppose that the commander of an air base in Georgia were to receive a letter from the Chief Justice of the Supreme Court, duly authenticated by the clerk of court, informing him that the Supreme Court has decided that the Constitution required that President Carter be executed, and that the commander of the air base was to perform this task by dropping a nuclear weapon on Plains the next time Carter was in residence. The order, of course, was to be kept under seal until it had been executed. I know of no one who would argue that such an order would be constitutional.

9. *Charles E. Hughes, Addresses* (1908), pp. 139–41. Hughes, of course, was not a member of the Supreme Court at the time he made this statement in a public lecture. But consider Justice Powell, "Constitutional Interpretation: An Interview with Justice Lewis Powell," *Kenyon College Alumni Bulletin* (Summer 1979), p. 15: "Yet, our independence does give the Court a freedom to make decisions that perhaps are necessary for our society, decisions that the legislative branch may be reluctant to make. The classic case that comes to mind is *Brown vs. Board of Education*. The Congress had adequate authority under the Constitution to enact the sort of legislation that has been adopted since *Brown*. But it was the Supreme Court that finally decided in 1954 that segregation in our society must come to an end. It also was the Supreme Court that made the difficult decision, one the Congress apparently did not want to make, to lower the voting age to 18. There was nothing in the Constitution that could have suggested that result. In the simplest of terms, the Court decided that when young people

were being drafted and asked to go to war and risk their lives at age 18, the time had come to extend to them the right to participate as citizens in the decisions that affected them so seriously." The whole interview is an extremely interesting one and it is unfortunate it was published in such an obscure source.

10. The next few pages are drawn from an article of mine: Gordon Tullock, "Constitutional Mythology," *New Individualist Review* (Spring 1965), 3:13–17.

11. *Marbury vs. Madison*, 5 U.S. (1 Cranch) 137, 177 (1803).

12. 5 U.S. (1 Cranch) at 178.

13. Hughes, *Addresses*.

14. 5 U.S. (1 Cranch) at 180.

15. 5 U.S. (1 Cranch) at 180. (Italics in original).

16. 5 U.S. (1 Cranch) at 180.

17. 74 U.S. (7 Wall.) 506 (1868). For another stirring illustration consider the Norris-Laguardia Act.

18. *Massachusetts vs. Mellon*, 262 U.S. 447, 488 (1923).

19. 5 U.S. (1 Cranch) at 178.

20. See William Letwin, *The Origins of Scientific Economics* (Garden City, N.Y.: Doubleday, 1964) for a somewhat similar theory. Letwin's general theme is that economics developed from a number of interested parties making arguments about economic policy. After a while, they began to realize that correct arguments may well be more persuasive than false arguments, and hence began the development of economic thought, simply in order to obtain a good argument for use in pressing their self-interest.

21. Remember President Jackson's statement, "John Marshall has made his decision, now let him enforce it"—Horace Greeley, *The American Conflict*, vol. 1 (Hartford, Conn.: O.D. Case, 1866), p. 106.

22. In particular, there was the prayer in the schools decision which was opposed by the overwhelming majority of the population. See Gallup Poll, AIPO Press Release, August 30, 1963.

23. As a matter of fact, one of the major duties of present-day congressional office staffs is dealing with the Social Security Administration for individual constituents. This means that there is an arbitrary administration, with the arbitrariness increased by the fact that, in some cases, congressional pressure leads to a reversal of the initial decision. Congressional pressure is inherently arbitrary, since congressmen cannot do anything significant about more than a very small minority of all possible Social Security complaints. In any event, many complaints are too small for the recipient to even bother calling his congressman. This particular pressure probably makes the administration less efficient rather than more.

24. Note that the investment of resources is individually rational to the two parties but not rational to the two parties taken as a group.

25. Not necessarily, of course. The famous case of *Johnson* vs. *Johnson*, in which the Supreme Court drew a distinction in the same case; or the more recent cases concerning capital punishment, in which the court changed its mind after further consideration, are examples.

26. As it happens, when I was working on this chapter I was in Basel, and a professor at the local university took me on a walk through the old city, which includes the old university buildings. One of them is still in use and is, in fact, a library and seminar room for their law school. It is indicative of the difference between law under code or under common law that this building, which contained the law library of an ancient and very famous law school, would fit into a small corner of the law library of even an undistinguished American law school. It is massively easier to master the law in a code country like Switzerland than in a common law country like the United States or England.

Index